JAMES WRIGHT

# JAMES WRIGHT

## The Poetry of a Grown Man: Constancy and Transition in the Work of James Wright

KEVIN STEIN

OHIO UNIVERSITY PRESS
ATHENS

**LIBRARY OF CONGRESS**
**Library of Congress Cataloging-in-Publication Data**

Stein, Kevin, 1954-
   James Wright : the poetry of a grown man : constancy and transition in the work of
James Wright / Kevin Stein.
      p.      cm.
   Bibliography: p.
   Includes index.
   ISBN 0-8214-0909-3
   1. Wright, James Arlington, 1927-   —Criticism and interpretation.   I. Title.
PS3573.R5358Z88 1989
81'.54—dc19                                                                                    88-23485
                                                                                                        CIP

Ohio University Press books are printed on acid-free paper. ∞

for my parents;
as always, for Deb and Kirsten

The kind of poetry I want to write is
    The poetry of a grown man.
The young poets of New York come to me with
Their mangled figures of speech,
But they have little pity
For the pure clear word.

I know something about the pure clear word
Though I am not yet a grown man.
—"Many of Our Waters: Variations on
  a Poem by a Black Child," 1972

# Contents

# Preface

American poetry has enjoyed (or suffered, depending on one's view) a curious polarization into resident parties mostly at odds with one another. Readers, critics, and occasionally even the writers themselves have been fond of dividing our poets into opposing camps—each, we are told, mutually repellent and exclusive, each seeking sanction as the true voice of American poetics. This dialogue, as chapter 1 will attest, has been both lively and continuous. And it is into this literary and aesthetic melee that James Wright entered in 1949, most probably, at the age of twenty-two, largely unaware of the history and vitality of the conflict.

Given the background of this division in American poetics, Wright becomes a compelling figure for study for a number of reasons. First, his work partakes of and achieves success at both poles of the dialectic, in what critic Charles Altieri calls the "lucid" and the "lyrical" modes of expression; examining his work, then, can help determine the representative qualities of each. Most significantly, Wright's late work attains freedom from the constraints of these modes, offering in the process an alternative to the poetics of polarity.

These arguments regarding Wright's own evolution as a poet often reflect the larger transitions many poets of his generation enacted in moving from the New Critical poem to a contemporary version that repeatedly rebelled against the former's rules of composition. One is tempted, therefore, to see Wright's transformation in style as representative of his generation's, and while this assumption is not entirely untrue, it is misleading. Wright's growth is more individual and personal than generic.

This study traces the unified growth of the entire body of James Wright's work. My aim is to examine the evolution of his poetry and to show (a) that the stylistic changes are frequently more apparent than actual, (b) that, nonetheless, Wright undergoes a continuing personal and aesthetic development, and (c) that the thematic transformation from despair to affirmation in Wright's poetry is based largely on his accepting the necessary combination of beauty and horror inherent in being human within a natural world.

Specifically, my thesis is that Wright's career may be divided into three interrelated stages of development. The first of these is a stage of containment in which he relies on traditional religious and rhetorical measures to separate the self from a world of experience; the second, a stage of vulnerability in which he enters the experiential world where the self is rewarded and equally threatened; and the last, a stage of integration in which his attention to the natural world enables him to balance his tendency to despair with an urge to affirm. Moreover, the particulars of Wright's stylistic and thematic evolution, I believe, derive from his quest to develop an individual relationship with a broad literary tradition he inherits equally from writers as various as Horace, Donne, and Trakl, and other less strictly literary sources such as his memory of the inhabitants of southern Ohio with whom he grew up. That he should seek and achieve a version of Emerson's "original relation to the universe" is Wright's primary goal as a writer. It demands attention to the lessons of nature, self, and literary tradition. The product of this kind of honest and personal relationship Wright referred to, albeit somewhat obliquely, as the "poetry of a grown man."

# Acknowledgments

Surely anyone who has undertaken the task of writing a critical study has, by the time of its completion, become indebted to not a few others whose help and advice were instrumental to finishing the job. These notes begin where they most assuredly must—with my sincere thanks to Mrs. James Wright for her gracious help throughout the period of my research. Because Anne Wright entrusted me with her late husband's unpublished work, especially the collection *Amenities of Stone*, my study offers an informed look at James Wright's redefinition of the poetic self. Thanks are also due to Roger Mitchell for his thoughtful remarks on the manuscript and his good-hearted prodding. Philip Appleman and Hayden Carruth read and commented on parts of my study, and Donald Hall aided my work immensely by consenting to a personal interview and offering his own account both of Wright's work and of the period in which Wright so remarkably altered it.

In addition, I acknowledge the generous support of the National Endowment for the Humanities' Travel to Collections Fund and of Bradley University's Board for Research and Creativity. Coupled with assistance from Bradley's College of Liberal Arts and Sciences and the Department of English and Foreign Languages, this funding has supported some of the research and revision of my manuscript.

I would be remiss if I neglected to thank the staff of the Kenyon College Libraries, particularly William Dameron and Allan Bosch, for their help in studying the James Wright Papers housed at Kenyon College.

Kathie Strum has devoted long hours to the expert (and patient) typing of this manuscript. Of the many friends whose suggestions have been invaluable, I give special thanks to Dean Young, Keith Ratzlaff, and Ralph Burns, with whom I read and discussed Wright's poetry at length. And I am most thankful for the sustaining gift of support and understanding that my wife Deb has given me.

I am grateful also to Wayne Dodd for his considerable encouragement and for permission to reprint "A Redefinition of the Poetic Self: James Wright's *Amenities of Stone*," which appeared originally in *The Ohio Review* (33 [1984]). I appreciate, too, the permission to reprint versions of two essays which have been incorporated in my study: "James Wright's 'A Blessing': Revising the Perfect Poem," which was printed in *Indiana Review* (8, no. 1 [Winter 1985]), and "The Rhetoric of Containment, Vulnerability, and Integration in the Work of James Wright," which was published by Ellwood Johnson in *Concerning Poetry* (20 [1987]).

Finally, I would like to thank the following publishers for permission to reprint the selections which appear in this work:

"The Horse" (excerpt), "To a Troubled Friend" (excerpt), "A Girl in the Window" (excerpt), "The Seasonless" (excerpt), "Erinna to Sappho" (excerpt), "A Fit against the Country" (excerpt), "Mutterings over the Crib of a Deaf Child"(excerpt). Copyright © 1971 by James Wright. Reprinted from *The Green Wall* (*Collected Poems*) by permission of Wesleyan University Press.

"A Note Written in Jimmy Leonard's Shack" (excerpt), "The Morality of Poetry" (excerpt). Copyright © 1957 by James Wright. Reprinted from *Saint Judas* by permission of Wesleyan University Press. "The Morality of Poetry" first appeared in *Poetry*.

"The Cold Divinities" (excerpt), "At the Executed Murderer's Grave" (excerpt), "On Minding One's Own Business" (excerpt). Copyright © 1958 by James Wright. Reprinted from *Saint Judas* by permission of Wesleyan University Press.

"Devotions" (excerpt), "At the Slackening of the Tide" (excerpt), "American Twilights, 1957" (excerpt), "Saint Judas" (excerpt). Copyright © 1959 by James Wright. Reprinted from *Saint Judas* by permission of Wesleyan University Press.

"Goodbye to the Poetry of Calcium" (excerpt). Copyright © 1959 by James Wright. Reprinted from *The Branch Will Not Break* by permission of Wesleyan University Press.

"By a Lake in Minnesota" (excerpt), "Snowstorm in the Midwest" (excerpt). Copyright © 1960 by James Wright. Reprinted from *The Branch Will Not Break* by permission of Wesleyan University Press. "By a Lake in Minnesota" first appeared in the *New Yorker*.

"Two Horses Playing in an Orchard" (excerpt), "Lying in a Hammock at William Duffy's Farm in Pine Island, Minnesota" (excerpt), "Miners" (complete poem), "Three Stanzas from Goethe" (excerpt), "Depressed by a Book of Bad Poetry, I Walk toward an Unused Pasture and Invite the Insects to Join Me" (excerpt), "Two Hangovers" (excerpt), "A Blessing" (complete poem), "Today I Was Happy, So I made This Poem" (excerpt). Copyright © 1961 by James Wright. Reprinted from *The Branch Will Not Break* by permission of Wesleyan University Press. "Miners" and "A Blessing" first appeared in *Poetry*.

"Twilights (complete poem), "Rain" (complete poem), "The Jewel" (complete poem), "Autumn Begins in Martins Ferry, Ohio" (complete poem), "Eisenhower's Visit to Franco, 1959" (excerpt), "The Undermining of the Defense Economy" (excerpt), "A Dream of Burial" (excerpt). Copyright © 1962 by James Wright. Reprinted from *The Branch Will Not Break* by permission of Wesleyan University Press.

"A Prayer to Escape from the Marketplace" (excerpt), "In Fear of Harvests" (complete poem). Copyright © 1963 by James Wright. Reprinted from *The Branch Will Not Break* by permission of Wesleyan University Press.

"The River down Home" (excerpt). Copyright © 1963 by James Wright. Reprinted from *Shall We Gather at the River* by permission of Wesleyan University Press.

Excerpts from *Two Citizens* by James Wright. Copyright © 1970, 1971, 1972, 1972 by James Wright, © 1986 by Anne Wright, executrix of the Estate of James Wright. Reprinted by permission of Anne Wright.

Excerpts from *To a Blossoming Pear Tree* by James Wright. Copyright © 1973, 1974, 1975, 1976, 1977 by James Wright. Reprinted by permission of Farrar, Straus and Giroux, Inc.

"May Morning" (complete poem), "A Reply to Matthew Arnold on My Fifth Day in Fano" (complete poem), "The Turtle Overnight" (complete poem), "Wherever Home Is" (excerpt), "Lightning Bugs Asleep in the Afternoon" (excerpt), "The Journey" (excerpt), and "A Winter Daybreak above Vence" (excerpt), from *This Journey* by James Wright. Copyright © 1977, 1978, 1979, 1980, 1981, 1982 by Anne Wright, executrix of the Estate of James Wright. Reprinted by permission of Random House, Inc.

Excerpts from "Spectral Lover," "Blue Girls," and "Agitato ma non Troppo" from *Selected Poems*, 3d ed. rev. and enl., by John Crowe Ransom. Copyright © 1924, 1927, 1934, 1939, 1945, 1962, 1963 by Alfred A. Knopf, Inc. Reprinted by permission of Alfred A. Knopf, Inc.

Excerpt from "Epidermal Macabre," copyright © 1932 by Theodore Roethke, and "The Far Field," copyright © 1962 by Beatrice Roethke administratrix of the Estate of Theodore Roethke. Both from *The Collected Poems of Theodore Roethke*. Reprinted by permission of Doubleday & Company, Inc.

Excerpt from *Essay on Rime* by Karl Shapiro. Copyright © 1945 by Random House, Inc. Reprinted by permission of Random House, Inc.

Excerpt from "James Wright: The Pure Clear Word, an Interview," by Dave Smith. Copyright © 1982 by the Board of Trustees of the University of Illinois. Reprinted by permission of the University of Illinois Press.

"My Heart at Evening" (complete poem) by Georg Trakl, translated by James Wright, from *Twenty Poems of Georg Trakl*. Copyright © 1961 by Sixties Press. Reprinted by permission of Robert Bly.

# 1 The Poetics of Polarization and the Work of James Wright

When James Wright published his first poem in a 1949 issue of *Hika*, the Kenyon College student magazine, he began in a small way not only to participate in American literary history but also to encounter its attendant pressures. These pressures, coupled with Wright's own artistic and emotional responses to them, shaped and colored his work throughout his career. No writer, of course, writes in a vacuum. None would want to. This is especially true of Wright, a poet possessing a lively intellect and an insatiable appetite for reading the work of others. In fact, the interrelated stages of containment, vulnerability, and integration in which Wright matures come into focus most clearly when placed against the backdrop of such a literary history.

## 1 The Polarization of American Poetry

Numerous critics have devoted a great deal of energy to analyzing the polarization of American poetics which Emerson himself ruefully chose to call a "schism." Just after the turn of the century, Van Wyck Brooks noted that American writing tended to divide itself into two divergent camps to which he applied the uniquely American titles, "Highbrow" and "Lowbrow."[1] The Highbrow camp, Brooks believed, mimicked the manners of the European upper classes, advocating a sophisticated and intellectual response to the activities of the world. On the contrary, the Lowbrows wore their American primitivism too proudly, displaying a wild, uncivil, and often rebellious attitude in their work. Brooks considered this dialectic to be a "deadlock" that forced the American mind to "drift chaotically" between the two extremes; only Whitman, in Brooks's view, had possessed the "middle" personality necessarily large enough to span and thereby resolve the dialectic.

Near the middle of the century, Philip Rahv also identified what he believed were the fundamental "polar types" of American literature, to which he applied the native terms: "paleface" and "redskin."[2] The paleface group—Henry James, Eliot, and the various New Critics—is characterized by its intellectual, often ascetic, and refined "estrangement from reality." On the other hand, the redskins—Thoreau, Whitman, and William Carlos Williams among them—share a largely emotional, sometimes unrestrained immersion in their environment, even when "rebelling against one or another of its manifestations"(2). The two parties, thus, display a basic disagreement regarding experience, the manner in which a human being interacts with his or her cultural and physical surroundings. The paleface stands apart from the proceedings, reflecting intelligently even while experiencing a flow of events, feelings, and attitudes. The redskin, though, rejects this Cartesian dualism and its attendant theory of separation and reacts intuitively, primarily emotively. At a deeper issue, the distinction expands still further: the paleface attempts to order what he experiences, while the redskin seeks to perceive a preexistent order. Implicit, of course, are conflicting judgments concerning the human (in)capacity to make orderly what appears to be a chaotic universe and, beyond that, the general trustworthiness of human perception.

Rahv considered the above polarity as a "split personality" or, worse, as a "blight of onesidedness" in the American mind. Others possessing variant critical viewpoints and purposes have nevertheless noticed a similar disjuncture. Roy Harvey Pearce labeled these two groups the "mythic" and the "Adamic," and D. H. Lawrence offered the terms "genteel" and "Indian" to describe this phenomenon. That is not to say that the poets busy writing American poetry were not aware of these choices between pedantic control and romantic abandon; Robert Lowell once characterized the option as the difference between "cooked" and "raw" poetry.[3]

However, not every commentator has regarded such a dichotomy as destructive; in fact, R. W. B. Lewis chose to call this situation a "lively and creative dialogue" between (using Emerson's terms) "the party of memory" and "the party of hope."[4] Mourning its decline in the New Criticism–dominated fifties, Lewis praised this dialogue as a (if not *the*) source of vitality in American letters.

Although Pearce contended that this dialectic had forced American poetry to the "point of no return" and that it had reached its fulfillment and conclusion in the work of the "mythic" Eliot and the "Adamic" Wallace Stevens, that simply has not proved to be the case.[5] More recently, Charles Altieri has traced the dialogue from its roots in Enlightenment ideology and asserted its reemergence—or continued presence—in contemporary writing.[6] Altieri calls the conflict between the "ideals of lucidity" and the "ideals of lyricism" the "longest-running play in our cultural history" (12). The pressures of Enlightenment reason forced artists and thinkers—confronted by the standard dichotomies of modern thought, such as that between fact and value—to assume "reflective stances" characterized by lucidity and lyricism. The lyrical poet was especially vulnerable to such an elevation of reason. In an age seeking rational and scientific explanation, what could not be objectified was distrusted. To claim a lyrical sense of transcendental knowledge not supported or provable by the laws of nature left the poet to be viewed as merely odd or eccentric, or as Altieri indicates, as standing "against the march of history" (13). Today, in his view, American poets still face these choices, or what he defines as the tension between the lucid poets, maintaining intellectual control while trying to reason their way to self-knowledge, and the lyric poets, maintaining a rhetoric of sincerity or naturalness as they emote their way to intensely epiphanic moments of transcendence.

## 2   The Poetics of Containment (or Lucidity)

Such a polarization, or a slight variation of it, indeed occupied much of modern poetry. Carried forward by the divergent figures of Eliot and Williams and their camps, the debate addressed more than the mere surface features of style. When Williams implied that "The Waste Land" had given American poetry over to the professors and remarked that it had destroyed his world like an "atom bomb," he was referring as much to the intellectual and aesthetic principles behind the work as to the content of the poem itself. Its ethos of ascetic self-control and its insistence on the relatively shabby prospects for modern society had bothered Dr. Williams, of course, but the poem's stiff intellectual underpinnings disturbed him more. For even though Eliot had praised Donne for his refusal to accept a dissociation of sensibility, some in Eliot's camp spoke as if Eliot had thoroughly separated thought from feeling in art and relegated emotion to the poetic scrap heap. Characteristic of those advocating Eliotic principles in 1927, John Gould Fletcher challenged "the importance of emotion in poetry" and asserted that "intellect and not emotion is the true basis of art."[7]

By the late 1940s Eliot's poetry and, in one form or another, his theory shared (and dominated) the poetic spotlight in America. Codified by academia and its scholarly journals, Eliot's poetics of lucidity kept Williams's lyricism mostly in the dark. When Wright entered Kenyon College in 1948, those forces that would influence his early work had evolved from Eliot's Impersonal Theory into a sometimes rigid New Critical approach. The hieratic had subjugated the demotic. The "lively" dialogue seemed remarkably quiet, nearly a monologue.

Wright first received national attention with the publication of *The Green Wall* (1957), chosen by W. H. Auden as the winner of the prestigious Yale Series of Younger Poets Award. As should be expected, both that book and his second, *Saint Judas* (1959), exhibited the influences of his teacher, John Crowe Ransom, and those ideals dictated by the dominant mode of the day: the need to compose a kind of metaphysical poem, formal in structure and decorous in every gesture. This was a thinking person's poem, intellectual and rigorous in its admiration for irony and paradox, a lucid or "paleface" poetry. Wright's work was well-received—and so was Wright—as a torchbearer of this version of the English literary tradition.

Initially, this mode extended by way of Eliot to the New Critics, a group Walter Sutton identifies as a "conservative counter-revolution" in American poetry.[8] Ransom, Allen Tate, Cleanth Brooks, R. P. Blackmur, I. A. Richards, and others combined to form a loose band of poets and critics who acknowledged the influence of Eliot's theories and posited a set of their own. Oddly enough, they had ignored the fantastic images of Eliot's early work, the Symbolist-inspired "bats with baby faces in violet light"; instead, they chose to concentrate on the prose criticism in which Eliot had called for an "extinction of personality" and reasserted respect for the metaphysical tradition in poetry. As Sutton argues, I. A. Richards helped provide a further critical basis for the group's theories by his revisionist treatment of chapter 14 of Coleridge's *Biographia Literaria* (1817). When Richards replaced Coleridge's "esemplastic imagination" as a reconciler of opposites and substituted irony—"a rational intellectualist quality"—he composed an altered formula for poetic engagement (152–53). The Romantic imagination thus became secondary to the rationalist intellect.

With the emergence of the Middle Generation of American poets in the 1950s, the formula—a controlled use of irony, paradox, and tension between opposites—became a form in itself. Richard Eberhart, Robert Lowell, Randall Jarrell, Howard Nemerov, Theodore Roethke, Louise Bogan, and Karl Shapiro wrote with distinction and established theirs as a generation to be reckoned with. As Shapiro said of Eliot, "His word was our poetic law."[9] Eliot's word—that is, his prose criticism and not so much his early Symbolist poetry—provided the common aesthetic groundwork for yet another generation of poets.

Wright had clear ties to both generations, having studied with Ransom and later with Theodore Roethke at the University of Washington. Though Richard Hugo and Carolyn Kizer also chose to work with Roethke at nearly the same time, Wright seems to have been the star pupil. Before his death, Hugo himself said that Wright was "one of the few students writing well in Roethke's classes."[10] Although at this stage of his career Roethke's notion of writing well still demanded the utter control of form and music, he had relaxed his attitude toward the necessity of authorial distance. However, his early poems, those of *Open House* (1941), nearly always seem exercises in containment, and not surprisingly, so do Wright's.

Using the seventeenth-century metaphysical poets as models (for those, Hugo tells us, are the ones that Roethke "pushed"), Wright learns to contain his raging against a world of disorder within a precisely wrought and musical poem (29). He juxtaposes dichotomous forces—the heavenly and the earthly, the physical and the spiritual, the human and the natural—within a poem bound rigidly by its intellectual control into what I call a poetry of containment.

In many of these poems, Wright retains a self-willed intellectual detachment, as if in doing so, he could also retain an emotional balance. For example, "A Fit against the Country" maintains a Cartesian duality between mind and matter. Though the body is lured to "fall" into nature, the mind insists on a logical dissociation from its surroundings. A similar tension between the human and the natural is contained by the reflective security of the past tense verb, which orders the poem "At the Slackening of the Tide," or by the rhetorical safety of the subjunctive mood, which lessens the emotional risks of "The Cold Divinities." Perhaps more importantly, the speaker of "The Horse" laments that modern humanity "has coddled the gods away." After comparing his vision of a mythical horse and rider with his memory of his own wife's fall from a runaway horse, the speaker lapses further into despair. The comparison proves chilling and ironic, for the wife's fall, surely a metaphor for the Christian fall from gace, reminds the speaker that as a result of original sin the human race is best suited now "to cough in a dish beside a wrinkled bed." This view of a Post-Lapsarian world, of a culture infinitely removed from its past grandeur reflects the general despair of a loveless, imperfect world. Wright must have been aware of the accepted mode's tenor of skepticism, an attitude succinctly summarized by Auden's admonition that the primary "purpose" of poetry is to "disenchant and disintoxicate."[11]

Wright often echoes the discontent with the modern world characteristic of the major figures of the day. Of course, Eliot and Ransom's shared admiration for the seventeenth-century mind reveals a deeper longing for the undissociated spirit they believed existed during the era of Donne. From the perspective of the twentieth century, that era appears enviably more unified, for it precedes Charles I, the Puritan revolt and its religious and political upheavals, the onslaught of the industrial age, and the horrors of world war.

Perhaps in the decade of the cold war, the policy of containment became as much a poetic as a political principle. Poets also conspired to separate themselves from the dangers of a disorderly and threatening world by composing a wall of rhetorical and intellectual defenses. For American politicians, the lesson of post–World War II existence may have been to distrust the Russians, but for many poets, the primary lesson seemed to involve not trusting one's emotions or the frightening world that made one vulnerable to them. The poem came to offer an insular, familiar, and more or less safe locale to reflect intelligently on the world and to order one's thoughts (and one's self) in measured lines. It was a form in which putting things in their places and keeping them there was not only an admirable but also an attainable goal. Most poets tried to write and liked to read poems that were not grossly unpredictable in form or content. Reading a poem that retained its composure and its respect for order assured them that at least one thing in a period of war, revolution, and hunger had not changed for the worse overnight. Respect for tradition and convention in a world seemingly hell-bent on destroying (or at least altering) both showed itself in the abandonment of modernist experiments and a return to conservative poetics, most notably in Eliot, the major figure of the day. Eliot's famous description of himself in *For Lancelot Andrewes* (1929) as a royalist in politics, a classicist in literature, and a member of the Anglo-Catholic faith (and Ransom's own version of that remark) defined a mind in search of a familiar continuity and order in which to reside. That residence may have seemed available only in art.

James Wright, however, serves to illustrate one significant problem with the generalized division of American poets into camps of "paleface" and "redskin." Once classified as, say, "paleface" and assigned to that camp, American poets simply refuse to stay there. Time and again these poets remind us that artistic endeavor is decidedly more dynamic than static. Beginning with the unpublished manuscript, *Amenities of Stone* (1961–62), and its successor, *The Branch Will Not Break* (1963), Wright markedly alters the basis, values, and goals of his work. Instead of a protective policy of containment, his work begins to evince a more vulnerable and expansive quality. Certainly, Wright was not the only one of his generation to undergo this transformation, for Adrienne Rich, W. S. Merwin, Galway Kinnell, Robert Bly, Louis Simpson, and others also changed their styles, rebelling against the literary status quo.

### 3   The Poetics of Vulnerability (or Lyricism)

To be sure, there had been attacks before: Charles Olson's "Projective Verse" (1950), Allen Ginsberg's "Howl" (1956), W. D. Snodgrass's *Heart's Needle* (1959), and Lowell's *Life Studies* (1959) had already fought implicit and explicit skirmishes with the reigning aesthetics. Karl Shapiro had waged a battle from the inside, as it were, with his treatise disguised as a meditation on verse, *Essay on Rime* (1945). Some years earlier Shapiro had perhaps best stated the manner in which laudable New Critical metaphysical theory had been transformed to mere technique:

> The yeast of criticism worked, and rime
> Declined to verbiage, decomposed to forms.
> (*Essay on Rime*, p. 65)

A number of poets not strictly Confessional, Beat, or Objectivist in the Williams tradition openly objected to the hierarchy of values expressed by the New Critical movement, an aesthetic which had only intensified the often stoic, intellectualist beliefs of Modernism. In theory and practice, these poets turned away from a restrained impersonalism to a romanticism that welcomed emotion and intuition, and this quickly became the dominant mode of the sixties. Bly, for example, departed from his early penchant for sonnets and arrived at the deep images of *Silence in the Snowy Fields* (1962); Rich and Merwin abandoned traditional metrics for free verse in *Snapshots of a Daughter-in-Law* (1963) and *The Moving Target* (1963), respectively. James Wright, too, published his important volume, *The Branch Will Not Break*, after a couple of years of struggling with poetic forms and values in *Amenities of Stone*.

The tension between the rhetoric of containment that dominated Wright's early work and his new insistence on forcing the poet-speaker out into the realm of experience manifests itself in the pages of *Amenities* and *Branch*. In 1962 Wright had surveyed the dominant mode of the day (surely including his own early work) and evaluated it harshly: "We endure a bloated body of verse which drops a shroud between the true feelings of a reader and the true character of the poet."[12] His metaphor implies that this body of verse is deceased, that some alternative must be found to revivify the rhetorical contract between writer and reader. Wright had a clear idea of how this might be accomplished. Although the new poems in *Amenities* and *Branch* do not cohere stylistically with his previous work (they are much more imagistic and elliptical, for example), this stylistic alteration is more properly described as a rhetorical transformation, one which enables the poet to convey to his reader a measure of emotionality and spirituality not possible in his previous mode. Perhaps, too, Wright had undergone a personal change that would allow him to see in himself and in the natural world surrounding him possibilities for a meaningful life far removed from that despairing vision of a man capable only of coughing into a "dish beside a wrinkled bed."

In poems such as "Milkweed," "Two Hangovers," and "A Blessing," he imagines a world in which human and natural interaction seems not only possible but ultimately rewarding. His feelings of elation at brief harmony with natural elements appear undisguised and unprotected by the irony that had served such a fortressing purpose earlier, and much like Altieri's version of the poet of lyricism, he risks asserting that truths exist beyond that which can be rationally or scientifically explained. For precisely this reason, Wright's poems—and Wright as poet—are most clearly vulnerable in this stage.

Using his imagination, unharnessed by logic and free to make the leaps of faith that Bly describes as a way into the "unknown part of the mind," Wright explores the so-called deep image that intertwines the inner and outer worlds, the poet's conscious and unconscious intelligence.[13] Many reviewers were not prepared for such a transformation in Wright's work; Louis D. Rubin, for example, referred to Wright's new image poems as mere "pictorial art" and bemoaned that he had "gone way off on a tangent."[14] To complicate matters for those reviewers who, like Rubin, had also expected a thematic continuation of Wright's previous mode, most of these image poems display a pronounced Pre-Lapsarian quality which contrasts greatly with the tone of his early religious themes. Both the lyricism of these images and their magical transformations which enable the speaker to "break/Into blossom" left him vulnerable to charges of innocence and childishness.

Wright did not always fare well under such attacks. And to be equitable, several of his deep image poems, such as "Eisenhower's Visit to Franco" and "The Undermining of the Defense Economy," offer poetic expressions quite different from what one may regard as celebrations of pastoralism. These poems pose social and political statements that indicate Wright's awareness of the wider rebellion that occurred in the sixties. But Wright's own personal and aesthetic deliberations appear to have been transmuted within his restless exploration of style in *Shall We Gather at the River* (1968), *Collected Poems* (1972), and *Two Citizens* (1973). Perhaps the Romantic vulnerability of *Branch*—which had drawn a few reviews similar to Rubin's—no longer seemed tenable to Wright. The speaker of these later collections is noticeably feisty and nearly always combative with his readers. At times he seems on the verge of punching out the "young poets of New York" for their "mangled figures of speech,"and he edges close to solipsism when he tells his readers to "Please leave the poem."

By the time that Wright reached *Two Citizens*, which, as chapter 5 discusses, has been regarded variously as the high or low point of his career, he was ready for a change. It is not implausible that he saw himself trapped within the confines of the present polarization of American poetics and sought a release into forms and values not bound by either set of artistic principles.

### 4    The Poetics of Integration (or an Alternative)

Wright, of course, is not the only poet or critic to seek or suggest an acceptable alternative to the dialectic between lucidity and lyricism in American poetry. Before discussing Wright's own integrational strategies for resolving the dialectic, two well-known contemporary poetic theories that attempt to do the same should be mentioned. The first is Robert Pinsky's call in *The Situation of Poetry* for the discursive poem, for "discourse, discursiveness, the sound of the writer ambling or running through his subject and speaking about it."[15] What Pinsky regards highly is a kind of thinking poem spoken with "all the virtues of prose," one that keeps its feet squarely on the solid ground of "great conscious art" (134, 175). Pinsky's idea of the "virtue" of prose, apparently, is that it avoids vague transcendental and lyrical excess and instead concerns itself with the conscious qualities of rational discourse as a way to human knowledge and understanding.

Obviously, Pinsky's aesthetic sees itself as a counter to the great "unconscious" art of the sixties and its lyric successors. In order to clarify the relationship between Pinsky's conception of discursiveness and the theory dominant in the sixties, it is helpful to recall that Bly's term for the lyric poetry of intuitive jumps between the conscious and unconscious mind is "leaping poetry." Comparing it to Pinsky's definition of the "discursive" aspect of the poetry he admires and advocates proves even more useful: "The word signifies going through or over one's subject  Whether digressively or directly, at a walk or at a run, the motion is on the ground and by foot. . . . Such a method tends to be inclusive; it tends to be the opposite of intuitive" (143).

Instead of "leaping," this poetry tends to "walk." Instead of intuition, it calls upon the intellect to direct the movement of the poem. It is "inclusive" not in the sense of an imagination that welcomes lyric possibilities, but in the sense of an intelligence that eschews elliptical presentation; that is, discursiveness fills in the gaps of association that a leaping poem—because it trusts the imagination to make the necessary connections—would leave vacant.

Altieri himself offers another alternative to the dialogue, urging upon our poets a reflective "self-consciousness" concerning rhetoric. He sees John Ashbery as illustrative of the "most promising of contemporary styles," a poet able to "distribute . . . traditional lyric emotions into a series of 'positions' " to which he can apply various rhetorical stances to qualify and undercut those very positions.[16] Altieri believes that this new style carries considerable aesthetic potential, for he asserts that Ashbery seeks to discover new lyrical possibilities "by giving the lucidity of self-consciousness and the duplicity of rhetoric their full play" (19). Altieri appears, therefore, to be proposing a new lyricism to be gained paradoxically through adopting a vigorous (and duplicitous) lucidity.

The new poetry that James Wright himself discovered in *To a Blossoming Pear Tree* (1977) and *This Journey* (1982) refuses the rhetorical basis of both Pinsky's and Altieri's suggested options. He rejects the duplicitous rhetoric that Altieri praises, labeling such a notion the mere "manipulation of words with the purpose of drawing unqualified attention to themselves and to the dubious charms of the manipulator." Wright prefers a definition of rhetoric that "retains its ancient meaning: a way to arrange words to convey a vision and evoke a true response in the feelings of the reader."[17] The rhetorical strategies of his final volumes seek integration rather than manipulation; his quest is to set himself firmly in the experiential world and communicate what he sees and feels and thinks to his reader. These integrated lyrics tend to be inclusive of others, not exclusive. They enable the fundamental lyric format of perception to be qualified—not overridden—by the conscious intelligence. Not unlike the kind of poet Altieri chooses to praise (although Altieri neglects to notice this alteration in Wright's work), Wright experiences an emotion, shows the ability to ride that feeling, and yet asserts the intellect as a kind of test of authenticity.

Though it functions as protection against bogus emotion, the intellect does not dominate the poem as it might in Pinsky's version of the discursive poem. Wright realizes that the real danger of extreme discursiveness is that its intellectualized "walk" can produce a merely pedestrian poem. His goal is to combine head and heart in the act of experiencing a particular state of being. Significantly, the "ancient meaning" of rhetoric to which Wright alludes is itself classical, in fact, Horatian. He finds its source in Horace's *Ars Poetica*, in Horace's definition of true art as that which incorporates both the intellect and the imagination in its creation. Moreover, for both poets, this art bears a great social responsibility: to communicate honestly one's private state in the belief that others may and ultimately do share it.

Secondly, unlike Ashbery's work, Wright's late poetry continually asserts the importance of things outside of the mind. A modern version of Thoreau's fully awake person, he remains "forever on the alert" to the world that surrounds him and to the other beings that share it. In this manner, his work abjures the idea expressed in the work of Stevens and Ashbery that mind creates nature, rejecting in the process the thinking of Berkeley, Kant, Hume, and Hegel. His view of the universe is much more in keeping with Alfred North Whitehead's philosophy of organism, for like Whitehead, Wright regards human and natural objects as equally real, and equally elements of the society of living things.[18] In poems such as "Well, What Are You Going to Do?" Wright espouses the interconnectedness of the human and natural worlds. Again, this rhetoric of innocence carries with it an inherent vulnerability, a posture Wright seems not to fear (or perhaps cultivates). Behind it is a view much like that which Hyatt Waggoner attributes to "visionary" poets who see humans as "participants in the world, neither objective observers of it nor homeless in it." Such an attitude, Waggoner points out, perhaps thinking of Ashbery, "runs counter to the poetry of 'idealism' that would make whatever is valuable in the world the by-product of our minds."[19]

Finally, Wright's exploration of the prose poem shows his willingness to try new methods of writing that might help him modulate between the poles of emotional immersion and intellectual distance. When he uses the freedom of the prose form to its best advantage, he deftly avoids both lyrical excess, a kind of self-reflexive bathos, and rational detachment, a refusal of the experiential world. In prose pieces such as "The Secret of Light" and "The Flying Eagles of Troop 62," Wright learns that "a rejection of a certain kind of rhetoric" inherent in poetry moves him to a prose lyric that can "reach over into some kind of rhythm, some closeness of life."[20] The results of such a rhetoric of integration prove considerable, for in "A Reply to Matthew Arnold on My Fifth Day in Fano," he is able again to become "briefly in harmony with nature before I die." Through the prose poem, as the discussion in chapter 6 illustrates, Wright escapes the debilitating rhetorical and stylistic prescriptions proposed by the disparate models of lyricism and lucidity, discovering in the process a personal and individual relationship to literary tradition, what he calls "the poetry of a grown man."

## 5   Conclusion

My point is that to see Wright as "defined mostly" by what he "reacted against," as Alan Williamson contends is common, shows symptoms of critical tunnel vision.[21] Such a view restricts Wright within the boundaries of the poetics of polarization he labored fervently to escape and dismisses without authority his final work with the integrated lyric— prose, fixed, or free in form. I have a notion that Wright's real influence on younger authors will in the future derive from this phase of his work, or bear at least as much significance as his remarkable accomplishments in *The Branch Will Not Break*. What his final poems, as well as his career in total, can offer us is an alternative to the aesthetics of polarization that have dominated American poetry for nearly 150 years. In fact, Warner Berthoff's impressive account of the weaknesses of contemporary writing, *A Literature without Qualities*, reserves special mention for Wright (along with Hugo, Ashbery, and a few others). Wright's *To a Blossoming Pear Tree*, Berthoff argues, is invaluable for its "patient continuation of a stubbornly developed integrity which is the more admirable for everything in contemporary life that conspires against it."[22] Though I do not presume to raise up James Wright as a twentieth-century Whitman, he does provide us a means of incorporating the best qualities of the lucid mode within a lyric poetry not fatally self-absorbed or fatuous. Wright's goal—and his achievement—is not a hopelessly enervated middle ground, but a lyricism more fully responsive to the pressures of contemporary life.

## 2 A Poetics of Containment:

Diction, Form, and Religious Theme in
*The Green Wall* and *Saint Judas*

The poems of James Wright's first two collections, *The Green Wall* (1957) and *Saint Judas* (1959), owe their ornate diction and conventional form not so much to this century as to the seventeenth. Although Wright cites Robert Frost and E. A. Robinson as influences (and critics such as Louis Simpson gladly concur), the most significant source of his early poetry lies in the work of several seventeenth-century poets.[1] Wright learns a technically flawless style from Ben Jonson, a delicacy of subject matter from Robert Herrick, and a fascination with the dialectic from John Donne.

However, these poets and their work amount to more than a mere literary indebtedness, for they provide Wright with a rhetorical means of addressing the religious themes of a loveless, material world. Owing his rhetorical strategies to Donne and channeling his thinking through the logical rigors of a cultivated poem, Wright chooses a formal language and an intellectual mode for one simple but compelling reason: He needs a sophisticated means to make bearable his Christian themes of separation and his overpowering sense of abandonment. In the decidedly Post-Lapsarian mood of the fifties, Wright's poetry—armored by his version of perfect form—recurrently confronts the vision of a world suffering the results of original sin: the detachment of humanity from nature, the separation of humans from each other, and the severance of the earthly from the heavenly. Wright, then, uses the received poetic language and forms of these seventeenth-century poets, revived in this century by T. S. Eliot and the New Critics, to construct a poetics of containment. In a modern world of evident and ubiquitous disorder, Wright views these forms as a way to impose order on his experience, to contain it within the impersonal verbal artifact that a certain kind of poem can become.

Still, no matter how much his work owes to the social, cultural, and aesthetic context of Auden's age of angst—and perhaps in spite of these influences—his early work shows, too, that Wright had misgivings about the attitude of containment that tends to distance the poet from both his poem and the outer world of experience. Auden himself notes in his introduction to *The Green Wall* that Wright's work displays a curiously expanded and unconventional notion of poetic subject matter. By choosing prostitutes and murderers as subjects, Wright implicitly rejects the reigning limits of decorous subject matter and the insular poem that results from them. He pushes his poetry, often tentatively at first, outward to experience, beyond the supposedly perfect symmetry of the contained poem and into the imperfect world that surrounds him. In addition, Wright uses the dialectic—often a dialogue of competing voices within the self—not merely to balance opposites but occasionally to subordinate the voice of despair to one of hope and acceptance. In this way, he brings to poetry a dialogic mode of discourse, showing, in the process, his desire for alternatives to the despairing themes and the authoritative modes of presentation prevalent in the day. A poem such as "Mutterings over the Crib of a Deaf Child" demonstrates Wright's aesthetic and personal dissatisfaction with the contained poem, for this poem, much like his later work, reveals his willingness to accept a Keatsian notion of a somewhat flawed but ultimately appealing world of experience.

\*   \*   \*

Wright employs a rhetoric of containment to distance himself from his pessimistic themes—and from the very experiences that compose them. In an age yearning for order and not finding it, he learns to impose one of his own through the suspension of opposites that structures the New Critical poem. Surely, Wright is not alone in this endeavor. Richard Wilbur, in fact, describes the source of the form and highlights the assumptions behind it: "Most American poets of my generation were taught to admire the English metaphysical poets of the seventeenth century and such contemporary masters of irony as John Crowe Ransom. We were led by our teachers and by the critics whom we read to feel that the most adequate and convincing poetry is that which accommodates mixed feelings, clashing ideas, and incongruous images."[2] By adhering to such aesthetic principles, the poet, it was believed, could create a timeless artifact, perhaps discover an apparent relief from the discomfitting themes of the day.

Although Wright uses form as a way to deal with religious issues, many contemporary readers more readily equate such New Critical practice with simple academic formalism, with a kind of intellectual show-and-tell. True, the witty and urbane intellectualizing of many lesser poets of that period often, as Karl Shapiro remarks, "decomposed to forms." This emphasis on forms, though, is understandable for an era which regarded quite seriously Eliot's notion that a "poet has, not a 'personality' to express, but a medium." The resultant separation of the poet from the poem showed itself in many ways: in impersonality, in ruminative distance, in a poetry detached from emotions. As Gerald Graff notes, these theories of form can easily extend the international fallacy to include the assumption that "language writes the poem, not the poet."[3]

Therefore, the form itself—its ironies and tensions between discordant attitudes—proffers the poet a freedom from pathetic self-absorption. By enabling the poet to deal with unsettling issues in an orderly fashion, it offers a means not only to display a mature sense of order and control but, more importantly, to achieve it. Thus, the form becomes a means of distancing the poet from his or her most vulnerable emotions or a way of imbedding them within the act of the poem at a sort of rhetorical arm's length. James Wright himself is quite forthcoming in explaining how he wields form to control despair in his early work: "Sometimes I have been very happy, but characteristically I'm a miserable son of a bitch. I tried to come to terms with that in the clearest and most ferociously perfect form that I could find and in all the traditional ways. That was partly a defensive action, because I hurt so much then."[4]

Wright was not alone in using form as a "defensive action,"for in much the same way, Adrienne Rich also describes how she manipulated form to shield herself in the early poem, "Aunt Jennifer's Tigers." By presenting Aunt Jennifer in the process of sewing "bright topaz" tigers into a tapestry, Rich structures a careful dialectic between the woman's "imagination, worked out in tapestry, and her life-style, 'ringed with ordeals she was mastered by' " (mostly those of a confining marriage). Rich interprets her strategy in this way:

> In writing this poem, composed and apparently cool as it is, I thought I was creating a portrait of an imaginary woman. . . . It was important to me that Aunt Jennifer was a person as distinct from myself as possible—distanced by the formalism of the poem, by its objective, observant tone—even by putting the woman in a different generation. . . .
>
> In those years formalism was part of the strategy—like asbestos gloves, it allowed me to handle materials I couldn't pick up barehanded.[5]

The formalism to which Rich alludes dictates the need for a thinking poem, objective in tone and impersonal in character. Once given "formal versification"—what Allen Tate referred to as "the primary structure of poetic order"—such a poem assured the reader and "the poet himself that the poet is in control of the disorder both outside him and within his own mind."[6] Those precepts call for the sort of poem John Gould Fletcher earlier had referred to in the *Saturday Review of Literature* as "antiromantic," one that refuses to revel in the chaos of the present moment but instead reflects intelligently from a cautious rhetorical distance.[7] Of course, Eliot and the New Critics after him found the source of such poetry in many seventeenth-century poets, especially the metaphysicals. Eliot's reappraisal of Donne, for instance, prompted much of the era's immersion in the seventeenth century. In fact, John Crowe Ransom states the consequences of Eliot's "The Metaphysical Poets" in large terms: "Its public effect has been to have just about upset the old comparative valuations of the great cycles of English poetic history: reducing the 19th Century heavily and the Restoration and 18th Century a little less, elevating the 16th and 17th Centuries to supreme importance as the locus of the poetic tradition at its full."⁸ This reevaluation can be stated in an admittedly brief summary: Eliot and the New Critics reacted against the easy self-centered emotionalism of decadent nineteenth-century romanticism and asked for a more universalist, mythic, and impersonal poem. Still, many contemporary readers of James Wright's early poetry are less attentive to these rhetorical goals than to the surface of a poetry that seems to them overwrought and affected, a strange relic of the Neo-Augustan age. They may wonder how the poet of *The Branch Will Not Break* (1963) and *To a Blossoming Pear Tree* (1977) could ever have written it.

To be sure, the language of Wright's first two volumes often seems spoken by what Dave Smith calls "the composite voice of his literary fathers."⁹ Although Wright shares Frost's sense of the ironic and Robinson's notion of human limitation, the voice that speaks his early poems clearly owes less to them than to the seventeenth century, for a carefully chosen poetic diction contributes to the air of preciousness that surrounds these early poems. Though Wright was raised in the mill and factory environment of Martins Ferry, Ohio, he mostly rejects that language he heard (and probably used) at home in favor of a learned, acquired manner of speaking more akin to seventeenth-century England than to twentieth-century Ohio. However, this is understandable: Like most poets of his generation, Wright learns first to work in the received methods of the day, those favored by the ruling orthodoxy.

Wright's early work appears schooled in the neoclassical style of Ben Jonson and his followers, the "sons of Ben." Jonson is a flawless technician capable of a restrained locution, as "On My First Son" demonstrates. Indeed, this poem serves as a fine example of the containment principle in application, for its formal control displays not a lack of emotion but a containment of it. However, he is also capable of a musical lyric, a kind of song. The opening lines of "Slow, Slow, Fresh Fount" reveal this lyrical quality:

Slow, slow, fresh fount, keep time with my salt tears;
Yet slower, yet, O faintly gentle springs!
(*Cynthia's Revels*, 1600)

In comparison, the opening of Wright's "To a Troubled Friend" displays a similar sense of rhythm, especially in its lilting melody punctuated with numerous commas:

> Weep, and weep long, but do not weep for me,
> Nor, long lamenting, raise, for any word
> Of mine that beats above you like a bird,
> Your voice, your hand.[10]
> (*The Green Wall*)

In particular, Wright's early work shares affinity with one of Jonson's followers, Robert Herrick. If Herrick could concoct exotic female subjects for his verses, so can Wright, but instead of Herrick's Julia, Corinna, and Electra, Wright chooses Sappho, Erinna, and Eleutheria. Such women were not, it is safe to assume, common subjects of discussion in Martins Ferry; they represent Wright's attempt to create a voice of refinement and erudition. Though he may be simply trying on another poet's voice, in *The Green Wall* Wright consciously avoids the language of his home and occasionally adopts Herrick's Cavalier appreciation of the female form. Here, it is useful to cite Herrick's brief "Upon Julia's Clothes":

> Whenas in silks my Julia goes,
> Then, then, me thinks, how sweetly flows
> That liquefaction of her clothes.
> Next, when I cast mine eyes, and see
> That brave vibration, each way free,
> O, how that glittering taketh me!

The subject of Wright's "A Girl in a Window" is not Julia or her clothes, but it could be. In fact, the ornate diction disguises the reality of the scene: that the speaker is a sort of Peeping Tom who is watching a woman undress in a window:

> Now she will lean away to fold
> The window blind and curtain back,
> The yellow arms, the hips of gold,
> The supple outline fading black,

> Bosom availing nothing now,
> And rounded shadow of long thighs.

The poem concludes in tribute and appreciation:

> Let us return her now, my friends,
> Her love, her body to the grave
> Fancy of dreams where love depends.
> She gave, and did not know she gave.

Wright's poem exhibits Herrick's courtly influence, for surely both poets are pleased by what the scene has given: a glimpse of feminine beauty. Further, Wright more than hints at his Cavalier sources when he assumes an urbane posture and directly addresses his readers as "my friends." Later on, Wright shows the richness of his wit when he turns a deft line break in "the grave / Fancy of dreams where love depends." In closing the poem by returning her body to the dark repository of dreams on which his purely imagined love "depends," Wright indicates that a thinking poet can enjoy this kind of scene without being taken in by it.

Significantly, Wright has at least two direct sources from which to learn the methods and manners of the seventeenth century: his teachers John Crowe Ransom and Theodore Roethke. Both admired the graceful, musical lyrics of the seventeenth century, and they passed on this admiration to their students. George Williamson, not without reason, labels Ransom and the New Critics a "curious example of a group which fled from Imagism and Chicago into the metaphysical seventeenth century."[11] True enough, though his poetic lovers are often refused the union which Herrick's lovers are granted, Ransom at times echoes many topics of Cavalier and metaphysical verse. His "Blue Girls" nearly paraphrases the carpe diem message of Herrick's "To the Virgins, to Make Much of Time":

> Practise your beauty, blue girls, before it fail . . .

It can be argued that even the chiefly British spelling of "practise" provides a clue to Ransom's literary allegiances. Likewise, his "Spectral Lovers" demonstrates both the Cavalier quality of his verse and the kind of dialectic favored by Donne. In the poem, two lovers contemplate a consummation of their love, but confronted with the paralyzing dialectic of honor and passion, the two become "frozen apart in fear." The result is a haunting stasis which leaves the two mere

> . . . spectral lovers,
> White in the season's moon-gold and amethyst,
> Who touch quick fingers fluttering like a bird
> Whose songs shall never be heard.

Ransom's theme of transience in "Blue Girls"and his dialectic suspension of opposites in "Spectral Lovers" are perhaps sources for the same items when they appear in Wright's work, but the musical quality of Wright's poetry comes from his study with Roethke. For Roethke, the true measure of a poem's appeal resides in its auditory textures. In the classroom, Roethke would occasionally read aloud for the entire period, and as Richard Hugo reminds us, Roethke's intentions for doing so were not "intellectual." Hugo, in fact, remembers that Roethke often could not explicate clearly the poems he read aloud, mainly, he believes, because Roethke "so loved the music of language that his complicated emotional responses to poems interfered with his attempt to verbalize meaning."[12] Finally, Hugo recalls most vividly Roethke's love of "verbal play" and his persistent suggestion to young writers: "Write like somebody else" (34).

Roethke's suggestion to seek "true 'imitation' " by writing like "somebody else" carries over into Wright's first two volumes. There, a certain delicacy of phrasing so asserts itself that Samuel Johnson's insistence on poetic diction, on a "system of words and phrases refined from the grossness of domestic use," seems to underlie many of Wright's more elaborate phrasings. In Johnson's neoclassical England, poets were expected to shun common words such as "rat," "cheese," or "milk" in favor of more decorous wordings. The rat, for example, might be a "whiskered vermin." In his first collection, Wright seems equally reluctant to use simple words such as "grapes"; they become, instead, "Mellifluous berries." For that matter, wine itself becomes "that sweet / Cluster of liquors caught in globes" in Wright's adopted language of poetry ("Erinna to Sappho"). Still further, his intention to

clothe simple things in complex, poetic verbiage turns winter snow-
storms into "this frigid season's empty storms" and snowflakes themselves into "flawless hexagons" ("To a Troubled Friend").

Such a strategy can result in a confusion of voices. For instance,
Wright chooses to end "The Seasonless," a poem concerning human
aging, with a question regarding a "lonely" old man in a winter park:

> And why should he, the lost and lulled,
> Pray for the night of vanished lives,
> The days of girls blown green and gold?

Miller Williams credits the final lines to the influence of Eliot; William
Matthews hears echoes of Housman and Frost—but few would see
these as Wright's own.[13] In this case Wright creates a poem of pleasing
music and meter but one in which these elements obscure the peculiar-
ities of his own voice.

Wright learns from these teachers not only the propriety of rhyme
and meter but also a certain decorum of language that stands in
marked contrast to that he had spoken in Ohio. He decides along the
way, it seems, that poets do not speak like the people back home. By
doing so, he may be seeking a bit of freedom from the past, a past
marked by economic necessity so grave that it prevented either of his
parents from continuing in school beyond the eighth grade. To acquire
other manners, to show other talents offers him both an escape and an
accomplishment that his parents can be proud of. In the process, of
course, Wright is also following Roethke's mimetic theory of learning:
"Imitation, conscious imitation, is one of the great methods, perhaps
*the* method of learning to write."[14]

Such decisions, though, involve a further choice regarding the self
presented in his poems— they require a persona somewhat cultured
and urbane, somewhat distanced from the hard-working folk of Martins Ferry. This choice never set well with Wright; the diction and even
the subject matter of *Saint Judas* reveal a tension between the urbane
persona (or mask) and his Ohioan roots. The pressures of this containment become obvious when one compares separate poems of the
collection. Even more remarkably, these pressures cause fluctuations
between the formal and the colloquial within the course of a single

poem, as the first stanza of "Devotions" shows when the speaker returns to the grave of a childhood enemy and remarks:

> I longed to kill you once, when I was young,
> Because you laughed at me before my friends.
>     And now the baffled prose
> Of a belated vengeance numbs my tongue.
>     Come back, before the last wind bends
> Your body to the void beyond repose.

The direct diction of the first two lines contrasts so sharply with the "baffled prose" of the last four that it is hard to imagine the same person speaking both. Note the highly wrought diction of the last four lines and note, also, the resultant lack of clarity. What is "the void beyond repose"? Is it death? If so, would a speaker who wants to "kill" someone be likely to resort to the formality of calling death the "void beyond repose"?

In addition to the confusion which results from such ornate phrasings, Wright occasionally bows to formalism by straining the natural language of his poems to facilitate an orderly rhyme scheme. "A Note Left in Jimmy Leonard's Shack" provides a good example of such an occasion. The poem is supposedly spoken by the kind of youth Wright would have known back in Martins Ferry, for the boy speaks in a mostly colloquial and sometimes profane manner. But rhyme appears to take precedence over the realistic presentation of this voice, and similarly, the voices of Wright's literary fathers take precedence over his own voice as a poet. The speaker and another boy have found Jimmy Leonard's brother dead—or drunk—at the river's edge. Mostly, the boy speaks in a believable, if profane, idiom:

> Well, I'll get hell enough when I get home
>     For coming up this far,

and later,

> Beany went home, and I got sick and ran
>     You old son of a bitch.

But the boy is also able to speak in a way that accommodates the poem's rhyme scheme, as the last line of the second stanza shows:

I hid behind the chassis on the bank,
   The wreck of someone's Ford.
I was afraid to come and wake you drunk;
You told me once the waking up was hard,
The daylight beating you like a board.
   Blood in my stomach sank.

The mere fact that "sank" is chosen to rhyme with "bank" and "drunk" is not an issue. After all, the poem makes use of a formal rhyme pattern, and rhyme, as such, must be regarded as a given. However, this rhyming should not interfere with or alter the boy's manner of speaking; as it is, poetic form dictates that the verb "sank" appear rather unnaturally at the end of the sentence. Surely, "Blood sank in my stomach" is more in keeping with the idiom of the speaker as it is presented elsewhere in the poem.

Athough these examples may seem slight, they reveal Wright's uncertainty about what kind of voice should speak his poems; he wavers from the formal to the colloquial, seemingly without direction. This inconstancy betrays Wright's larger uncertainty about the form he uses to write these poems, for the disparity between the old and new form does not escape him. For Wright, the aesthetic question of choosing between traditional and experimental forms adopts an urgency derived from what can best be described as the question's moral ramifications. This dialectic becomes the topic of one of the more significant poems in *Saint Judas*, "The Morality of Poetry."

The poem is a kind of argument with the self, a debate between traditional "rules of song" and notions of organic form that move naturally "with lunar tides." It is a fine example of the sort of dialogue that Jurij Lotman defines in *The Structure of the Artistic Text* as an internal dialogue taking place between two versions of the self, what Lotman refers to as an earlier and a later version.[15] Because the self is always evolving, in such a poem we see the process of this alteration—the argument—in a temporal framework granted by the poem itself. In "The Morality of Poetry," the speaker argues with himself about the proper means of writing poems: Should he adhere to preset, conventional verse forms, or should he trust to free verse and organic composition in which the poem apparently makes itself as it goes? At root, the question invokes a larger and—for Wright—curiously moral issue. He wonders, Is it a lapse of moral responsibility for the poet to immerse himself in the disorderly pleasures of experience?

"The Morality of Poetry" begins in the past tense. By the opening of the poem, the speaker has been standing on the beach for some while, contemplating the poem's epigraph from Whitman: "Would you the undulation of one wave, its trick to me transfer. . . ." From watching the "sheer outrage" of the constantly moving sea, the speaker has come to decide that those waves (and by expansion all natural processes) represent only a vacant "nothingness," that any aesthetic based on such a "trick" of apparent order is actually disorderly—and poetically irresponsible.

Certain of the necessity for rigorous intellectual and formal control, he sends forth his "rules of song" to Gerald Enscoe, to whom the poem is dedicated:

> Summon the rare word for the rare desire[ . . . ]
> Before you let a single word escape,
> Starve it in darkness; lash it to the shape
> Of tense wing skimming on the sea alone. . . .

When the second ellipsis appears in the poem, it signals a break in the poem's movement. Reflecting on what he had just said, the speaker dismisses it as mere "cold lucidity." Wright's invocation of the word "lucidity" begins to delineate the real topic of the poem, for Wright has fashioned his own version of Charles Altieri's description of the lyricism/lucidity dialectic. He has asked himself: In writing this (or any) poem, should I remain intellectually removed or instead react with intuitive immersion? Moreover, the question Wright is asking expands itself still further, I suppose, to a conflict between the urge to create and communicate intellectualized order and its counterurge to discover and express lyrical perceptions of order.[16]

This point of the poem serves as a sort of fulcrum, and it is no accident that the tense of the poem changes from past to present, for at this juncture, the speaker rejects a poetry of preconception for a poetry of process. Such a process can only be expressed in a present tense awareness of both natural objects and the human self. The speaker, once distant from the "nothingness" of his surroundings, "now" feels immersed in these surroundings, and a competing voice declares his altered perception:

> Mind is the moon-wave roiling on ripples now.
> Sun on the bone-hulled galleons of those gulls
> Charms my immense irrelevance away,
> And lures wings moonward.

This moon, "woman or bird," becomes a spiritual presence and a corrective force, for she causes the speaker to reevaluate his insistence on the supposed superiority of the lucid mode by "flaunting to nothingness the rules I made." Following his intuition (not his rational mind), the speaker decides to "let all measures die" in favor of a more organic means of composition:

> Where the sea moves the word moves, where the sea
> Subsides, the slow word fades with lunar tides.

Although Victoria Harris believes that the speaker concludes the poem in "intellectual control of his lyric . . . in passive articulation about—rather than active participation in—the scene," the poem reveals otherwise.[17] Though the lines remain in iambic pentameter, the speaker, excited to the frenzy of "a mindless dance," discovers a new basis for his work. Its sources are the elements of the natural world (the sun, moon, and waves), given expression in organic form, in the "trick" of the "undulation of one wave." Seemingly from the midst of the sea itself, the speaker's "voice" comes shoreward, partaking of a kind of Dionysian ecstasy that rejects the "intellectual control" which Harris would assign it:

> I send you shoreward echoes of my voice:
> The dithyrambic gestures of the moon,
> Sun-lost, the mind-plumed, Dionysian,
> A blue sea-poem, joy, moon-ripple on wave.

Linking humanity, nature, and a kind of numinous presence in nature, the speaker overcomes the voice of existential separation that colors the poem's opening section. In place of "careful rules of song," he chooses the "dithyrambic gestures of the moon" and gives himself over to the "joy" of imagined unity with nature. Furthermore, the speaker's urge to unify the human and the natural shows itself in the very language he uses; it results in numerous hyphenated nouns such as "sea-poem."

Wright begins to redefine his conception of how one writes poems, and the dialectic—or dialogue—provides the means to do so. The basis of Wright's poem is an awareness of competing or alternative definitions of what true poetry amounts to, definitions that implicitly involve how one writes it. My point is that Wright's poem retains the scaffolding of such an argument and shows us the process of qualification and questioning about the act of writing a poem that might otherwise have been hidden or discarded before publication. And "The Morality of Poetry" is not Wright's only poem that employs this dialogic mode of presentation; many of his poems, both early and late, show this tendency. In fact, "Mutterings over the Crib of a Deaf Child," a dialogic poem to be discussed later in this chapter, reveals quite clearly the conflict between Wright's competing voices of despair and affirmation—one of the central themes of his work throughout his career. An attention to the dialogic imagination at work in Wright's poetry may inform our reading of it, enabling us to see the manner in which he argues matters of aesthetics, ontology, and epistemology through such a format.

I have spent this space detailing the movement of "The Morality of Poetry" because it is at once representative and unique. It reflects the book's tendency to employ a dialectic format, in this instance debating the proper goals of poetry by setting lucidity and lyricism in opposition in Wright's own version of the polarization discussed earlier. Such a move parallels his perhaps less intentional but equally revealing fluctuation between formal and colloquial diction. On the other hand, Wright's questioning of the propriety of formal versification can be seen as an act of insubordination, a refusal to accept Ransom's authoritative pronouncement that only "meters confer upon the delivery of poetry the sense of a ritualistic occasion." According to Ransom's line of thinking, metrical poetry possesses the spiritual and metaphysical power normally associated with religious experience: "The nearest analogue to the reading of poetry according to the meters . . . is the reading of an ecclesiastical service by the congregation." Wright must have been conscious of this purposeful linking of morality and aesthetics. As David Antin has argued, the use of regular meters had become such a moral issue for the fifties that "the loss of meter" became "equivalent to the loss of a whole moral order"—just the sort of issue to which this poem's very title alludes.[18]

*   *   *

By questioning the superiority of a rhetoric of containment that separates the poet from the world and urging instead a rhetoric of immersion derived from direct contact with the experiences of nature, Wright implicitly connects the act of writing poems with the act of living in the present moment—surely a romantic notion. Wright may see the intellectual distance that underlies the "cold lucidity"of containment as isolating the poet from the natural world, thereby preventing the poet from being a participant in it. Given the post-Edenic temper of the day, however, Wright remains fearful of absorption in nature. Not only may such absorption be considered naive, but it may also be assumed untenable in light of Christian doctrine. The Christian fall from grace had seemingly secured a separation of the human and the natural, and to wish otherwise was to subject one's work to charges of juvenilia.

In this way, Wright's deliberations regarding poetic form oddly lend themselves to his most compelling religious themes, evoking questions such as how should a man or woman fallen from God interact with or relate to the natural surroundings? Are intimations of harmony with nature misleading and destructive? For Wright, answers to these questions are hard to come by. First, Wright lacks the romantic zeal which allowed Emerson in "Self-Reliance" to dismiss with aplomb such worries about the possible Satanic source of his intuitions: "They do not seem to me to be such; but if I am the Devil's child, I will live then from the Devil." Second, Wright's version of the containment principle would not often permit him to address these issues in an emotionally charged "mindless dance." On the contrary, Wright relies on the voice of containment derived from his "ferociously perfect" form to provide a safe means of approaching these religious themes.

A splendid example of this technique is the opening poem of *The Green Wall*, "A Fit against the Country,"a poem Steve Orlen astutely labels "British in its reserve," one "about its ideas rather than its experiences."[19] This poem, much like "The Morality of Poetry," can be considered a dialogic text in which two versions of the self argue; however, one voice—that which urges comfort in the natural setting—remains silent or unvoiced even though its impulse to unification clearly provides a basis for the poem's tension. The controlled tension inhering within this unique form of dialogue can be sensed in the opening description of a natural setting carefully detailed in iambic trimeter:[20]

> The stone turns over slowly,
> Under the side one sees
> The pale flint covered wholly
> With whorls and prints of leaf.
> After the moss rubs off
> It gleams beneath the trees,
> Till all the birds lie down.
> Hand, you have held that stone.

> The sparrow's throat goes hollow,
> When the tense air forebodes
> Rain to the sagging willow
> And leaves the pasture moist.
> The slow, cracked song is lost
> Far up and down wet roads,
> Rain drowns the sparrow's tongue.
> Ear, you have heard that song.

> Suddenly on the eye
> Feathers of morning fall,
> Tanagers float away
> To sort the blackberry theft.
> Though sparrows alone are left
> To sound the day, and call
> Awake the heart's gray dolor,
> Eye, you have seen bright color.

Part of the "reserve" that Orlen notes in the poem is surely produced by the "one" of the second line, a way of distancing the poet from the speaker and the speaker from these very experiences. At a safe intellectual distance, the speaker can refer not so much to himself as a composite of mind and body, but to his hand, ear, and eye, that have separately experienced the elements of nature here presented. The poem's use of the past tense is significant. As Madeline DeFrees points out, the "contact of man with nature is always seen in this poem as a completed act, something over and done with."[21] The poet exchanges immediacy for rational intelligence—and for detached rumination couched in a lush poetic diction that dispels the unpleasantness of the poem's theme. This accomplished artifice, for example, finds expression in pleasing off-rhymes such as, down/stone, tongue/song, and dolor/color.

In the fourth stanza, Wright moves closer to his real concern. The speaker, aware of what it means to be "ravished out of thought," recalls what the unvoiced speaker, perhaps the body itself, had been urging all along—a sensual delight in and a tempting allegiance with "the dark tang of the earth":

> Odor of fallen apple
> Met you across the air,
> The yellow globe lay purple
> With bruises underfoot;
> And, ravished out of thought,
> Both of you had your share,
> Sharp nose and watered mouth,
> Of the dark tang of the earth.

However, the speaker addresses all five bodily sensors as if they were somehow isolated from his mind. In doing so, he evinces a profound Cartesian dualism representative of New Critical poetics, a dualism that assumes a distrust of the body and a reliance on objective reason. Even though the speaker's body seems enticed, his mind remains alert and detached from what it sees as a deathly (or devilish) attraction. In fact, the final stanza is nearly a poetic paraphrase of Jonathan Edwards's warning to his Puritan congregation: "This world is all over dirty."

Yet, body, hold your humor
Away from the tempting tree,
The grass, the luring summer
That summon the flesh to fall.
Be glad of the green wall
You climbed across one day,
When winter stung with ice
That vacant paradise.

Perhaps through this form, Wright hopes to balance head and heart in the kind of indissociability of thought and feeling that Eliot finds in Donne. Wright, however, does not maintain this balance, for the poem itself operates on a Cartesian dialectic separating mind and body and subordinates the voice of unification to that of alienation. In the end, Wright has produced a fine poem, though it is a lyric dominated by the containment principle, one which betrays the act of mind necessary for such control and which leaves both poet and speaker estranged from a world of experience. This dependence on intellectual modes for the presentation of religious or emotional subjects is characteristic of the work of the metaphysical poets and the New Critics that influenced not only Wright's early work, but that of Lowell, Jarrell, Eberhart, and a host of others as well. And as George Williamson reminds us, "Metaphysical poetry springs from the attempt to resolve emotional tension by means of intellectual equivalents" (158).

Behind this effort is the Christian notion of the "fall" from "paradise" to which Wright alludes in the poem. Wright's early poems reject the romantic conception of human beings as innately good. Whether by religious orthodoxy or its secular embodiment, nearly all of the writers of this generation deny the state of being that makes Romanticism what it is, that is, the belief that humans can be whole again, or in other words, free of sin. Certainly, Eliot's acceptance of the doctrine of original sin differentiates his version of Modernism from the Romanticism of Whitman, Blake, or his own contemporary, William Carlos Williams. Considered in this light, the New Critics' yearning for objectivity, reason, and impersonality may derive, as Gerald Graff argues, from an overpowering belief in original sin (135). Graff's contention accounts for the New Critical acceptance of Cartesian dualism as the basis for sophisticated art and for its attendant moral suspicion of intuition and the body. Such a distaste for the bodily is evidenced in Roethke's early poem "Epidermal Macabre." Although he would later reshape his attitude considerably, in *Open House* (1941) Roethke makes this pronouncement:

> I hate my epidermal dress,
> The savage blood's obscenity,
> The rags of my anatomy . . .

By expansion, this dissonance between mind and matter can be made to demand a corresponding separation of the mind from the matter and the experience of the natural world. The sense of alienation from nature with which Wright imbues "A Fit against the Country" becomes even more accentuated in other poems of these first two collections. He seems to have acknowledged the elemental sense of difference Ransom states this way in "Agitato ma non troppo":

> I will be brief,
> Assuredly, I know my grief,
> And I am shaken; but not as a leaf.

As one might expect, many of Wright's poems discuss the possibility (or impossibility) of reconciliation between the human and the natural, and these poems, too, often take on religious implications. In Wright's work, the separation from nature is a banishment that achieves its full measure as punishment only when one is most conscious of the loss. As such, human consciousness is more of a punishment than a virtue or reward. Indeed, he often isolates this idea, thereby managing (as Eliot said of Donne) to "arrest it, to play catlike with it, to develop it dialectically."[22] Wright's "The Cold Divinities" illustrates how he uses a subtle dialectic format to address this religious theme. While watching his wife and child play near the sea, one voice of the speaker waxes romantically in his description of the scene. A close reading, however, reveals that this five-stanza celebration is set in the past tense and in the subjunctive mood. Here are key examples:

> I should have been delighted to hear
> The woman and the boy,
> Singing along the shore together,

and later,

> I should have been delighted for the gaze,
> The billowing of the girl,
> The bodying shirt, the ribbons falling.

The past tense phrasings indicate that these incidents have been carefully observed and carefully ordered, shown from the perspective of a later contemplative moment as if a distance from the experience had provided a key to understanding. James Seay describes this method as a "strictly 'logical' ordering of images and ideas after the fact of discovery."[23]

However, the most significant clue to the dialectical or dialogic nature of the poem is its use of the subjunctive mood. No matter what the initial voice of the speaker says he "should have" felt, seen, or heard, the competing voice which ends the poem will elucidate what he really discovered: in this case, the "clear enduring face" of the sea and "her cold divinities of death and change." Elsewhere, Wright provides a useful gloss for this poem, and for that matter, for much of *The Green Wall* and *Saint Judas*. In a review of Robert Penn Warren's *Promises*, he displays his realist's attitude toward nature: "Indeed, what makes reality in nature seem hideous is that it is both alluring and uncontrollable. Once man is committed to it in love, he is going to be made to suffer."[24]

At this point in his career, Wright often views the source of this suffering as humanity's naïve insistence on seeking solace in the natural world, in natural and regenerative process. In "At the Slackening of the Tide," Wright's assumptions seem almost naturalistic in their portrayal of an unconcerned nature. The speaker of the poem has seen "a woman wrapped in rags" helplessly watch her child drown in the ocean. Horrified by what he has witnessed, the speaker looks to the natural world for some consolation. Instead he finds:

> Lonely for weeping, starved for a sound of mourning,
> I bowed my head, and heard the sea far off
> Washing it hands.

This image of nature, much like Pilate, divesting itself of responsibility for human suffering reflects many of the dominant religious themes of Wright's first two collections. Surrounded by an alluring but uncaring natural world, human beings assume an almost Christlike role as victim.

In total, these poems and others like them effectively counter the romantic hopefulness of "The Morality of Poetry." They would appear to bring Wright to an emotional and intellectual dead end. Other than the relief achieved through a suspension of dissonant values within his poems, what comfort can Wright assent to in this world? At this time, he does not accept an Emersonian merging with natural cycle. His poetry seems equally unaccepting of the salvation through Christian redemption that Lowell's "Colloquy in Black Rock" offers; Lowell's kingfisher, echoing Eliot's own fisher king, simply cannot pierce the protection that Wright's irony and detachment provide. It is easy to see why Wright would characterize himself at this point in his literary life as a "miserable son of a bitch."

\*　　\*　　\*

Of course, much of Wright's work reflects the despairing mood of the day, a fashionable despondency that leaves no room for Emersonian optimism. In 1955 R. W. B. Lewis castigated this mode for its overt one-sidedness:

> In it irony has withered into mere mordant skepticism. Irony is fertile and alive; the chilling skepticism of the mid-twentieth century represents one of the modes of death. The new hopelessness is, paradoxically, as simple-minded as innocence. . . .
> (*The American Adam*, p. 196)

Wright, however cut off from the heavenly and the natural, does not permit this skepticism to become deadly in his work. Shunning the narrow constraints of what Dickey in a review of *New Poets of England and America* had nastily labeled "The Outlook," Wright admits the imperfect world of experience into his poems. Side by side with Sappho and the garden of Eden, Wright places murderers, prostitutes, and hunted criminals. The expansive range of this subject matter most certainly drew the attention of Auden, the acknowledged master of the age of angst, who, Louis Simpson asserts, "whatever his predilections" simply could not "overlook the real merits of this work" (459). What compels such attention is another of Wright's poetic acts of insubordination. By forcing his poetry outward to experience and beyond the accepted limits of the dominant mode, Wright begins to fashion a poetry more responsive to the actualities of contemporary existence and less confined by the rhetorical and intellectual strategies of the era.

Wright's decision to address the real events and lives of those not previously considered proper poetic subjects is not naïve Wordsworthianism. In fact, it demands an awareness of our common guilt—another vestige of original sin, no doubt—and mandates the acceptance of social outcasts as a way to overcome it. In "On Minding One's Own Business," his allegiances include:

> All hunted criminals,
> Hoboes . . .
> And girls with rumpled hair.

Later, he willingly embraces those apt to be rejected from society's fold in "Reading a Newspaper on a Beach," a sonnet included in *Amenities of Stone*, the unpublished volume meant to follow *The Green Wall* and *Saint Judas*. There, Wright declares his love for:

> Boys without fingers, ladies without eyes,
> Pale adolescent girls with ruined lives,
> Sots, drudges, snarling dogs and crying wives,
> And men who crumble when a woman cries,
> I know you live. Acknowledgment I make . . .[25]

In a kind of Whitmanian gesture, Wright announces his support for those unsupported by society; for those withheld human brotherhood, he implores God in "American Twilights, 1957":

> Have mercy on man who dreamed apart.
> God, God have pity on man apart.

Although Wright dedicates "American Twilights, 1957" to the convicted murderer Caryl Chessman, he probably has in mind those equally "apart" from society: Betty the prostitute, Maguire the fugitive, Jimmy Leonard the drunkard, or George Doty the murderer. Doty is the subject of two of his most memorable early poems, "A Poem for George Doty in the Death House" (*The Green Wall*) and "At the Executed Murderer's Grave" (*Saint Judas*).

In a provocative act of inclusion (or expansion), Wright offers Doty as a figure representative of all human beings. Considering Doty's isolation behind physical, emotional, and spiritual walls, Wright arrives at a metaphor for the modern human condition. Paradoxically, it offers him, also, a means of breaking out from his own wall of formal and ironic containment, for in "At the Executed Murderer's Grave," his mode of containment begins to give way to a centrifugal urge. Structurally, though the poem still carries the universalist feel of New Critical statement, its manner is personal and direct. Often set in iambic pentameter and laced with an occasional rhymed couplet, the language of the poem is rather spare and rough compared with much of Wright's early work, and it *is* consistent. The poem exemplifies his approach to the sticky moral issues of guilt and innocence and does so without invoking the defensive measures of containment. Though the poem is set in traditional form, its tenor and manner show that form is not necessarily confining, that a formal poem can be expansive and responsive as well.

Furthermore, the apparent confusion in regard to whose voice is speaking this poem never applies. From the first stanza, in fact, from the very first line, it is clear that the speaker is Wright himself, that the "I" of the poem must be identified with the poet:

> My name is James A. Wright, and I was born
> Twenty-five miles from this infected grave,
> In Martins Ferry, Ohio, where one slave
> To Hazel-Atlas Glass became my father.
> He tried to teach me kindness, I return
> Only in memory now, aloof, unhurried,
> To dead Ohio, where I might lie buried
> Had I not run away before my time.
> Ohio caught George Doty. Clean as lime,
> His skull rots empty here. Dying's the best

Of all arts men learn in a dead place.
I walked here once. I made my loud display,
Leaning for language on a dead man's voice.
Now sick of lies, I turn to face the past.
I add my easy grievance to the rest . . .

Wright attends to the matter of Doty's uniqueness by dispelling it altogether. He equates himself with Doty by implying that he, too, might have committed crimes (or sins) punishable by death. Moreover, Wright claims the "past," his Martins Ferry heritage, and does so in the language of that area, not of Augustan England. Note the use of simple but vigorous verbs such as "run," "rots," and "turn"; the brief and understated simile "clean as lime"; and the general lack of elaborate adjectival phrases. Though other versions of the poem were not always so direct, this passage displays a simple, but not simplistic, colloquial diction.[26]

Thematically, "At the Executed Murderer's Grave" presents Wright's own attitude toward the moral ambivalence of the modern world. For if Doty's crimes seem abhorrent to Wright ("Doty, you make me sick"), Wright also admits a human compassion for him:

Doty, if I confess I do not love you,
Will you leave me alone? I burn for my lies.

Wright believes this human compassion to be necessary, though its proper object is the living: "I do not pity the dead, I pity the dying." Later, he reaffirms and clarifies this idea in "I Regret I Am Not Able to Attend," where he says, "True pieties have to do with the living, / Who are afraid."[27]

Wright bases this need for compassion and understanding on two factors. First, nature, though alluring, cannot provide a solution to or any consolation for humanity's existential condition. To romantics, Wright says, "Nature lovers. . . . To hell with them." Second, Wright believes it foolish to impose labels of guilt and innocence on human beings, for we share in a flawed humanity. In "The Accusation," he calls this moral egalitarianism the "scarred truth of wretchedness." The truth, as Wright sees it, is that we all contain a bit of Doty. When he is enveloped by the "last sea" on the judgment day,

Wright asserts that "they could not mark my face / From any murder-er's." By accepting his own faults and reminding us of ours, Wright proposes that humans should view with considerable humility the flaws of others; we are of the same "Dirt of . . . flesh."

Later on, the sonnet "Saint Judas" insists on this attitude, for it finds the capacity for selfless acts even in the most hated of humans, Judas, the betrayer of Christ. For after he had "bargained the proper coins, and slipped away," Judas came upon a "victim beaten, / Stripped, naked, and left to cry." Moved to compassion, Judas "held the man for nothing in my arms." The figure of Judas that Wright imagines is not the one we have come to expect—a vile, self-centered man who gives in to weakness. Instead Judas is capable of an apparently selfless act; he is capable of extending human compassion. "Banished from heaven" as he was, Judas could not hope to gain spiritual redemption, yet he per-forms a humanly redemptive act by holding the man "for nothing"— not even, we take it, for money. The apocryphal story reveals more about Wright than Judas. In his view, the resonance of human guilt and innocence tends to be muted, so that Doty, Chessman, and even Judas become representative figures capable of instructing us all in the reality of being human. Thus, the answer to a portion of the epigraph to *Saint Judas*—"They answered and said unto him, Thou was alto-gether born in sin, and dost thou teach us?"—is simply, yes.

That Wright is able to reach such a resolution within a sonnet dem-onstrates that the form itself need not become a containment device, a means of protecting the vulnerable self. It is not the supposed con-straint of form but rather how the poet chooses to operate within it that achieves enclosure—or expansion. Clearly, the expansiveness of his early work is evident in the internal form of the poem itself. Wright's playfulness with form creates a sonnet more expressive of his own personality, yet one that works within an established mode. By manipulating the internal form of the poem to the advantage of increased expansiveness, Wright causes the poem's effect to be predi-cated largely on a reversal of expectations, on the irony that exists between the common image of Judas and that of the poem—a "Saint" who performs a compassionate deed despite the fact that it will do him no monetary or spiritual good. The poem postulates that even in the worst of us, flawed and given over to evil, there exists a redemptive element, human compassion. Therefore, Wright employs irony, a standard tactic of New Critical poetics, to link Judas with the remainder of humanity, to unify not contain, to establish commonality not difference.

Much of Wright's early work mediates between the disparate poles of human limitation and human possibility. Most often, the voice of limitation subordinates or altogether silences its counter, as evidenced by several of the poems discussed in this chapter. But one poem, in particular, provides a clue to Wright's changing personal attitudes and demonstrates the kind of affirmation that will characterize his late work. "Mutterings over the Crib of a Deaf Child," written in iambics and rhymed in a formal pattern, is composed of alternating stanzas of intense dialogue (or perhaps argumentation) between two distinctively different voices of the self. While the speaker apparently stands above the child's crib, one of the speaker's competing voices bemoans both the limited life available to such a child and the difficulties the parents will encounter merely caring for it. The second voice, however, counters each familiar argument about the child's inability to hear the school bell ringing or his mother's voice calling him to breakfast with a patient explanation of how the child will learn to make do with his diminished resources. Finally, the first voice, clearly exasperated, concludes with the question: "But what will you do if his finger bleeds? / Or a bobwhite whistles invisibly / And flutes like an angel off in the shade?"

To this, the second voice, echoing the tone of Wright's late work, responds with a Keatsian acceptance. He seems confident that natural beauty and human solace—however often unseen or unheard—may be felt through "the skin,"through a compassionate human touch:

> He will learn pain. And as for the bird . . .
> I will putter as though I had not heard,
> And lift him into my arms and sing
> Whether he hears my song or not.

In coming to terms with the various manifestations of separateness issuing from original sin, Wright finds a way out of the narrow skepticism that Lewis denigrates and discovers a means to escape from the poetics of containment that had protected him from the dangers of experience and from its rewards. In "Erinna to Sappho" he is moved to say that the "ditch of earth" and the human body are "where we belong, if anywhere." This kind of resolution, coupled with that of "Mutterings," shows Wright moving toward an acceptance of what Keats described as "Negative Capability": "I mean Negative Capability, that is, when a man is capable of being in uncertainties, mysteries, doubts, without any irritable reaching after fact and reason."

Wright will continue to explore the possibilities of the dialogic text, a poetry that incorporates the competing voices of the self within the spatial and temporal boundaries of a single poem. As he matures, however, the thematic resolution of these poems will more often resemble "Mutterings over the Crib of a Deaf Child" than "A Fit against the Country." On the dust jacket of *Saint Judas* Wright had announced, "To me poetry in this age is the act of stating and examining and evaluating the truth." This effort leads him to an awareness of the human condition that need not resolve itself in a static suspension of opposites within the poem—or in utter despair.

A function of Wright's achieving Negative Capability will be his renewed exploration of other forms, other voices, other possibilities for poetic expression. Wright is surely a restless poet whose style and approach undergo continual self-evaluation. Many critics believe that Wright simply rejects the conventional poetics of Herrick, Jonson, and Donne, that he in some vague way passes beyond them. It is more accurate, both to Wright and to that literary tradition, to argue that he subsumes this tradition within his expanding embrace of poetic possibility. Wright has begun, though tentatively and perhaps in small measure, to develop the individual relationship to literary tradition that will mark his best work throughout his career. A poetry of containment based on the balance of dissonant forces—like that which Wright fashions after Ransom and the New Critics—is one way of dealing with religious themes of separation and loss. There are others. Though the voices of these poets make themselves heard occasionally throughout Wright's career, he does not return to the use of irony, paradox, and the dialectic as a means of protection and detachment. Unlike Ransom, whose poetry Allen Tate believes operates on the assumption of the "vulgarity of the present and the purity of the past," Wright does find value—if not purity—in the present.[28] Much like Lowell, Wright explores the present moment with his eyes open to new opportunities and new sources for expression.

## 3   A Redefinition of the Poetic Self:
*Amenities of Stone*

Readers and critics of James Wright have been left with two options as they hope to understand the marked changes that occur between the traditional poems of *Saint Judas* (1959) and the free-verse image poems of *The Branch Will Not Break* (1963). One can pore over *Saint Judas* and count unmetered lines, look for instances of colloquial language (they do exist), and circle images striking for their beauty and imagination. This kind of textual comparison seeks to find early indications of Wright's eventual movement to a lyrical and metrically free style. The second option involves looking for answers in the particulars of Wright's poetic relationship with Robert Bly and in his poetry translations, especially those of Georg Trakl, whose work he came across while on a Fulbright Fellowship in Vienna during 1952–53. The first of these options possesses inherent textual limitations, and the second, while more promising, has not worn well with some critics, such as William Matthews, who have tired of its familiar "story" about Wright's *The Branch Will Not Break* that revolves around the influences of Trakl and Bly.[1]

Fortunately, there now exists a third choice, one informed and aided by the discovery of Wright's unpublished book-length manuscript *Amenities of Stone*. Recently uncovered among Wright's various papers, *Amenities of Stone* falls chronologically between *Saint Judas* and *The Branch Will Not Break*, that period which has drawn so much critical attention. Accepted in 1961 by Wesleyan University Press, *Amenities* illuminates the nature of Wright's poetic transition between *Saint Judas* and *Branch*.

An emphasis on Wright's evident movement from traditional forms, from rhyme and meter, and from a dependence on irony and paradox deflects attentions from more fundamental changes in his attitude toward himself as a poet and toward what poetry should reach for. *Amenities* shows Wright in the process of a redefinition of poetic self, a redefinition which involves the search for a true lyric voice free of rhetorical niceties, the reevaluation of the relationship between the poet and a world of natural objects, and the acceptance of the intuitive mind as a source of meaning and order. Certainly, Wright at that time dropped the trappings of rational intelligence as Robert Bly has noted,[2] but this detachment from poetry dominated by reason assumes a larger and more pervasive alteration in Wright's poetics. The poet of wit and reason attempts to impose order on his world; the poet of the arational imagination seeks only to perceive order, trusting to numinous relationships among natural objects. For James Wright, *Amenities of Stone* documents this process of transition.

Though his early work was lauded by W. H. Auden and Thom Gunn among others, Wright was excoriated by some who found only limitations in his traditional style. Wright, apparently, did not let these castigations go unnoticed. He reacted with a string of letters to James Dickey when Dickey's review of the anthology *New Poets of England and America* (1957) relegated him to dubious membership in the poetic "School of Charm."[3]

Furthermore, in September of 1960, Wright scrawled on a tentative table of contents for an earlier manuscript version of *Amenities*, entitled *Now I Am Awakened*, a bibliographic citation for Richard Foster's article "Debauched by Craft: Problems of the Younger Poets."[4] Foster's stinging assessment of *New Poets of England and America* attacks the choice of traditional poems in which a heavy dose of rhyme, metrics, wit, and poetic mannerism clouds honesty and meaning. In particular, Foster cites Wright's work as mere "exercises in 'style'—in tone, diction, even metrics." He further singles out Wright's "To the Ghost of a Kite" for the "pompous and heavy poetic mannerisms it affects" (9). Reading Dickey and Foster, as Wright did, would surely have intensified his own doubts about his past work.

Doubting a poem's worth was not uncommon for Wright. He was not one easily satisfied with what he produced, be it a single poem or a collection of verse. Between 1959 and 1963 Wright did not work on *Amenities* alone; in fact, he tinkered with no less than six separate manuscripts in that period, placing side by side and in myriad combinations some 113 different poems in that four-year span.[5] Various tables of contents reveal that twenty-eight of the forty-five poems in *Branch* originate as early as the previously mentioned 1960 manuscript, *Now I Am Awakened*, and the March 1961 draft of *Amenities*. Thus, it would seem Wright's struggle was equally a matter of learning to write in some new style and a slow process of eliminating from his manuscript those poems that did not stylistically cohere with the deep image poems which later formed the crux of *Branch*.

What Anne Wright found amongst the collected cardboard boxes of James Wright was a typescript of sixty-seven poems divided into three sections. Numerous handwritten and typed tables of contents give account of Wright's endless reworking of that manuscript. A second draft of *Amenities* dated 5 March 1961 and prefaced by a handwritten title page and table of contents appears to be the version accepted by Wesleyan for publication and release in January 1962. But that was not to be.

This March 1961 draft of *Amenities*, forefather as it is of *Branch*, displays Wright's awareness of his changing poetic style. Two of *Amenities*'s three sections consciously separate metered and free-verse poems. The first section of fourteen poems, subtitled "Academic Poems," is mostly rhymed and metrically regular (and contains two sonnets).[6] Only two poems from this section appear later in *Branch*, both greatly revised.[7] Forty-eight poems compose the second section, "Explorations," from which over twenty would be included later in *Branch*. Wright added a third grouping of five poems, subtitled "Fictitious Voices," though none of these survives in *Branch*.

*Amenities of Stone* reflects the ferment of American poetry some twenty-five years ago. In *Amenities* Wright's traditional poems, which bear an "orthodoxy" Donald Hall believed derived from Eliot and the New Critics, confront those of a "new kind of imagination" seeking to establish itself preeminent in contemporary poetics.[8] For James Wright, who admits remarking to his publisher after *Saint Judas*, "I don't know what I'm going to do after this, but it will be completely different," *Amenities* reveals the specifics of this "completely different" poetic stance.[9] Though *Amenities* shows Wright's gradual disassociation from the poetry of rhyme, meter, and paradox, it more importantly discloses his reassessment of the role and function of the poet: The poet has become an equal in a world of natural objects—his or her function is not to impose order but rather to perceive it. A look at the poems of *Amenities of Stone* supports these contentions.

The early Wright stood not on the shoulders of but side by side with the poets of a previous generation. His first two books, *The Green Wall* (1957) and *Saint Judas* (1959), represent an extension of prevailing New Critical aesthetics, and the poems of the "Academic" section of *Amenities* are of the same vein. For example, "The Thieves" makes use of contraries to provide meaning informed by rational intelligence. The initial stanza sets both the scene and the essential irony:

> Now let the summer die, for those
> Lean ponies nibbling under boughs
> Will fleshen over ground and plump
> The silken shoulder and the rump.
> Thieving the orchard, they invade
> The earth, to ply the ancient trade
> Of living while the seasons die;
> They whinny at the evening sky.[10]

In eight lines of iambic tetrameter, Wright juxtaposes an earth moving toward a kind of death with the two ponies going about "the ancient trade / Of living." Everything in the scene conspires toward a mood of bleakness and death—except for the two ponies. The "seasons die," but these thieves, or so we think of them, fatten themselves for winter "over ground" (pointedly not underground). In them life seems oblivious to an encircling death. The poem further intensifies its irony:

> Oh, soon enough some man will come
> And curse the fence, and drive them home.
> Then, neighing softly through the night
> The mare will nurse her shoulder bite.
> Yet, lightly fair, through lock and mane,
> She gazes over the dusk again,
> And sees the gathering stallion leap
> In grass for apples half-asleep.

He stands alight on slender knees,
Lithe in his winter dream of trees.
Apples will fall and fall this day,
And wind will brush the rinds away.
Yet light is left before the snow,
And apples hang on sprays so low
His mouth can reach them, small and sweet,
And some are tumbling to her feet.

Of course, the thieves' brief pleasure will be ended by the owner of the orchard; limits and fences will again be imposed. But for now, in a time of abundant harvest, apples fall and revitalize with their death the still blossoming lives of the ponies. Up to this point the irony is predictable; however, the last stanza underscores who the real thieves are:

The living flourish still. His haunch
Rears in delight beneath the branch,
Where now, for her delicate sake,
The wires drag and the fences break.
Beyond the fence the summer grieves,
But only wind and snow are thieves,
Marauders sacking fruit and thief
To the last wilderness of leaf.

Whereas the title and the first stanza would have us believe the ponies are thieves stealing in the "trade of living," the real thieves—wind and snow—will soon reduce both apples and thieves to nothing. Ironically, the true thieves of this poem (and of the world in general) prove to be the passage of time and its agents, the wind and snow. Irony, a rational element, provides the tension upon which the poem operates.

In working his way through *Amenities* to *The Branch Will Not Break*, Wright eventually dealt with such poems of tension, irony, and rational thinking simply by discarding them. Such poems seemed aesthetically out of place among the deep image poems which compose *Branch*. Devoted to its theme but troubled by its rhetorical excess, Wright worked and reworked "The Thieves," at one point angrily noting on a February 27, 1960, draft of the poem: "The last stanza is still not quite right. Cut out all the abstractions like 'The living flourish,' and clarify—i.e. purify—the grammar. . . ." Significantly, by No-

vember 24, 1961, he had begun not only to "purify" the language of
the poem but also to think of himself as sharing the orchard with the
two horses; he tried numerous titles meant to indicate his sense of
unity with them, for example: "The Thieves All Meet at the Same
Moment in an Orchard" and "The Thieves Are Gathered Together in
the Orchard." Still, clearly frustrated by the lengthy and unwieldly
process of revising the poem, he also, "late at night," began to believe
that "the solution is probably to *omit* this poem entirely."

Nevertheless, only two days later, November 26, 1961, Wright was
able to rescue "The Thieves" by eliminating its ironic message, and
instead, focusing on the interconnectedness of the human and natural
worlds. Titled "Two Horses Playing in the Orchard," this revised version of "The Thieves" appears later in *Branch* as the only rhymed poem
in the collection.[11] Because the poem is rhymed and metrically regular,
it would seem ostensibly out of place among the free-verse, image
poems of *Branch*. However, its similarity lies not in form but rather in
its attitude toward nature, in its way of looking at a world of other and
equal objects. Further, the looseness and playfulness of the altered
title reflects Wright's movement away from the well-wrought poem
and its necessary sampling of irony.

In the *Branch* version, the first stanza vanishes entirely—and with it
the ironic premise of the poem. The second and third stanzas of the
original, here the first and second, are substantially unchanged. It is
the third (final) stanza that clearly elucidates Wright's changing allegiances. In *The Green Wall*, a spiritual or emotional wall separates humankind from nature; here Wright acknowledges and rejoices in his
connection with it:

> Too soon a man will scatter them,
> Although I do not know his name,
> His age, or how he came to own
> A horse, an apple tree, a stone.
> I let those horses in to steal
> On principle, because I feel
> Like half a horse myself, although
> Too soon, too soon, already. Now.[12]

The speaker so identifies with the horses that he lets them in "to steal" their brief pleasures until they are driven from the orchard, a kind of Eden with similar consequences. Feeling "like half a horse" himself, the speaker likewise faces a perfunctory eviction from the world of the living; that is the basis of commonality between them. Rather than the discursive manipulation of irony shown in "The Thieves," the speaker in "Two Horses" makes use of intuited feeling to disclose a union between humankind and nature.

Wright's evolving poetic stance, then, would seem to have less to do with dropping the supposed encumbrance of rhyme and meter and more with reevaluating the relationship of humanity and nature. That Wright groups his rhymed and metered work under an "Academic" heading says one thing, but that he also includes free-verse and un-rhymed poems in this section says quite another. What distinction does Wright make between academic and nonacademic poems? Another poem from the "Academic" section of *Amenities*, "I Regret I Am Unable to Attend," offers a helpful reference point:

> True pieties have to do with the living,
> Who are afraid.
> I think the dead, if they feel anything,
> Feel just fine. They would just as soon
> Be left alone,
> Thank you. They have enough of a good thing.
>
> So I am not coming back there
> (At 3 p.m. Aug. 22 dark suits please)
> When you plant her.
> I think I am afraid of the dark deputies
> Who are always taking down names and addresses
> In the county boneyard
> Of my hell, where my friends, such as they were,
> Are.

What makes "I Regret I Am Unable to Attend" unacceptable to the poet of *Branch* lies in the internal mechanics of the poem. With the

exception of "dark deputies," the poem is expressed in lucid and expo-
sitional language foreign to the lyric speaker of, say, "A Blessing."
Wright flirts with colloquialisms such as "plant" and "boneyard," but
the speaker seems more at home with the "true pieties" of a discursive
voice. In fact, rational intellect predominates the poem. That the
speaker twice repeats "I think" is just the point. All meaning emerges
from the poet as thinker, former, and shaper.

The poem is that of a New Critic in all but its external form. Wit, not
image or imagination, orders it. Thus, its internal form, the manner of
its development is essentially rational. When the poet as thinker crafts
such witticisms as the wordplay between "were" and "are," thinking
man becomes *poeta sapiens*. The poem is what the poet thinks.

Wright distinguishes "I Regret" as an academic poem not for its
outer form, but rather for its inner mode of development, for its rational underpinnings. Some distinction, therefore, need be made between internal and external form, as the above poems indicate. *Amenities* shows Wright gradually eschewing the role of logical orderer for
that of intuitive perceiver, and a further comparison of poems from its
"Academic" and "Explorations" sections can help delineate this movement.

In a *Paris Review* interview in 1975, Wright told Peter Stitt that he
regarded himself "primarily as a craftsman, as a Horatian."[13] Wright's
characterization of himself as a classicist finds support in a poem such
as "To a Shy Girl," a sonnet from the "Academic" section of *Amenities*.
Written in iambic pentameter and Italian in format, the sonnet off-
rhymes through a strained *abab, cdcd, efgefg* scheme and displays the
fancified language and rhetoric of an English tradition—not of
Wright's native Ohio:

> I see the broken hooves of fire decline
> Out of your hair, as fawns in running trees
> Dapple a grove and fade in sudden sun.
> Water and redwing fix a broken gaze.
> I see the breath of forest air dissolve
> Out of your bones, as I have come upon
> Femur and skull in fern the hunters leave:
> Nearly so frail as you, frail skeleton.

Your bones so light, your hair so near to fire,
The lashes limp as rain, the hands so small,
Your fingers flutter back to you like plumes.
Now, though your small mouth quicken out of fear,
I lean to touch you, but my fingers fail:
I cannot hold the mountain in my arms.

Simile dominates the poem. The girl's hair shines "as fawns in running trees," her lashes are "limp as rain," and her fingers "flutter . . . like plumes." The poet describes the girl's small body through mental comparisons easily rendered in simile. Moreover, the diction presents these comparisons in luxurious terms, replete with "fawns" and "dapple" groves. These images result from the rational associations of a classic, gentrified speaker trying to explain what he sees through what he thinks.

More striking, though, is the artifice consciously at work in the poem. The somewhat surprising ending exists as such only because—from the beginning—the poet asks the reader to chance the final leap, a leap not of imagination but rather of conscious intelligence, one carefully prepared for by the craftsmanship that precedes it. That in the end the speaker paradoxically cannot lift this "slight" child reveals the poem as an artifact fashioned by irony and paradox, in which an imposed order and meaning reside.

"To a Shy Girl" and other poems like it did not survive to appear in *Branch*. These purely rational and highly rhetorical poems seemed so fixed and constraining that after *Saint Judas* Wright himself said he felt he "had come, for personal but also for artistic reasons, to something like a dead end."[14] Perhaps he received a clue to the source of his discontent through his association with Robert and Carol Bly. As is common with Wright, who kept honest and meticulous notes on the drafts of many poems during this intensely productive period, his comments on a worksheet for the poem fragment "Two Images of One Place" reveal his own conception of his poetic problems: "It occurs to me that my first . . . letter to the Blys was a cry of longing: 'What must I do to be saved?' Answer: 'Cut the rhetoric.' Okay, I fight on."[15]

One way to accomplish this was through his translations of Pablo Neruda, Federico García Lorca, Cesar Vallejo, and Georg Trakl and

through his artistic collaborations with the Blys. Gradually, Wright
came to realize "that the tradition of poetry which I had tried to master, and in which I had come to a dead end, was not the only one. . . .
that poetry is a possibility, that, although all poetry is formal, there are
many forms, just as there are many forms of feeling."[16] The shape of
his future work would resemble "Twilights" more than "To a Shy
Girl."

> The big stones of the cistern behind the barn
> Are soaked in whitewash.
> My grandmother's face is a small maple leaf
> Pressed in a secret box.
> Locusts are climbing down into the dark green crevices
> Of my childhood. Latches click softly in the trees.
> Your hair is gray.
>
> The arbors of the cities are withered.
> Far off, the shopping centers empty and darken.
>
> A red shadow of steel mills.

Of course, rhyme and meter have vanished. So have irony and
paradox—the tenets of New Critical aesthetics. Robert Bly in his essay
"The Work of James Wright" has noted the disappearance of these
accoutrements of discursive reasoning. But that is not the entire point.
A more fundamental transition has occurred in Wright's poetic sensibility: Gone is his insistence on imposing order and fixing meaning.
The poet has taken on the role of perceiver not rational orderer, and
the poem's voice, the source of its images, and its manner of exposition
display this newly defined poetic self.

Certainly, the common language of the poem is closer to Wright's
own than the gentrified speaker of "To a Shy Girl." Wright said later in
"Many of Our Waters: Variations on a Poem by a Black Child" (*Collected
Poems*, 206–12) that "The kind of poetry I want to write is / The poetry
of a grown man." To do so necessitated speaking like one. *Amenities of
Stone* shows Wright learning to trust in the music of natural speech.

In a poem such as "Twilights," the basic element, however, becomes
the image, not diction or tone. The relaxed language allows an expres-

sion of meaning solely through image, and it is here that Wright's redefinition most startles the reader. The opening presentation of the whitewashed stones "of the cistern behind the barn" perhaps leads the reader to expect another imagist piece, another red wheelbarrow beside white chickens. But Wright's images insist on intertwining the inner and outer worlds. They are not content with merely painting pictures.

Wright mingles internal and external reality in deep images that transcend a subject-object dichotomy. His "grandmother's face is a small maple leaf / Pressed in a secret box" of his memory. Locusts crawl down "into the dark green crevices" of his childhood recollections. Thus, the speaker feels so immersed in these remembered images that temporal distance subsides and his grandmother appears so near he can say to her, "Your hair is gray."

A distance between an object and a person ruminating about that object predicates the poetry of wit and reason. That a person should think rationally requires such separation. But poems similar to "Twilights" admit of no such detachment because the natural world imaginatively interpenetrates the inner and emotional life of the poet. As in "Two Horses Playing in the Orchard," human being and object are equals in a poetic stance that will not tolerate a subject-object dichotomy.

Further, the final two stanzas of "Twilights" are composed entirely of images without a carefully threaded narrative to supply a logical movement from one form of twilight to another. Meaning surfaces intuitively through these deep images: the pastness of youth, the diminishment of rural life in the face of "shopping centers" and "A red shadow of steel mills," the industrial age. When Robert Kelly partially defined deep-image poetry by saying, "The fundamental rhythm of the poem is the rhythm of the images," he no doubt had in mind a poem that develops in the manner of "Twilights."[17]

This mode of reaching understanding signals a poetry of and about process. The poem unfolds as an act itself; its truth lies in awareness through process. Unlike "To a Shy Girl," the poet of "Twilights" has not presupposed the poem's intended conclusion. When W. H. Auden said that "rhyme, meters, stanza forms, etc. are like servants" which secure "an orderly household," he spoke as much for a generation of formalists as for himself.[18] In *Amenities,* James Wright, whom Auden had chosen as the 1957 Yale Series of Younger Poets award winner, has begun to turn away from poetry as a rational construct of imposed order and, instead, has freed himself to explore a poetry of possibility.

That is not to say Wright never met failure in his exploration of this poetry of possibility. As the earlier quotation from Wright suggests, all poetry—even that which is supposedly "free"—is formal. Wallace Stevens believed that every poem is essentially experimental. Surely Wright, as every other poet, occasionally botched an experiment.

"Written during Illness," a poem from the "Explorations" section of *Amenities,* is just such a poem. Wright apparently agreed; he chose to omit it from *Branch.*

> I look out the window.
> Two starlings mutter in a half-bare maple tree.
> Underneath, a girl sits, alone, her calves folded
> Neatly under her.
> She tastes her pencil thoughtfully,
> And gazes across the lawn as the trees
> Turn gray with twilight.
> I touch my face with my hand,
> And turn to arrange my books. It is the end
> Of summer at last, and the sun entirely gone.
> My hair
> Is turning gray.

The poem vacillates between an intrusive speaker's narrative sign-posting and a simple listing of images, and that vacillation betrays a central weakness of the poem: The speaker cannot decide whether to provide a structure for what he sees or simply to let that scene speak for itself. "I look out the window" accomplishes nothing but its offering of a narrative framework for the subsequent images. That the speaker sees takes precedence over what he sees; the image does not tell its own story.

In September 1960 Wright noted at the bottom of a tentative table of contents for his unpublished book, *Now I Am Awakened,* "Restrict yourself to one or two pronouns in every poem." He was, perhaps, reacting against the misuse of the personal pronoun. Much of the new poetry displayed a debilitating egoism in its absorbing concern with the "I" of the poem. In his new poetry, Wright sought to avoid this self-absorption and its elevation of the speaker to the level of seer, thinker, and most importantly, orderer. In "Written during Illness," he seems to fail.

Just as the reader of this poem becomes interested in the girl and the descending twilight as objects in themselves, the speaker interrupts to redirect the poem to other concerns—his face and his books. This reminder of what the topic of the poem is (the speaker and not the girl) makes the supposedly jarring ending rather logically predictable. The speaker's aging is no surprise, coming as it does on the heels of the twilight and the end of summer. The use of too many pronouns and a corollary elevation of seer over what is seen imply too great a dependence on the "I think" mode of "I Regret I Am Unable to Attend." Wright is not yet ready, or perhaps not yet skillful enough in his new form, to allow image alone to convey meaning.

But this is no denigration of Wright. "Written during Illness" and "I Regret" demonstrate there is more to the new poetry than simply its free-verse structure. Internal form, a poem's manner of development must also change from the rational to the intuitive. Wright's "Lying in a Hammock at William Duffy's Farm in Pine Island, Minnesota" supports this contention. The poem appears in *Amenities* exactly as it does later in *Branch*:

> Over my head, I see the bronze butterfly,
> Asleep on the black trunk,
> Blowing like a leaf in green shadow.
> Down the ravine behind the empty house,
> The cowbells follow one another
> Into the distances of the afternoon.
> To my right,
> In a field of sunlight between two pines,
> The droppings of last year's horses
> Blaze up into golden stones.

> I lean back, as the evening darkens and comes on.
> A chicken-hawk floats over, looking for home.
> I have wasted my life.

In "Lying in a Hammock" every pronoun (until the final one) emphasizes not the seer but the object seen. For example, the physical beauty of the sleeping butterfly is no less important than the human act of seeing it; natural beauty and the perception of beauty are equals.

The speaker's attention to the seemingly spiritual orderliness of the natural world brings him, then, to a discomfitting realization. The butterfly which seems made of precious bronze and the horse droppings which "blaze up into golden stones" appear capable of marvelous transformations that elude the speaker. Unlike the hawk "looking for home" (not "a home," but simply "home," implying one exists), the speaker has no emotionally secure center, only a swinging hammock at someone else's farm. In the face of such natural almost spiritual order, the speaker journeys to what Bly calls a "wounded area."[19] In a world of apparent order and meaning, a speaker who feels bereft of both could painfully conclude, "I have wasted my life."

The poem unfolds without logical connectors to explain the significance of the presented images. Its structure is alogical and arational—a kind of stream of consciousness process of awareness. "Written during Illness" and "Lying in a Hammock" share a similar outer form, and each concludes with a statement of expanded awareness that the speaker has garnered from attention to his surroundings. But unlike "Written during Illness," "Lying in a Hammock"makes use of a different internal form in which meaning emerges only through a series of images, a meaning informed by imagination and intuition.

"Lying in a Hammock" represents Wright's effort to transcend a subject-object dichotomy. This effort is reminiscent of Emerson's *Nature* (1836) as a way of seeing natural facts as emblems of a desirable and parallel order in humanity. Here, Wright shares Emerson's belief in nature as purveyor of lesson and model. In "Lying in a Hammock," transient happenings inform the speaker's immanent revelation, for the poet lives in and with a natural world in which he perceives, not imposes, order and meaning.

This disparity between his traditional work and his new style did not escape Wright; his separation of the "Academic" poems from those of "Explorations" indicates as much. Furthermore, the four-year span between *Saint Judas* and *The Branch Will Not Break* may be accounted for in Wright's wrestling with the obvious dichotomy which surfaces in the poems of *Amenities of Stone*, that is, how to reconcile placing a poem such as "To a Shy Girl" in the same book as, say, "Twilights."

Thus, Wright confronted the dilemma of how to deal with such a marked change in his work. Retrospect tells us that Wright chose to make a clean break from the poetry of his past by suppressing *Amenities* and including in *Branch* only those poems of the new format. But *Amenities* shows that he contemplated at least one other option: to provide a more or less graceful transition between his variant styles by combining them in one book, thus underscoring a continuity more than a fragmentation of stylistics. "His Farewell to Old Poetry," an unpublished poem from *Amenities*, documents Wright's attempt to do so.

Intended to bid his solemn good-bye to the tradition of poetry that had up to that time served him well, "His Farewell to Old Poetry" was to be placed either in the final section "Fictitious Voices" or on the flyleaf of *Amenities*. (See page 212.) But Wright once considered an even more audacious role for "His Farewell." On a 1961 draft of the poem, he wrote a note to himself that questioned whether his "Farewell to Poetry" should be "written in *prose?*" and concluded by urging, "try it."[20] The radical gesture of printing in prose his good-bye to poetry must have seemed appealing and ironic to Wright, especially since the poem mourns the disappearance of "All the old echoes" that had inspired his early, classicist work. By June 1961, however, he had scrapped that idea in favor of a more traditional form, nearly an elegy, that begins with a brief epigraph from *Tristam Shandy* lamenting the uncontrollable passage of days *"more precious . . . than the rubies."*

### His Farewell to Old Poetry
*more precious . . . than the rubies*

I have been here, alone, all afternoon,
Dreaming, of maple leaves I walked beneath
Some years ago, with Philip Timberlake,
Who is dead. We paused together once beside

The Ohio river flowing past the town
Of Marietta, where the trees, he said,
Held in green shadows many noblest men,
And we might hear their voices quietly.
Now he is buried, but he was the first
To tell me how the Muse survived in trees.
Now I must leave you, Jenny of strange names,
Jenny of maple leaves. . . .

Philip Timberlake, Wright's teacher at Kenyon College (to whom *Saint Judas* was dedicated), first introduced Wright to the "many noblest men" of English tradition that influenced Wright's early work; for Wright, their voices and "the Muse survived in trees." Here, for the first of many times, Wright invokes Jenny, a woman of "strange names" (one of which is surely the muse) who represents in this instance the classical tradition of poetry. When Jenny the muse had "Vanished without goodbye," her absence precipitated a further disappearance:

2

Jenny, Sir Walter Ralegh and John Donne
Brood in the trees, but they say nothing now.
They sang delicate melodies to your voice
When I was young, but now I grant them rest . . .

The poets of an English, classicist tradition "say nothing now," a matter that the speaker later attributes to his inability to hear the muse Jenny:

Now that I cannot hear your voice, I lose
All the old echoes, Jenny, maple leaf.

Thus cut off from the muse, the speaker turns from the poetry of a beloved past and concludes with a brief but emotional third section that includes the book's title. These lines, some of which appear also in "Three Letters in One Evening" (another poem from *Amenities*), curiously surface eleven or so years later in "October Ghosts," a poem addressed to Jenny in Wright's *Two Citizens* (1973):

3

Now my amenities of stone are done,
God damn me if I care whether or not
Anyone hears my voice, now you will not.
We came so early, we thought to stay so long.
But it is already midnight, and we are gone.
I know your face the loveliest face I know.
Now I know nothing, and I die alone.

It would seem that Wright had contemplated what would be "completely different" in his poetry and concluded, not without struggle, that his "amenities of stone were done," that the smooth and decorous veneer of formal poetics had become, finally, so inflexible and constraining as to resemble stone. Without the muse, without Timberlake or Donne or the tradition they represent, Wright laments, "Now I know nothing, and I die alone."

By the time these lines appear in "October Ghosts," Wright will have further evolved as a poet. He will have accomplished the unlearning he refers to in a letter to Madeline DeFrees as "leaping outside of every technical trick I had learned."[21] In *Two Citizens*, a book acknowledged by many critics as the fruition of Wright's movement to common language, Wright pointedly ends "October Ghosts": "Now I know nothing, I can die alone."[22] Eleven years more work will enable Wright to complete his technical unlearning. The slightly revised line displays his feeling of emancipation; Wright the formalist now "*can* die alone" (emphasis added). Donne and Ralegh can lie at peace.

Although Wright believed his "amenities of stone" finally done, he was, of course, wrong. He never fully bid "His Farewell to Old Poetry." *This Journey* (1982), a collection published posthumously, contains a smattering of rhymed and metrically regular poems (for example, "With the Gift of an Alabaster Tortoise" and "Your Name in Arezzo"), as did the "New Poems" section of *Collected Poems* before it. In fact, Donald Hall remembers that James Wright was "constantly attracted to metrical verse. . . . and was always dabbling in it."[23] Wright simply stopped showing his metrical pieces to those who disapproved (such as Bly), and when he did show them at all, he asked, "Please don't tell Robert."[24] But no matter. Wright told Dave Smith in 1980 that he disliked the assumption that with *The Branch Will Not Break* he had "calculated . . . to be born again."[25]

More than Wright realized or perhaps cared to admit, *Amenities of Stone* reveals a poet in the process of a redefinition of the poetic self. He may have suppressed *Amenities* for just that reason, wishing to keep to himself the process of such a transition, one evidently painful for a poet and academic so steeped in the English literary tradition he was ostensibly abandoning.

Whatever Bly's role in Wright's poetic transition, Wright himself had to make the decisions and live with the results. While working on *Amenities* and the versions that followed, he reevaluated the rhetorical basis of his art, risking not only his hard-earned aesthetic principles but also his own spiritual and emotional identity. On a May 21, 1962, draft of "Holding a Pearl in My Hand, April 1962," Wright's handwritten comments detail the process of such a poetic redefinition through his response to Bly's suggestion that he delete the poem "Saturday Morning" (published earlier in the *New Yorker*) from the book that would eventually become *Branch*:

> I had *already* deleted it! The fact was the clearest sign so far that I am learning what the new poetry *is*, and also that I have obtained at least enough emotional strength to feel reassured about deletions. I was afraid last summer that [my] withdrawl of the previous version of the manuscript from Wesleyan might be just another . . . self-destructive move on my part. Well, the dread I felt was real—but I am so glad, so relieved. . . . Because the book that is still emerging from the deliberate wreckage of the old one is what I most deeply wanted to write in the first place. It is not a 'great' book; but it might yet be a *true* book. I've kept it hidden— fallow. . . . there are times when it's necessary to *let the book grow alone.* [26]

In a handwritten note dated 5 January 1962, well after Wright had decided to suppress *Amenities*, he indicated additions to the still-emerging manuscript. Among the changes was the addition of a sequence of poems titled, "Apprenticeships," five poems written by poets Wright presumably considered his masters. Frost and Robinson, whom Wright had cited as influences in a note to *The Green Wall*, don't appear. Neither does his teacher at Kenyon College John Crowe Ransom. Instead, Goethe, Guillén, Trakl, Vallejo, and Rilke (in Wright's translations) have taken their places. Frost and Robinson could not appear in this new list of masters because Wright had chosen a means of study—apprenticeship by translation—that necessarily excluded them.

Ten years later, long after the critical furor which resulted from his change of poetic styles, Wright would include four of these poems in the "Some Translations" section of *Collected Poems*: Goethe's "Anacreon's Grave," Guillén's "I Want to Sleep," Trakl's "De Profundis," and Vallejo's "Our Daily Bread." One should not overlook the placement of these translations—they neatly separate the formal poems of *The Green Wall* and *Saint Judas* from the experimental poems of *Branch* and its successors.

In his apprenticeship to the above poets, Wright had encountered a tradition so unlike the one dominant in England and America that he had earlier been moved to remark he had "decided to abandon . . . 'nineteenth century poetry'."[27] Whatever his intentions, the actual process was a protracted one and the abandonment never fully accomplished. He never recanted his love for his old masters, though he certainly did modify and expand his poetic sensibilities. Here *Amenities of Stone* proves quite useful in understanding Wright's transition, for this collection of poems, even its very structure, discloses his movement from a poetry of detached classical wit to one of sympathy and engagement.

More than a simple rejection of rhyme, regular meter, irony and paradox, Wright's transformation in *Amenities* is predicated on a more pervasive alteration in his attitude concerning a poet's task and place in the world. Wright admits of an alternative poetics based on the imaginative and intuitive mind. In redefining the poet's place as an equal object in a world of natural objects, he rejects a subject-object dichotomy and refuses to separate the poet from a universe of process. Finally, Wright affirms a poetics in which meaning emerges not through a rational imposition of order but rather through intuitive perception, thus extending a kind of Emersonian romanticism to contemporary poetics.

*Amenities of Stone* reveals the process by which Wright, a poet of vision and integrity, furthers what he considers the purest of artistic purposes: the need "to grow" and "go on discovering . . . new possibilities of writing."[28]

# 4 A Poetics of Vulnerability:
*The Branch Will Not Break*

In his introduction to the 1962 edition of *Contemporary American Poetry*, Donald Hall describes the main emphasis in our poetry since Eliot: "For thirty years [1925–55] an orthodoxy ruled American poetry. It derived from the authority of T. S. Eliot and the new critics; it exerted itself through the literary quarterlies and the universities. It asked for a poetry of symmetry, intellect, irony, and wit. . . . [it prescribed] the thinkable limits of variation."[1]

Although these limits were narrow, their enforcement was decidedly more de facto than de jure. For the most part, the poetry that these quarterlies published (and applauded) was of a kind: intelligent, urbane, and accomplished—but often predictable in its sameness. The chorus of voices characteristic of early Modernism had subsided to a sort of solo in which the speaker may change but never the voice.

Although James Wright's first two collections are in accord with this prescription, *The Branch Will Not Break* (1963) reveals the extent to which he reevaluates his personal and aesthetic stance between *Saint Judas* (1959) and *Branch*.[2] Turning from Donne and Jonson, from the well-wrought poem he had learned to write from his neoclassical masters, Wright embraces foreign sources, most notably Georg Trakl and Cesar Vallejo, and redefines both the manner and tenor of his work. He momentarily abandons traditional forms in favor of a kind of free-verse image poem; along the way he rejects ornate diction in favor of colloquial language. More importantly, he reassesses humanity's separation from nature, a pervasive religious theme in his first two books, and contrarily affirms the possibility of a kind of unity and transcendence through nature. Such a movement exemplifies the increased vulnerability of the speaker (and the poet) in Wright's new work.

One measure of this heightened vulnerability is the way Wright begins to dissolve the distance between the poet and his poem. As *Amenities of Stone* demonstrates, Wright chooses to shape his new work from the actualities of experience, to create poems of process in which act and deed take precedence over thought and word. In his redefined poetics, the image surrounded by "white spaces" of silence (and not by a rhetoric of containment) becomes a means to communicate with his reader. This is a poetry of reticence, cleansed of verbal clutter.[3]

As should be the case, much has been written about the alteration in Wright's poetry between the publication of *Saint Judas* and that of *The Branch Will Not Break*.[4] And with the recent discovery of *Amenities of Stone*, there now exists a much fuller understanding of both the larger process of Wright's transformation and its particulars. Still, many of these essays, concerned as they are with the surface features of Wright's stylistic alteration, have largely overlooked the elements of constancy in this period of his work. Chief among these elements is Wright's active social and political consciousness. In fact, many of the poems of *Branch* show how his earlier regard for those at odds with society takes on a much wider aim. Wright now addresses the plight of workers and housewives, and he vilifies the questionable values of America's military-industrial complex.

What is most striking about Wright's social and political work is the poetic form he uses to pursue these issues: a lyric composed primarily of images, often "deep images," far removed from his previous highly rhetorical mode. In fact, one may attribute the relative lack of attention given the issue of Wright's poetry of social commentary to his use of the image poem as a mode for making such statements. Many readers, perhaps, are too concerned with assessing the nuances of Wright's new style to notice the constancy of his themes. This chapter, as a consequence, will begin by discussing the importance of the image in his redefined poetics and citing his models for such a poetry, then move on to examine the varied purposes to which Wright applies this new aesthetic.

*1   The Deep Image: Lyricism and Social Consciousness*

The form and manner of Wright's first two collections closely follow
the poetic prescription laid down by the New Critics. Thematically,
they accept a dualism of mind and matter and the severance of the
human from the natural; they show a preoccupation with original sin
and the fallen state of humankind and evince a pervasive mood of despair. Formally, these poems display the era's retrenchment to conventional form, to what Ransom defined as "traditional poetic labour" or
"the determinate metering of a determinate discourse."⁵ Structurally,
they make use of irony, paradox, and the dialectic. For Ransom, irony
is "the ultimate mode of the great minds," one that rejects but still
acknowledges the "romantic mystery which is perhaps the absolute
poetry." Cleanth Brooks, not to be outdone, boldly asserts that "the
language of poetry is the language of paradox."⁶ In this line of thinking, romanticism is seen as a function of the unsophisticated or imma-
ture mind; the sophisticated mind, on the other hand, writes an ironic
and "metaphysical" poetry, what Ransom praises as the "most original
and exciting, and intellectually . . . most seasoned" poetry possible.⁷
Whether in protection of the vulnerable self or in adherence to the
dominant mode, Wright's early poems tend to subordinate imagination to intellect; they regard the rational mind as the sole orderer of
experience.

To recall Hall's term, such an "orthodoxy" of technique became, in
itself, debilitating; it became both the foundation and the medium of
the voice of despair. The "thinkable limits of variation" had been reduced to experiments in rhyme and meter, in irony and paradox. As
early as 1945 Karl Shapiro had asked pertinent questions of this ruling
aesthetic:

> Where is the literature
> Of nature, where the love poem and the plain
> Statement of feeling? How and when and why
> Did we conceive our horror for emotion,
> Our fear of beauty? Whence the isolation
> And proud withdrawal of the intellectual
> Into the cool control-room of the brain?

> At what point in the history of art
> Has such a cleavage between audience
> And poet existed?[8]

By the late 1950's the limits of the contained poem to which Shapiro alluded had become even more confining. Robert Bly preferred to call these limits a kind of "jail," and he described the influence of the New Critics in this way: "American Twentieth-Century poetry had fought for its freedom, and it soon showed an irresistible desire to be locked up again. In the very next generation after Eliot and Pound, American poetry voluntarily turned itself in. Tate and Ransom went through town after town asking, 'Does anyone know of a good jail near here?'[9]

Regardless of their agreement or disagreement with Bly's brash and impassioned argument, by 1960 or so Wright, Hall, W. S. Merwin, Galway Kinnell, Louis Simpson, Adrienne Rich, and a number of other poets had had enough of this orthodoxy. Wright's unpublished *Amenities of Stone* reveals the process of his own transformation, how he came to "lose / All the old echoes."

However, the loss of the "old echoes" of this tradition allows Wright to look elsewhere, particularly to Georg Trakl, to whose work he had been introduced in 1952 while on a Fulbright Fellowship in Vienna.[10] Although Trakl's poetry is neither rhymed nor regularly metered, neither formal quality amounts to his greatest influence on Wright's work. Instead, Wright is most affected by Trakl's voice, his means of speaking a poem wholly through its images.

Trakl uses the image as a form of poetic communication; it carries the emotion and meaning of a poem in an expansive, though some-times veiled, manner. Of Trakl's poems, Wright says:

> One does not so much read them as explore them. They are not objects which he constructed, but quiet places at the edge of a dark forest where one has to sit for a long time and listen very carefully. Then, after all one's patience is exhausted, and it seems that nothing inside the poem will ever make sense in the ways to which one has become accustomed by previous reading, all sorts of images and sounds come out of the trees, or the ponds, or the mead-

ows, or the lonely roads—those places of awful stillness at the center of nearly every poem Trakl ever wrote.[11]

The same can be said of many poems in *Branch* which reveal themselves only after long and attentive reading. These poems operate—as Wright says of Trakl's—in an arational manner quite distinct from "the ways to which one has been accustomed by previous reading." Admittedly, reading Donne and Jonson, Tate and Ransom leaves one unprepared for the associational leaps of Wright's and Trakl's poems. One sure way to amplify the associational or intuitional quality of a poem is to emphasize the abrupt movement between its images, deleting, in the process, the discursive thinking that might have lead the poet from one image to another. For a poet schooled in the traditional poetics dominant in the fifties, this effect can be difficult to achieve. Wright had been trained to fill in these gaps of logic; these transitions often, in fact, provided the best opportunity for a thinking poet to assert his sophistication and sense of order. Translation, on the other hand, especially translating a poet whose work subscribed to an aesthetics widely removed from Wright's own, offers the perfect occasion for Wright to learn the method of such associational leaps, and later, to adapt it to his own poetry.

In reading and translating the poems of Trakl, Wright came upon a method of translation that proved instructive, and equally effective, as a method of composition. At the bottom of his translation of Trakl's "Lamentation," he clarified the proposition and reminded himself to "explain the principle to Bly: to translate the image *as image*, not as a mere equivalent abstraction. In a real ~~poet~~ poem, each word is a physical world."[12] Wright's principle of translation clearly elevates the image to supreme importance, requiring, as he later indicates, that the image must be translated in an "imaginative" rather than a "literal" fashion. That Wright crossed out "poet" and inserted "poem" shows how he has begun to equate the two, how the act of language which makes a poem and the act of selfhood have become nearly identical in his mind. Note, too, that the act of language and of selfhood occurs in a physical, not merely a mental or rhetorical, world. The experiential world has become the primary locus of personal and poetic reality.

Consider Wright's own translation of Trakl's "My Heart at Evening," a poem composed almost entirely of images and sounds:

> Toward evening you hear the cry of the bats,
> Two horses bound in the pasture,
> The red maple rustles,
> The walker along the road sees ahead the small tavern.
>
> Nuts and young wine taste delicious,
> Delicious: to stagger drunk into the darkening woods.
> Village bells, painful to hear, echo through the black fir
>    branches,
> Dew forms on the face.[13]

The title leads one to believe that the poem will present the speaker's emotional response to the descent of evening. However, instead of containing a bathetic series of "I" clauses, the poem itself is nearly without a persona. Although the "you" of the first line may refer to the speaker in a sort of veiled first-person use of the second-person pronoun, the speaker has already begun to distance himself from the potential for solipsism inherent in the "My Heart" of the title. This "you" could just as easily refer to any reader of the poem. Such a gesture, of course, is expansive, and its actions show themselves even more subtly in the fourth line, where the "you" gives way to a more universal "The walker." In removing himself from the poem, the speaker indicates that his presence is less important than the images and sounds presented. It is, after all, this twilight world and not his discourse about it that the speaker wants to shape the movement of the poem.

Toward the poem's conclusion, the speaker acknowledges a desire for unification with the darkening woods and bemoans the interference of a human element in this process of immersion; because they disturb his reverie, the village "bells" become "painful to hear." The poem concludes with the speaker, or at least the speaker's mental dream state, alone in the woods. Dew forms—not as one would expect, on "my face" or "your face"—but on "the face"; for the speaker's face (and his heart, we assume) has become one with the face of the woods.

Thus, the subject-object dichotomy, that is, the distance between the human subjective perceiver and the object perceived, is resolved. The poet himself has dissolved into the landscape.

This dissolution of the poet-speaker, of course, enacts a kind of romantic merging of opposites, but it also contributes to the poet's successful handling of a potentially troublesome subject. While the topic of the poem—a unification with the natural—carries inherent vulnerability, the poem's manner of presentation lessens those risks. At the point of the poem's epiphanic moment, both poet and speaker seem curiously absent; both have diffused into the natural setting, leaving only the poem's images to speak the act of immersion which closes the poem. Therefore, the final image not only conveys the act of merging so integral to the poem but also enables the poet to avoid self-reflexive bathos.

The beauty—and the real difficulty—of such a poem is that it requires the reader to assume the poet's expansive but delicate state of being. It is true that the writer of a poem adhering to New Critical principles might fall prey to a "cleavage" between poet and audience through an excess of erudition or wit (as Shapiro implies). However, the poet of an image poem might also do so by a less than effective manipulation of image or by a too effective concealment of the speaker. Shunning overt statement, narrative, and often the musical phrase in such a poem, the poet must rely on the artfully perceived and presented image as the medium of thoughts and feelings.

Wright largely succeeds in avoiding this pitfall in *Branch*, but occasionally, he asks his readers to make intuitive leaps too broad for even the most athletic imagination. A poet can easily lose readers by describing the moon as "Hunting for hidden dolphins / Behind the darkening combers / Of the ground" ("By a Lake in Minnesota"). The last three stanzas of "In Ohio" also show this tendency:

> The sun floats down, a small golden lemon dissolves
> In the water.
> I dream, as I lean over the edge, of a crawdad's mouth.
>
> The cellars of haunted houses are like ancient cities,
> Fallen behind a big heap of apples.

A widow on a front porch puckers her lips
And whispers.[14]

Briefly stated, the poem's images display either passive natural description or energetic human imagination, but they do not successfully interrelate the two. How the poet's dream, the cellars of haunted houses, the apples, and the widow are connected remains mysteriously unclear because the speaker, who remains mostly absent from the poem, has not sewn the intuitive thread which joins these elements. The reader might make unkind connections between the "crawdad's mouth" and the old woman's "puckered" lips, but certainly that is not the point of the poem. In a number of these poems Wright uses mystery to his advantage, but here readers might find themselves wishing that the old woman would speak up, for what she is whispering at the poem's close might tell more than her silence.

The great majority of these poems succeed, however, and Wright's short poem "Rain" exemplifies how he has assimilated what he learned from Trakl's work:

It is the sinking of things.

Flashlights drift over dark trees,
Girls kneel,
An owl's eyelids fall.

The sad bones of my hands descend into a valley
Of strange rocks.

Rain, the ostensible topic of the poem, is addressed only in the poem's first line. However, the mere suggestion of rain establishes the context for the subsequent images; rain descends, sinks into the ground, and thus penetrates a dark and mysterious place akin to the human unconscious. The flashlights in dark trees evoke the mystery of nightfall; the kneeling girls offer a pose of religious meditation; and the owl drops its eyelids in introspection, looking to the inner self for knowledge and instruction. Finally, the persona allows himself to enter, well after the movement of the poem has set up this atmosphere of attention and introspection. In keeping with the poem's verbal and spatial development, the speaker also descends, this time to a land-scape of subjective awareness which is "strange" to him. In the pro-cess, the speaker equates his unconscious (his inner life) with a natural element, thereby momentarily eliminating the distance—if not the distinction—between the human and the natural. The poem succeeds largely because the series of images that establishes the movement of the poem is given a clear reference point in the speaker's own inner life.

Wright learns to explore the imagination as a poetic tool from trans-lating not only Trakl but also Cesar Vallejo. In Vallejo Wright discov-ers an alternative to both the formal excellence of Richard Wilbur and the rebellion of the Beats. In identifying "what a poet in the United States may hope to learn from Vallejo," Wright proposes his own ver-sion of the poetic polarity discussed earlier: "Current poets in the United States seem to be perishing on either side of a grey division between century-old British formalism on the one hand and a vandal-ism of anti-poetry on the other. In Vallejo we may see a great poet who lives neither in formalism nor in violence, but in imagination."[15]

By translating Vallejo, Wright examines the imagination of a poet writing in another language, and in doing so, he is forced to find En-glish equivalents for that poet's imagination and the idiom in which he expresses it. The more or less simple idiom which Vallejo uses in his poems must surely have affected Wright's own poetry, for Vallejo's influence is, at times, quite obvious. Consider Wright's short image poem "The Jewel":

> There is this cave
> In the air behind my body
> That nobody is going to touch:
> A cloister, a silence
> Closing around a blossom of fire.
> When I stand upright in the wind,
> My bones turn to dark emeralds.

Now, note the similarity of "The Jewel" to Wright's own translation of the third stanza of Vallejo's long poem, "Have You Anything to Say in Your Defense":

There is an empty space
in my metaphysical shape
that no one can reach:
a cloister of silence
that spoke with the fire of its muffled voice.[16]

The two poems, it should be said, share no thematic similarity and Vallejo's is much longer, but the language and images are remarkably similar. My point is not that James Wright stole from Vallejo, but that Wright—moved by his translation of Vallejo—composed a poem in his own idiom using Vallejo's as a source of inspiration. Notice how Wright adapts the lines to his own emerging colloquial voice: "metaphysical shape" becomes simply "body"; "that no one can reach" becomes a tougher, more Ohioan, "That nobody is going to touch." Curiously enough, William Matthews, a fine poet and dependable critic, cites these first lines of "The Jewel" as examples of Wright's plain speech, for they use "a kind of speech I heard and spoke as a boy in Ohio."[17] Apparently, Wright comes home to Ohio by way of Vallejo.

The above poems and others like them fulfill Bly's call in "Looking for Dragon Smoke" for a poetry of associational leaps, not mere juxtaposing of images. This type of poem makes use of what Robert Kelly and Jerome Rothenberg term the "deep image."[18] In "Notes on the Poetry of Deep Image," Kelly asserts: "Poetry cannot exhibit naked perception. The clothed percept is the image."[19] These images are drawn from both the conscious and unconscious to link inner and outer realities, and they occur in the poem, as it were, in process—as they are perceived by the poet. What results is a new thing, an image not wholly based on inward or outward experience, but rather a mingling of the two faithful to both realms. The effect is to create a poetry of immediacy and revelation, a poetry not amenable to more conventional, more rational modes of writing and explication. In fact, Kelly argues, "Only the superior rationality of the dream is an effective impetus for the movement of the deep image" (16).

Frequently, critics are tempted to cite these qualities of the poems in *Branch* as examples of how Wright abandons the manner of his past work and, thereby, to praise or to condemn him for these choices. What remains unnoticed, however, is the fashion in which Wright applies these techniques to his earlier proclivity for writing a poetry of social statement. By choosing murderers, prostitutes, and drunkards as subjects for his early poems, Wright insists on admitting them into the fold of society and, in the process, enlarges the ground of acceptable poetic subject matter. It is easy to forget that Wright's early efforts at composing a poetry of social relevance were uncommon for those writing in the dominant mode. As Bly proposes in "A Wrong-Turning in American Poetry," American poets since Eliot had carefully avoided the political or social poem, preferring a poetry of rigorous (and often protective) intellectual control.[20] In reading Vallejo and Neruda, Wright discovers an energetic poetry of social and political commentary that values pertinence and emotional depth as much or more than artifice. From Vallejo Wright learns a means to address social issues in a lyric poem and in a manner more in keeping with "Rain" than his earlier attempts, for example, in the Doty poems. Those attentive primarily to the matter of Wright's evolving poetic technique, therefore, might easily overlook the larger thematic issue of the constancy of his social consciousness. A careful look at "Miners," however, shows both the intuitive connectedness of a typical deep-image lyric and the social awareness that characterizes Wright's work:

1

The police are probing tonight for the bodies
Of children in the black waters
Of the suburbs.

2

Below the chemical riffles of the Ohio River,
Grappling hooks
Drag delicately about, between skiff hulks and sand shoals,
Until they clasp
Fingers.

3

Somewhere in a vein of Bridgeport, Ohio;
Deep in a coal hill behind Hanna's name;
Below the tipples, and dark as a drowsy woodchuck;

A man, alone,
Stumbles upon the outside locks of a grave, whispering
*Oh let me in.*

4

Many American women mount long stairs
In the shafts of houses,
Fall asleep, and emerge suddenly into tottering palaces.

Both the poem's redefinition of the term "miners" and its social commentary begin in the first stanza. The poem's images of descent commence there, where children metaphorically drown in the "black waters / Of the suburbs." Together with the subjects of the second stanza, these children represent victims of the American culture and economy, for like the polluted Ohio itself, they are both the products and the victims of capitalistic theory and industrial greed. In the zone of death that Wright has portrayed through image, the only redemption is a grappling hook.

Descent, thus, becomes a means of release, and death is its object and end result. Though the third stanza offers an obvious connection to the Appalachian coal miner trapped in economically and physically destructive work, the final stanza makes clear that the poem addresses not only the coal miner's hope for transcendence but also the dreams of many Americans for a similar spiritual escape. In the upper right-hand corner of a worksheet of "Miners," Wright reminds himself of (and, unknowingly, clarifies for his reader) the crucial thematic element that forces the poem's ostensibly disparate images to coalesce into a single, unified work: "Two kinds of miners here: 1. real miners, a social class, a depressed social class, 2. spiritual miners."[21] Wright suggests that these "American women" also live and work in a mine of equal desperation. Because their "sleep" is a form of release, their ascent is the first positive movement of the poem, raising them through dream into "tottering palaces." In a life of the imagination, in a precarious ascent to dream (that is also a descent into the unconscious), they find a place of value unlike the "shafts" they inhabit. The combined images of the poem, therefore, propose a redefinition of the term "miners": that all Americans are miners of a sort, forced to flee the polluted earth in search of spiritual beauty or release which can be found, apparently, only in death or dream.

What is perhaps most startling about the poem's manner of posing social commentary is its lack of a specific speaker or persona to give voice to it. Much like the speaker of Trakl's "My Heart at Evening,"the speaker of "Miners" disappears into the landscape that he portrays, essentially empowering the poem's images with the role of speaker. Rather than offering a single speaker relating his personal feelings of loss, Wright's strategy, thus, objectifies the speaker so that he shares in each act of desecration and the attempt to flee it. The effect is to universalize the speaker's intuited and personal despair by objectifying it in images drawn from others' lives, a tactic not far removed from Eliot's objective correlative and a result not unlike the universal expression sought by New Critical aesthetics. Apparently, then, Wright chooses dissimilar techniques to achieve a similar result, therefore signifying both a continuity and a transition in his work. Moreover, the intuitive connectedness of the images gives the poem its formal structure, though a form different than that of, say, a sonnet. Wright himself considers "Miners" a clear example of how the deep image is used as a formal device in free-verse poems: "I think it's ["Miners"] extremely formal. . . . The images are all parallel to one another. It's as formal as the end of Lincoln's Gettysburg Address. I don't mean it's as good."[22]

Though perhaps a bit defensive in the above remarks, Wright indicates that free verse really is not "free," that it operates, instead, on standards established by the intuitive, form-discovering mind. This emphasis on the imagination and on the image as its expression reduces the importance of a rhetoric of containment and its accompanying verbal clutter. If the image itself is to carry the emotional and intellectual meaning of the poem, the presentation of the image must not be gaudy or meretricious. It must be expressed in language that emphasizes the image itself and not its verbal presentation.

This idea accounts for the simple diction of the poems in *Branch*. It explains, also, why the "mellifluous berries" of *The Green Wall* ("Erinna to Sappho") become simple "grapes" stolen from heaven in "A Message Hidden in an Empty Wine Bottle That I Threw into a Gully of Maple Trees One Night at an Indecent Hour." Not even a drunken poet is likely to say, "The unwashed shadows / . . . Are sneaking across the pits of strip mines / To steal *mellifluous berries* / In heaven."

The "white spaces" produced by the simplicity of language and image in Wright's "Autumn Begins in Martins Ferry, Ohio" allow room for the reader to enter the poem and engage it, to live within its open spaces:

> In the Shreve High football stadium,
> I think of Polacks nursing long beers in Tiltonsville,
> And gray faces of Negroes in the blast furnace at Benwood,
> And the ruptured night watchman of Wheeling Steel,
> Dreaming of heroes.
>
> All the proud fathers are afraid to go home.
> Their women cluck like starved pullets
> Dying for love.
>
> Therefore,
> Their sons grow suicidally beautiful
> At the beginning of October,
> And gallop terribly against each other's bodies.

In brief, the poem's strength is its ability to pose a vigorous social statement while leaving so much unspoken. The poem, in fact, operates on a kind of alogical syllogism through which Wright is able to use the methods of logic to call into question the values of American culture that emphasize youthful athletic competition as a precursor to the capitalistic competition of adulthood. As the speaker must realize, to dream of heroes in our society, whether in athletics or business, is to dream of the wealthy. The speaker, apparently Wright himself, holds a great empathy for the poor, for those driven to the refuge of "long beers," made pallid by the "blast furnace" of their workplace, for those fathers who realize that for them the American dream has been irreparably "ruptured."

Though the connection between the despair of the parents and the violent actions of the sons does not follow altogether logically, as the "therefore" would suggest, still, the speaker's syllogism achieves seamless closure. Having seen the "ruptured" dream of their fathers and mothers, the sons passionately partake of their own "suicidally beautiful" ritual of competition, each hoping he, unlike his father before him, will achieve momentary glory—for this is their last chance at it. By succeeding this evening on the football field, they try to reassure themselves that they, too, will not be defeated by the economics of hard labor that dominate Martins Ferry. Because their abandon on the field is a function of their fear, the final image of the young men's bodies thrown "terribly against each other" indicts a society whose cultural values and class distinctions seem askew, somehow as tilted as "Tiltonsville."

Within his image poems, Wright often reversed the stereotypical associations of light and darkness to startling effect in his celebrations of nature, a technique of considerable importance to his poem "A Blessing." Using the same strategy, however, enabled Wright to attack the nation's emerging military-industrial complex without risking the overt and moralistic tone of liberal rhetoric. He was acutely aware of the pitfall of preachiness into which so much political poetry stumbles headlong, and his remarks on a September 1961 draft of "Eisenhower's Visit to Franco, 1959" underscore his determination to avoid it: "I must be careful not to yield too easily to *talk* and *statement*."[23]

In the poem Wright juxtaposes the goodness of natural things, such as "dark red" wine, with the "glare of photographers" who take pictures of Eisenhower and Franco "embracing" while the fleet of "clean new bombers" that Eisenhower has sent to support the dictator descend in the "shine of searchlights." Wright imagines the good darkness, which throughout *Branch* serves as a symbol of beauty and mystery, to be dangerously imperiled by the harsh, unforgiving, and paradoxically evil adulation of light: "The American hero must triumph over / The forces of darkness." Although these images effectively convey the mood and tenor of his political theme in "Eisenhower's Visit to Franco, 1959," Wright once did not altogether trust them to perform adequately; one version (of the many) extant drafts of the poem concludes with this angry but rather flat example of "talk" or "statement": "I am ashamed of my country."[24]

Avoiding such statements and relying instead on the image, Wright discovered a new mode and a new vitality for his poetry of social consciousness. Further, in a volume often regarded solely as a celebration of nature and the self, these example prove that a lyric need not always address the beauty and terror of the individual life but may also deal passionately with our culture and its various pressures. Having learned from his study of Trakl and Vallejo, Wright composes an expansive lyric that evokes a broad social statement, not mere pathos or self-absorption. By building on a foundation of images and enacting a diffusion of the speaker within those images, he allows the poem's silences and clear language to carry a discomfitting message within an essentially lyric format.

## 2   The Natural World: Silence and Attention

Up to now, I have discussed Wright's experimentation with image and idiom and the constancy of his social consciousness, demonstrating how these represent another step in his efforts to discover alternatives to the contained, "square poem" of the 1950s.[25] Perhaps more startling, however, is his reconsideration of the relationship between the human and the natural. In the past Wright had thought of nature as composed of "tempting" and "luring" elements that "summon the flesh to fall"; his was a thoroughly Post-Lapsarian view of nature. Yet, in Branch attention to nature yields knowledge—intimations of order, meaning, and possible transcendence—that accentuates the vulnerable position of a poet who thinks himself in harmony with the natural world. Suddenly, Wright can imagine and inhabit a Pre-Lapsarian world not tainted by original sin.

Again, Wright's model for this poetry of attention is Trakl. In the "silence and speechlessness" of Trakl's poems, Wright finds a poetry significantly different from the highly wrought rhetoric of his own first two collections; he finds "a poetry from which all shrillness and clutter have been banished" (Wright, "A Note on Trakl," 83). He discovers a poetics of reticence and applies its principles to his own work.

Trakl teaches Wright the value of attention and patience, and these virtues express themselves in a poetry of stillness and vision. "A single red maple leaf in a poem by Trakl," says Wright, "is an inexhaustibly rich and wonderful thing, simply because he has had the patience to look at it and the bravery to resist all distraction from it" ("A Note on

*Trakl,"* 83). In "Beginning" Wright urges himself to "be still," for he has learned from Trakl the importance of listening:

> I stand alone by an elder tree, I do not dare breathe
> Or move.
> I listen.
> The wheat leans back toward its darkness,
> And I lean toward mine.

The poem represents a "beginning"; in it Wright begins to put into practice his new theory of attention, and the poetry which results is calm and deliberate. As the speaker turns toward knowledge of his inner self, of his "darkness," he has found in nature a means to personal understanding.

In a similar fashion, Wright's "Lying in a Hammock at William Duffy's Farm in Pine Island, Minnesota" reveals the speaker in the process of recognition. In the apparently harmonious natural environment that surrounds him, the speaker perceives a model for living based on attention. Wright considers the poem's provocative final line, "I have wasted my life," a "religious statement, that is to say, here I am and I'm not straining myself and yet I'm happy at this moment, and perhaps I've been wastefully unhappy in the past because through my arrogance or whatever, and my blindness, I haven't allowed myself to pay true attention to what was around me."[26]

To accomplish this religious attention to the natural world, Wright evidently believes some other things must be left behind. In "A Prayer to Escape from the Market Place," he indicates one element of the poet's publishing life he would like to abandon:

> I renounce the blindness of the magazines.

Later, he reveals another desire, to abandon further the constraints of responsibility:

> I want to lie down under a tree.
> This is the only duty that is not death.
> This is the everlasting happiness
> Of small winds.

The escape which the poet envisions for himself requires an immersion in the experience of nature and a relinquishment of the city for the quiet of the country, where among "the fountains of hills" he will "hunt the sea, to walk on the waters" ("Snowstorm in the Midwest"). This sea that the poet seeks is an interior one. It had existed undiscovered within the poet of *The Green Wall*, but now the poet knows where to look and from whom to ask assistance. Wright's translation of Goethe amounts to a signal poem in the manuscript, for it gives voice to his prayer for the healing waters of self-understanding:

> Oh Father of Love,
> If your psaltery holds one tone
> That his ear might echo,
> Then quicken his heart!
> Open his eyes, shut off by clouds
> From the thousand fountains
> So near him, dying of thirst
> In his own desert.
> ("Three Stanzas from Goethe")

Seeking harmony within himself and within the natural world, Wright's most fervent wish is to resolve the subject-object dichotomy that divides the human from the natural. His quest, of course, is at the heart of Romantic ideology, and as Charles Altieri points out, this Wordsworthian desire is common among contemporary poets.[27] It is a miracle not far removed from Christ's "walk on the waters," and Wright wants no less.

Wright's method for accomplishing this miracle is rooted in attention to natural elements. Through attention to these numinous objects, the poet can learn to see himself and his place in the natural world, as Wright does in "Depressed by a Book of Bad Poetry, I Walk toward an Unused Pasture and Invite the Insects to Join Me."[28] Here, he shuns the human for the natural, watching ants who are so "frail" that he "can see through them":

> I close my eyes for a moment, and listen.
> The old grasshoppers
> Are tired, they leap heavily now,

Their thighs are burdened.
I want to hear them, they have clear sounds to make.

Wright's object is to make his poetry more natural, to allow it to take on what Emerson calls "an architecture of its own," like that of a plant or an animal. Unlike the verbal clutter of his early work—what he elsewhere calls his "loud display" ("At the Executed Murderer's Grave")—these grasshoppers have "clear sounds to make." Wright, thus, discovers not only an aesthetic clarity in nature but also value and solace where he previously saw only "the cold divinities of death and change."

It is useful to recall that the poet who is now beginning to feel in harmony with nature had been, in *The Green Wall*, more than content with a separation from it:

> Be glad of the green wall
> You climbed across one day,
> When winter stung with ice
> That vacant paradise.

Such a fundamental alteration redefines Wright's poetic stance and should not be overlooked for its effect on the methods and tenor of his work. Perhaps "Two Hangovers," a poem set near the middle of *Branch* (the twentieth of forty-three poems), best illustrates this transition in the poet's relationship with the natural. The poem appears in two distinctly different parts.[29] In the first section, the speaker, consumed by despair, uses his imagination to transform natural elements into expressions of that despair. A portion of the first section follows:

### NUMBER ONE

> I slouch in bed.
> Beyond the streaked trees of my window,
> All groves are bare.
> Locusts and poplars change to unmarried women
> Sorting slate from anthracite
> Between railroad ties:
> The yellow-bearded winter of the depression
> Is still alive somewhere, an old man

Counting his collection of bottle caps
In a tarpaper shack under the cold trees
Of my grave.

I still feel half drunk.
And all those old women beyond my window
Are hunching toward the graveyard.

The speaker's means of dealing with outer experience is to recast it to suit his somber mood. Hung over by both drink and despair, the speaker stares at the "bare" groves of trees outside his window, lacking even the courage to rise from bed. In this state of mind, the speaker transforms the "locusts and poplars" to "women / Sorting slate from anthracite." Thus, he imbues nature with human failure; he insists on making a human "depression"also a natural one. Moreover, the speaker's posture, his "slouch in bed" shows his resignation to his own "grave" within the larger "graveyard" that the entire earth has become for him.

Later, deeper in the grips of such despondency, the speaker rejects the most archetypal symbol of hope: the sun. Even it displays the taint of human weakness and failure; it is "drunk," like the speaker, and unable to convey any message of reassurance, for today its language of hope is spoken in "Hungarian." The speaker cannot (or does not want to) understand it. Such a poet insists on viewing the natural world through the dark lens of his own solipsistic despair. In fact, he modifies the outer world of experience to accommodate the vision he imposes on it. Even a sparrow betrays the natural world by singing the praises of its victimizer, the Hanna Coal Company. Its song and the "filaments of cold light bulbs" combine to make a "cold" and inhuman music. It is no wonder that the speaker's response to such world, one he perceives as wholly uncaring and unredemptive, is simply to "turn it off," to return to the sanctity of his dreams and withdraw from experience. By this point, the reader, who could well have tired of the speaker's self-centered and single-handed transformation of the earth into useless detritus, may simply be gladdened that the speaker has ended his harangue.

However, the second section of the poem shows a far different view of the natural world. This time, what the speaker sees encourages rather than discourages him, largely because he does not impose his own despair on it:

NUMBER TWO:
I TRY TO WAKEN AND
GREET THE WORLD ONCE AGAIN

In a pine tree,
A few yards from my window sill,
A brilliant blue jay is springing up and down,
Up and down,
On a branch.
I laugh, as I see him abandon himself
To entire delight, for he knows as well as I do
That the branch will not break.

Unlike the sun who spoke "Hungarian," this jay's message of the resiliency inherent in the natural world is understood by the speaker. Structurally, this section remains uncluttered by image and the speaker's personal associations; the interaction of man and animal composed the entire sequence of events. Because the speaker is attentive and receptive to this jay, he is able to recognize the commonality of humankind and nature which amounts to their collective strength—a piece of knowledge the bird "knows as well as" the speaker. Though the world may be composed of old women masquerading as trees, they are resilient, nearly unbreakable entities.

Such a way of thinking and seeing amounts, also, to a significant alteration in the speaker's (and the poet's) relationship with nature. He no longer fears being taken in, sinfully fooled, as it were. Now nature, in the figure of this bird, provides the means to the fulfillment which has eluded the speaker. This is a transcendent jay, for he has found a way to "abandon himself," to give himself over to "entire delight." By his actions, the jay reveals that the path to transcendence lies through delight, not despair. Appearing halfway into the volume, "Two Hangovers" signals an end to the tone of uncertainty that dominates the first half of the collection. In the space of this one poem, the poet moves from hopelessness to hopefulness.

Hope alone is not the end result of the Wright's redefined relationship with nature; he finds even greater promise. Such attention reveals that "it is impossible to die" ("Today I Was Happy, So I Made This Poem"), a stunning assertion for a poet as enthralled with death as Wright was in the first two volumes. Now at ease with the cycles of life and death, the poet seems to have found what he was seeking, something far different than the "terrible oak tree darkening with winter" of the collection's opening poem. Instead, in spiritual agreement with an eagle rejoicing "in the oak trees of heaven," the speaker can say, along with that eagle, *"This is what I wanted."*

Certainly, the use of the past tense "was" in the poem "I Was Afraid of Dying" further demonstrates Wright's substantial transformation. No longer fearful of death—the ultimate effect of original sin—the speaker finds the healing waters he was seeking and does so in the midst of "damp fields." He feels reassured merely by "trying to keep still, listening." As a result of such attention, what Thoreau called being "forever on the alert," the speaker's reevaluation of the relationship between humankind and nature issues its reward. By the final poem of the volume, "A Dream of Burial," the "hunching" old women have been transformed yet again:

> A parade of old women
> Sang softly above me,
> Faint mosquitoes near still water.

Likewise, the poet himself is transformed: he has become the redemptive "still water" that can solve "the whole loneliness" of the collection's opening poem. He earns self-knowledge, discovers joy, and most importantly, accepts a sense of possibility.

### 3   Vulnerability and Its Rewards

This is the same possibility that the speakers of "Lying in a Hammock" and "Two Hangovers" first notice but cannot fully realize: the possibility of a transcendent joy. Wright's feeling of unity with natural elements comes to its best expression in "A Blessing," a poem which also substantially resolves the subject-object distance. Here, Wright acknowledges humanity's ties with the natural world and rejoices in that awareness.

Wright's "A Blessing," is not only the best of the poems in *Branch* but also exemplary of Wright's transformation from a poetry of aesthetic and religious orthodoxy to a poetry of attention. Further, a comparison of the published version with its unpublished revision establishes the craftsmanship that characterizes Wright's newer work. It establishes, also, that in a free-verse poem, as in other forms of verse, the alteration of a few words or the deletion of a few lines can significantly transform the poem—for good or ill. Free verse, as Wright indicates, is not at all free of form or structure. Though Wright moves from rhyme and regular meter, from irony and paradox, he retains his concern for craft. Perhaps most importantly, a comparison of the two drafts sheds light on the real tensions involved in Wright's redefinition of the poetic self, for it shows his hesitancy to embrace a poetrics of vulnerability.

Wright's "A Blessing" has received widespread critical acclaim. Norman Friedman, in fact, goes as far as to say that "for sweetness, for joy, for precision, for rhythm, for eroticism, for structure, for surprise—for all of these things, this poem is nearly perfect."[30] Most readers of contemporary poetry would assent to Friedman's high praise. It is easy to see why:

> Just off the highway to Rochester, Minnesota,
> Twilight bounds softly forth on the grass.
> And the eyes of those two Indian ponies
> Darken with kindness.
> They have come gladly out of the willows
> To welcome my friend and me.
> We step over the barbed wire into the pasture
> Where they have been grazing all day, alone.
> They ripple tensely, they can hardly contain their happiness
> That we have come.

They bow shyly as wet swans. They love each other.
There is no loneliness like theirs.
At home once more,
They begin munching the young tufts of spring
    in the darkness.
I would like to hold the slenderer one in my arms,
For she has walked over to me
And nuzzled my left hand.
She is black and white,
Her mane falls wild on her forehead,
And the light breeze moves me to caress her long ear
That is delicate as the skin over a girl's wrist.
Suddenly I realize
That if I stepped out of my body I would break
Into blossom.

In late 1960 John Frederick Nims accepted "A Blessing," under the title "The Blessing," for *Poetry* magazine. But the story is not that simple. Before Nims could publish the above version, he had to contend with James Wright, for Wright had, in the meantime, decided to revise his "nearly perfect" poem. The following is the revision that Wright sent to *Poetry* for Nims's approval.

## JUST OFF THE HIGHWAY TO ROCHESTER, MINNESOTA

Twilight bounds softly out on the grass.
They have come gladly out of the willows
To welcome my friend and me
We step over the barbed wire into the pasture
Where they have been grazing all day, alone.
And the eyes of those two Indian ponies
Darken.
I would like to hold the slenderer one in my arms,
For she has walked over to me
And nuzzled my left hand.
She is black and white,

Her mane falls wild on her forehead.
At home once more,
They begin munching the young tufts of spring
    in the darkness.
I think
That if I stepped out of my body I would break
Into blossom.[31]

That any truly good poem should require meticulous reworking is not surprising, but that Wright should feel it necessary to revise "The Blessing" so markedly is really quite startling. "The Blessing" is simply the superior version. As we shall see, the act of revision has a great deal to do with Wright's reluctance to open himself entirely to charges of naïveté. However ingenuous the published version may appear, Wright was clearly aware of its risks.

Asserting that many contemporary poets derive from the Romantics has become a workable scholarly truth, for these poets also recognize and seek to overcome a kind of subject-object dichotomy that isolates the individual from the natural world. Wright's "The Blessing" moves with surety to a resolution of this dichotomy, a resolution found in the poem's brief but consequential transcendent moment. "The Blessing" is the better poem because—unlike its revision—it subtly prepares for the speaker's final moment of epiphany.

Though several lines are rearranged in the revision, the significant alterations can be generalized as follows: Wright makes the first line the title of the poem, changes "softly forth" to "softly out on," drops the phrase "with kindness," recasts "Suddenly I realize" as "I think," and, finally, deletes six lines (9–12, 20–21) from the poem. What results from this revision is a poem composed primarily of passive description. The speaker's interaction with his environment is reduced, and with it, the appealing Romantic texture of the poem is flattened.

The title "The Blessing" seems more in keeping with both the emotion and the tenor of the poem. It provides the suggestion of a sacred gift transferred from one to another, and it introduces the tone of awe and religious splendor that colors the simple actions that follow. The grounding in place and time, so important to the poem's lyric intensity,

Wright achieves nicely enough in the opening of "The Blessing." The speaker has escaped the human community (except for his friend) and stands "off the highway," away from the linear strictures of human time and travel. The time of day is twilight, a sort of magical period when light and dark mingle to create a fascinating other, one that is wholly neither.

The speaker of "The Blessing" further establishes the Romantic atmosphere of the poem with his personification of the twilight as it "bounds softly forth on the grass." The personification itself and the language of its presentation both accentuate the vulnerability of the speaker who is enthralled by the natural elements that surround him. That speaker is vulnerable simply because—in the decidedly rational climate the New Critics had established by 1960—he allows his intuition and imagination to operate freely in the poem and to lead him to a felt unity with nature. Also, by choosing the somewhat archaic "forth," Wright confirms his debt to the Romantics (a move not as fashionable then as it is now). Finally, in terms of the poem's music, the repetition of smooth "f" and "th" consonant sounds produces a more gentle lyric effect than the clash of vowels in the "softly out on" phrasing in "Just off the Highway."

In the Romantic setting of "The Blessing," common distinctions break down. The ponies' eyes "darken with kindness" in a manner that repudiates the stereotypic association of darkness with evil and foreboding. This yoking of opposites, of darkness and kindness, eludes the speaker of "Just off the Highway," who says only that the ponies' eyes "darken." These early lines of "The Blessing" prompt a poetic reassessment of reality. In this poem common distinctions are not always to be trusted, suggesting that a close (Emersonian or Traklian) attention to nature is one means to greater perception.

Another movement toward redefinition occurs in both versions when the speaker and his friend "step over the barbed wire" that separates the human from the natural. They transcend the barrier that prevents any real communication between the two, and in doing so, they prefigure both the ecstasy and the peril of the poem's conclusion. In "The Blessing" version, four significant lines—which Wright curiously deletes from its revision—detail the further evolution of this process:

They ripple tensely, they can hardly contain their happiness
That we have come.
They bow shyly as wet swans. They love each other.
There is no loneliness like theirs.

The radical awareness of an incompleteness in nature is a quality
Wright praises in the poetry of René Char, of whom he says, "For this
poet, nature, so richly presented, is yet incomplete without man."[32]
Here, the speaker attributes human qualities to the ponies; they can be
shy, happy, lonely, and most of all, they can love. Moreover, their fullest pleasure seems to come not only from the love of "each other" but
also from the love of the two people who "have come" to visit them.
"There is no loneliness like theirs" because nature remains inchoate
without the human.

Thus, in these four lines of "The Blessing," Wright rejects duality in
favor of unity. He allows the speaker to begin to resolve the subject-
object dichotomy that divides the human from the natural. These feelings of unity originate when the speaker notices the ponies as more
than objects, when he comes to see them as creatures with whom he
shares both a physical and emotional landscape; they come to fruition
when the speaker experiences the poem's final transcendent moment.

Both versions further present the ponies as figures of unification.
They partake of a spiritual communion, "munching the young tufts"
of a revenant spring enveloped, again, in "darkness." One pony in particular represents a merging of the opposites discussed earlier, for she
is "black and white." A composite of light and dark, she has "nuzzled"
the speaker's hand, and for her part, has eliminated a portion of the
subject-object distance.

In "Just off the Highway," however, this encounter is somewhat
incomplete, for the speaker does not, in turn, touch the pony. In the
following lines which were deleted from the revision, the speaker of
"The Blessing" remarks:

And the light breeze moves me to caress her long ear
That is delicate as the skin over a girl's wrist.

Compelled by a "light" wind in darkness, subject and object interact, as
equals, in a world made intensely alive. There is no arrogant insistence

on rational and intellectual detachment from nature. The speaker, in fact, collapses all distinctions when he calls upon a human element, the skin of a girl's wrist, to describe the softness of the pony's ear.

As a result of this brief touch with the natural, the speaker of "The Blessing" suddenly accepts the possibility of transcendence. This realization evokes both terror—he would certainly "break" if he did so—and wonder—he would become pure, natural "blossom":

> Suddenly I realize
> That if I stepped out of my body I would break
> Into blossom.

Such a moment of insight informs the speaker of both the risk and the potential reward inherent in numinous experience. Manuscript evidence would have it that Wright does believe an individual can experience these revelations immanent in nature. Wright's handwritten notation on the manuscript copy of "Just off the Highway" indicates as much. To the right of the poem's final three lines—its moment of epiphany—he writes simply, "It is possible." (See page 215.)

Note, though, how the phrasing of "Just off the Highway" clouds this aura of possibility:

> I think
> That if I stepped out of my body I would break
> Into blossom.

The phrase "I think" lacks the suddenness of insight shown in "The Blessing" and betrays a sense of uncertainty. Or worse, the final lines seem prompted by the bland and wholly out-of-place action of rational thought in a moment of arational and intuitive knowledge. Thus, the imagination seems shackled by the ruminative.

It is clear, then, that Wright's revisions alter more than the poem's surface. "Just off the Highway" lacks the heightened lyric quality and the full resolution of the subject-object distinction which characterize "The Blessing." As a result of the deletion of six significant lines, the revision does not properly prepare for the revelation of its final lines. In contrast, the structure of "The Blessing" subtly establishes a context for the poem's conclusion. The speaker's subjective awareness results from the gradual reduction of the distance between human and natural object that precedes it. These are the elements of "joy," "eroticism," and "structure" that Friedman praises. Without them, the poem falters.

In revising "The Blessing," perhaps Wright sought to temper the Romantic vulnerability of the poem. After all, "The Blessing" was a large break from the detached formalism which dominates *The Green Wall* and *Saint Judas*. In the poem he implicitly rejects the era's obsession with original sin, those beliefs that separate the human and the natural in a kind of Post-Lapsarian world of disjuncture. In "The Blessing," he imagines a Pre-Lapsarian world and assumes a momentary wholeness that to some may appear unsophisticated, merely jejune wishful thinking. In "The Rise and Fall of James Wright," Edward Butscher, for example, disparages Wright for his "almost innate sentimentality" and his simplistic quest for "romantic oases" in the modern world.[33] By revising the poem as he did, Wright shows his awareness of these cultural and aesthetic pressures. Whatever his intentions, these revisions display the courage and inventiveness that characterize Wright's work throughout his career. "Just off the Highway" should not be construed as evidence that Wright was inept at revision.

In this instance, Nims evidently urged Wright to retain the Romantic risks that produced a compelling poem. On December 13, 1960, Wright noted on the manuscript copy of "Just off the Highway" that Nims "still wants to print the previous version." Below that on the same page, Wright indicated to himself, "Okay. See how it looks in print." And with that, "The Blessing," Wright's "nearly perfect" poem, came to appear in *Poetry*.[34]

Obviously, Wright was convinced by what he saw in print; he included "The Blessing" in *The Branch Will Not Break* (which at one point was titled *The Blessing*) under the slightly altered title, "A Blessing." Here, Wright shows his talent at revision. Through this simple change of article, he implies that the sort of transcendent moment which forms the basis of the poem is more than an isolated occurrence, and indeed, is likely to happen again.

"A Blessing," then, represents Wright's poetry of possibility, a poetry rooted in a close attention to the natural world. Moreover, it reveals the distance between the poet of aesthetic and religious orthodoxy and the vulnerable, Romantic poet of *Branch*. Written in free verse, the poem makes use of plain language; Wright's choice of the colloquial "slenderer" measures just how far he has come in that regard. Also, the poem's structure deftly prepares for, and thereby emphasizes, its startling final image, its transcendent moment. Finally, the poem affirms a harmony with nature that results from an Emersonian or Traklian attention to natural things. That Wright would not long retain this Romantic joy (or its forms) is not altogether surprising. The poem, like the whole of *The Branch Will Not Break*, represents another step in the continuous exploration that is the sustaining gift of James Wright's poetry.

# 5 The Jenny Poems:

*Amenities of Stone, Shall We Gather
At the River*, "New Poems,"
and *Two Citizens*

Few will dispute that James Wright alters his
poetic stance in the important and beautiful collection *The Branch Will
Not Break* (1963). Peter Stitt, in fact, argues that Wright's *The Branch
Will Not Break*—much like Roethke's *The Lost Son*, Lowell's *Life Studies*,
and Berryman's *Homage to Mistress Bradstreet*—shows the poet putting
"on a distinctive voice."[1]

However, so much has been made of this one (albeit significant) alteration in style that the transformations which occur after *Branch*
have been largely ignored—or rejected.[2] In either case, the loss is a
considerable one, for Wright is not a poet satisfied with stasis in style
or content, and the books that immediately surround the publication
of *Branch* attest to that.

Grouped together, *Amenities of Stone* (1961–62), *Shall We Gather at the
River* (1968), the "New Poems" section of *Collected Poems* (1972), and *Two
Citizens* (1973) may be regarded as Wright's Jenny poems, for Jenny, his
lover-muse, plays a large part in his movement from despair to affirmation. These collections reveal Wright's continuing quest to resolve
the distance which separates the human and the natural worlds, something he achieves in *Branch* and thereafter struggles to sustain. Secondly, they display Wright's use of various traditional and experimental poetic forms and his awareness of the possibilities inherent in this
variety of poetic voices. Most importantly, these poems show Wright
seeking a reconciliation of extremes, a way to deal with the joy and
despair that alternately dominate his work.

In these Jenny poems, Wright confronts the question of what one should do with this brief life in the face of death and its agent, despair. The question is not a unique one, nor, perhaps, is Wright's eventual answer. But as Wright moves toward an affirmative and compassionate response, he offers the reassurance he gains from a child's advice: "Take care now, / Be patient, and live" ("The Old WPA Swimming Pool in Martins Ferry, Ohio," *TC*).[3]

It is appropriate that this advice be given by a child, for the innocence and knowledge of a child come to Wright in *Two Citizens* and bring him to the beginnings of a poetry of affirmation. As I have indicated earlier, Wright's career may be divided into three interrelated rhetorical and thematic phases: one characterized by containment, another by vulnerability and possibility, and the last by integration and affirmation. Wright himself seems aware of these phases in his own and other poets' work and views them as essential to an artist's growth. In fact, his analysis of Whitman's career serves reasonably well to illuminate the transitions of his own:

> He [Whitman] becomes a great artist by the ways of growth which Nietzsche magnificently describes in the first speech of *Thus Spake Zarathustra*: The Three Metamorphoses of the Spirit. The spirit that truly grows, says Nietzsche, will first be a camel, a beast of burden, who labors to bear the forms of the past, whether in morality or art or anything else; then he will change into a lion, and destroy not merely what he hates but even what he loves and understands; and the result of this concerned and accurate destruction will be the spirit's emergence as a child, who is at last able to create clearly and powerfully from within his own imagination.[4]

The parallels to Wright's career are obvious. The form and manner of his first two books, *The Green Wall* (1957) and *Saint Judas* (1959), clearly owe much to such writers as John Donne and Robert Herrick. This is Wright's "camel" phase, during which he carries forward the traditions of the past. Through his work on the unpublished collection *Amenities of Stone* and its successor *The Branch Will Not Break*, Wright rears up like a lion to destroy those principles to which he had once adhered.

Furthermore, a kind of formal variety—or perhaps confusion—characterizes the latter half of this phase. Here, Wright destroys "not merely what he hates but even what he loves and understands." *Shall We Gather at the River* (1968), "New Poems" (1972), and *Two Citzens* (1973) display this uncertainty, for Wright both attacks and defends traditional verse forms, all the while writing both regularly metered and free-verse pieces. It is obvious that Wright desires the kind of aesthetic freedom and possibility that would enable him to write both kinds of verse, and perhaps achieving that freedom amounts to "the poetry of a grown man," which he so fervently seeks.

Near the conclusion of *Two Citizens*, Wright emerges "as a child, who is at last able to create clearly and powerfully from within his own imagination." This third phase is fully realized later in *To a Blossoming Pear Tree* (1977) and *This Journey* (1982), the two collections which are the subjects of chapters 6 and 7. However, a key characteristic of this third stage first appears in *Two Citizens*: the child's innocence and unquestioning affirmation of life, a point which I will discuss later in this essay. For now, it will be useful to examine the manner in which Wright struggles to sustain the joy in nature he discovered in *Branch*.

*1 "I want to be lifted up. . . ."*

The final poems of *Branch* posit a world where transcendence through natural things stands as a possibility come to fruition. Through his interaction with two Indian ponies, the speaker of "A Blessing" is drawn into a wondrous and dangerous communion with natural elements, and the subject-object distance separating the human and the natural is wholly eliminated. After *Branch*, Wright's desire for transcendence remains, but its realization proves infrequent. In fact, *Shall We Gather at the River*, the darkest of Wright's collections, opens with a plea for such unification. It is a prayer that goes mostly unanswered:

I want to be lifted up
By some great white bird unknown to the police,

> And soar for a thousand miles and be carefully hidden,
> Modest and golden as one last corn grain,
> Stored with the secrets of the wheat and the mysterious lives
> Of the unnamed poor.[5]
> ("The Minneapolis Poem")

The passage evokes both Wright's yearning for spiritual transcendence and his familiar identification with the neglected and downtrodden members of society. Here, not only does the speaker wish for unity with the natural but he also proposes to become a natural thing, "modest and golden as one last corn grain."

More importantly, the stanza contains a phrase crucial to the understanding of these three volumes: "I want to be lifted up." In these collections, Wright conjoins rising and transcendence into a religious act so appealing that he continually and passionately seeks it. Moreover, the honesty of "I want" typifies the emotional authenticity of these works, for Wright does want, does feel inadequate and incomplete, and he is brave enough to say so in these poems. What he wants is a kind of spiritual, natural transcendence; it is his means of getting beyond the pain of human suffering to an understanding of it, for "The sea can stand anything. / I can't" ("The Poor Washed Up by Chicago Winter," SW).

Immersion in nature brought such relief in *Branch*. In *Shall We Gather at the River*, Wright attempts similar tactics:

> Sometimes I have to sleep
> In dangerous places, on cliffs underground,
> Walls that still hold the whole prints
> Of ancient ferns
> ("Living by the Red River," SW).

The results, however, prove far different. Seemingly foredoomed to failure, these attempts to commune with the natural often vitiate the solace Wright had discovered there. Where he once found reassurance, he now encounters a troubling reminder of his human frailty. An early version of "Late November in a Field," a poem Wright began more than six years before *Shall We Gather* was published and one meant to be included in his unpublished manuscript *Amenities of Stone*, illustrates his quest for this sort of spiritual affirmation. The poem's first two lines, which do not appear in the version printed in *Shall We Gather*, indicate clearly what type of situation prompted Wright to seek "a blessing" from nature:

> Yesterday I spoke harshly to someone
> Who was kind to me.
> Today I am walking alone in a bare place,
> And winter is here.
> Two squirrels near a fence post
> Are helping each other drag a branch
> Toward a hiding place; it must be somewhere
> Behind those ash trees.
> They are still alive, they ought to save acorns
> Against the cold.
> Frail paws rifle the troughs between cornstalks
>     when the moon
> Is looking away.
> The earth is hard now,
> The soles of my shoes need repairs.
> I have nothing to ask a blessing for,
> Except these words.
> I wish they were
> Grass.[6]

It is not surprising that he is more troubled than rewarded by watching two squirrels apparently "helping" each other prepare for the perils of an imminent winter. Threatened by the same "cold" environment and offered assistance by a caring friend, the speaker had reacted with angry words instead of thanks. Though such an exchange may seem trivial, for a poet who regards his language as conjunct with his selfhood it represents an unforgivable act of violence. Wright understands well enough that words can be weapons; the desire that his words might become "grass" is in itself a wish for silence, a poet's most severe punishment.

In spite of all that conspires against it, occasionally, a form of transcendence does occur, as in "Listening to the Mourners":

> Now I am speaking with the voice
> Of a scarecrow that stands up
> And suddenly turns into a bird.

Nevertheless, even this momentary transformation into a bird capable of a timely rising produces an epiphany more discomfitting than transcendent. As a result of it, the speaker's perception is elevated only enough for him to "hear myself weeping."

*Shall We Gather at the River* indisputably represents the emotional nadir of Wright's work; in "New Poems" and *Two Citizens* he gradually regains a comforting relationship with nature in which rivers and trees play an integral role. Born along the Ohio River in Martins Ferry, Wright sees the Ohio as the Styx, as both the river of human death and the river of spiritual rebirth. On one hand, it is a cause of violent death: "Under the enormous pier-shadow, / Hobie Johnson drowned in a suckhole" ("The River Down Home," in *SW*). On the other, it is a means of revivification: "Close by a big river, I am alive in my own country, / I am home again" ("RIP," *SW*). Though the river may seem only a "Tar and chemical strangled tomb" ("Three Sentences for a Dead Swan, *SW*), Wright still believes the Ohio possesses healing qualities:

> Oh my back-broken beloved Ohio.
> I, too, was beautiful, once,
> Just like you . . .
> This morning I feel like that old child
> You gathered so often
> Into your rinsing arms,
> And bathed and healed,
> I feel lonesome,
> Sick at heart,
> Frightened,
> And I don't know

Why.
*Help.*[7]
("Many of Our Waters: Variations on a Poem by a Black Child," *Collected Poems*)

By beseeching the river for *"help"* and fully expecting to receive it, Wright reaffirms his belief in nature's healing powers. Likewise, Wright comes to envision trees as a helpful source of spiritual, almost transcendent beauty. Much like emissaries from a more perfect world, these trees both reveal to us our essential humanness and offer us knowledge of what we might become if given the understanding necessary to transcend it. In fact, trees often become elements of nature transformed to ideal, feminine beauty. For example, the speaker of "Blue Teal's Mother" (*CP*), in spite of his evident sensitivity to the incredulity and cynicism of his imagined reader, relates the magical story of what happened one night when "a bulk tree got in my way":

Never mind what I thought when dawn broke.
In the dark, the night before,
I knew perfectly well I could have knocked
The bulk tree down.
Well, cut it up, anyway.

I didn't hurt it.
I gathered it into my arms.
You may not believe this, but
It turned into a slender woman.
Stop nagging me. I know
What I just said.
It turned into a slender woman.

This mystical encounter in an apparently transcendent natural environment brings the speaker to self-knowledge; from it he realizes that "I, too, live, / Even in my pain."

Trees, in particular, are capable of mysterious transformations. The speaker of "A Secret Gratitude" (*CP*) even claims to know a girl "Who could turn into a laurel tree / Whenever she felt like it. / Think of that."

Even more importantly, as agents of transcendence trees provide the sought-after means to "escape from" the body:

> I rose from my body so high into
> That sycamore tree that it became
> The only tree that ever loved me.
> ("Son of Judas," *TC*)

What such an escape becomes, paradoxically, is a source of revelation about the body's value: "Now I've discovered my body was alive / After all."

Now more at home within his own body, no longer assenting to the Puritanistic disgust of the flesh expressed in Roethke's early poem "Epidermal Macabre," Wright also more fully understands the complex relationship between the human and the natural. Admirably, he refuses to sentimentalize the connection, as is shown in "A Secret Gratitude" when the speaker and a group of men spot several deer. In the moment of vulnerability for these deer, he realizes the potential of humanity to create or destroy: "We are men. / We are capable of anything. / We could have killed every one of those deer. . . . / We can kill anything. / We can kill our own bodies."

Suddenly made aware of his human malevolence toward natural things and toward his own body, Wright learns to appreciate the delicate connections among living things of all types. It fosters the kind of regard for life that Wright admires in his Aunt Agnes who once saved a goat from stoning when she "gathered the goat, / Nuts as she was, / Into her sloppy arms" ("Ars Poetica: Some Recent Criticism," *TC*). Agnes may have been "nuts," but she was sane enough to recognize and respect the sanctity of all earthly life.

Perhaps "Northern Pike" best shows Wright's mature awareness of the relationship between humankind and the natural. The poem, another example of a dialogic text, opens with an argument already in progress. This argument, however, one which concerns the morality of eating a Northern which the speaker and his friends have caught to feed themselves, is the speaker's argument both with himself and with his reader:

All right. Try this,
Then. Every body
I know and care for,
And every body
Else is going
To die in a loneliness
I can't imagine and a pain
I don't know. We had
To go on living.

There is considerable distance between the poem's conclusion and the marked emotional dejection and separation from the natural world characteristic of *Shall We Gather at the River*. In this instance Wright comes to accept the complex interrelationship of the human and natural worlds. Though the men "would just as soon . . . let / the living go on living," they eat the fish to sustain their own lives. By doing so, they reenact a kind of Eucharistic feast that enables the speaker to reach a spiritual epiphany: "There must be something very beautiful in my body. / I am so happy."

Finally, through experiences like this one, Wright is able to maintain, although tenuously, the joy in nature he first discovers in *The Branch Will Not Break*. Wright's appreciation of the natural world, though, is more complex than one might at first imagine; in it he finds a means to sanctify the beings of the visible, physical world, but he also discovers here a means to escape these physical entities for the tempting realm of spiritual life. His admiration for the natural, therefore, is both an acceptance of the beauty one can see and touch—and a refusal to be limited to that.

Wright, however, does not sustain all of the major breakthroughs of that collection in his later work. In *Branch* Wright almost exclusively uses a colloquial voice to speak his free-verse poems, but in the volumes following *Branch* Wright occasionally returns to a formal voice and to regular metrics. The gesture amounts to more than a curious about-face; through it Wright demonstrates his dissatisfaction with the limits of free verse and signals his own search for a poetics possible of admitting a variety of forms and voices.

2  *"The kind of poetry I want to write is*
      *The poetry of a grown man."*

Although Wright is often a quotable poet, perhaps the most remarked-on of his statements occurs in the "New Poems" section of his *Collected Poems*. The statement appropriately opens Wright's discussion of his awareness of his poetic (or unpoetic) language and delineates his movement from a formal to a colloquial voice:

> The kind of poetry I want to write is
>     The poetry of a grown man.
> The young poets of New York come to me with
> Their mangled figures of speech,
> But they have little pity
> For the pure clear word.
>
> I know something about the pure clear word.
> Though I am not yet a grown man.
> And who is he?

The final question is a useful one, and not only Wright has asked it. Readers and critics alike wonder just what establishes a poet's work as that of a "grown man." Evidently, Wright thinks the prospect has something to do with avoiding the "mangled figures of speech" that dominate (and some say mar) his own first two collections. It has something to do with "the pure clear word," an Horatian concept in Wright's thinking. Although Horace's insistence on rhyme, meter, and formal control contributes to the formalism of the first two books, these are the elements of Horace's *Ars Poetica* that Wright's early masters—Ben Jonson (who translated the *Ars* into couplets in 1604), Alexander Pope, Samuel Johnson, and for that matter John Crowe Ransom—most emphasized. Now, Wright more and more comes to see the principles of clarity, honesty, and precision as Horatian. As Dave Smith reminds us, Horace was (like Wright) a poetic "innovator" concerned with honest and direct expression.[8] When Wright eventually recognizes that his initial preoccupation with regular meter and elevated language is a misreading of Horace's truest lesson, he acknowledges the importance of simplicity in good writing. In "Prayer to the Good Poet," a poem which asks Horace to welcome Wright's deceased father into heaven, he indicates just that:

> Quintus Horatius Flaccus, my good father,
> You were just the beginning, you quick and lonely
> Metrical crystals of February.
> It is just snow. (*TC*)

Indeed, those "metrical crystals" were just the "beginning" for Wright. They were the mode of his early, adopted voice, the voice he modeled after his formal masters. They had led him to an elaborate and ornate verse, which in *The Green Wall* had insisted those snowflakes were "flawless hexagons" ("To a Troubled Friend"). Now, "It is just snow." Furthermore, that Wright believes he "is not yet a grown man" underscores the importance of the growth process in the art of writing poetry. Perhaps Wright understands that he still resides in the second of Nietzsche's three metamorphoses of the spirit; he understands that growth and change await him and should be welcomed.

Wright begins such a transition in *Shall We Gather* by declaring, "To speak in a flat voice / Is all that I can do." Such a declaration tempts critics to seize upon it as evidence of Wright's altogether altered style. However, a close study of the poem in which these lines appear reveals something quite different:

SPEAK

> To speak in a flat voice
> Is all that I can do.
> I have gone every place
> Asking for you.
> Wondering where to turn
> And how the search would end
> And the last street light spin
> Above me blind.
>
> Then I returned rebuffed
> And saw under the sun
> The race not to the swift
> Nor the battle won.

Liston dives in the tank,
Lord, in Lewiston, Maine,
And Ernie Doty's drunk
In hell again.

And Jenny, oh my Jenny
Whom I love, rhyme be damned,
Has broken her spare beauty
In a whorehouse old.
She left her new baby
In a bus-station can,
And sprightly danced away
Through Jacksontown.

Which is a place I know,
One where I got picked up
A few shrunk years ago
By a good cop.
Believe it, Lord, or not.
Don't ask me who he was.
I speak of flat defeat
In a flat voice.

I have gone forward with
Some, a few lonely some.
They have fallen to death.
I die with them.
Lord, I have loved Thy cursed,
The beauty of Thy house:
Come down. Come down. Why dost
Thou hide thy face?

Wright's poem is a dark quest for reassurance, a search for a spiritual light. It is a plea for God to reveal order and meaning, to reveal His "face" to the distraught speaker. But is the prayer, as the speaker contends, entirely spoken "in a flat voice"? Surely not.

The music of the poem is far from flat. Written in iambics, the eight-line stanzas alternate three lines of trimeter with one line of dimeter. Also, the stanzas are rhymed *a b a b, c d c d*, and they make use of such exact rhymes as do/you and sun/won. But the accomplished off-rhymes warrant more attention: voice/place, tank/drunk, and baby/away show a trained poetic ear. Actually, the poem proves to be a tightly constructed and quite melodious piece. It is anything but flat.

In addition, the speaker's voice shows confidence and control. In the second stanza of his invocation to God, he deftly juxtaposes the lessons of Ecclesiastes with some more modern examples. Here, Sonny Liston is accused of throwing a prize fight and the familiar figure of George Doty reappears. Later, Jenny, to whom *Shall We Gather at the River* is dedicated, makes her first published appearance in Wright's work, this time as a prostitute who abandons her child. Wright's ability to draw upon these diverse subjects gives the poem its emotional and intellectual breadth.

As the poem moves toward its conclusion, the last stanza displays a marked alteration in language and tone. The language becomes imploringly biblical and quiet. Suddenly, "Thy," "dost," and "Thou" appear as naturally as "drunk" and "damned" did earlier. The poem evokes its emotional plea by use of music, rhyme, regular meter, and varying levels of language. As a piece of poetic artifice, it is a tour de force. Though Wright surely can speak "in a flat voice" when he chooses, that is certainly not "all" he "can do."

In fact, occasional passages from these three volumes recall the formal language of his earlier work. Although Wright contends, "I am not one of the English poets" ("At the Grave," *TC*), he can still sound like one. Note the inversion and overt poeticism of these following lines from *Shall We Gather*:

> Oh the voice lovelier was
> Than a crow's dreaming face,
> His secret face, that smiles
> Alive in a dead place.
> Oh I was lonely, lonely:
> What were the not to me?
> ("For the Marsh's Birthday")

The inversion employed in the first line, the repetition in the fifth, and the poetic breathlessness and vagueness of "the not" in the sixth all could qualify this as the work of a number "of the English poets." During these years, and for that matter throughout his career, Wright refuses to drop altogether the ways of the past—they are as real and earned to him as are his newer aesthetic principles.

This paradox can be easily shown by comparing two poems from Wright's "New Poems." In the first, "A Way to Make a Living," Wright seems to have decided to abandon rhyme and regular meter, for these elements have come to represent a kind of "graveyard" of poets inhabited by "the polished / Dead of whom we make so much." Wright admits the choice he had to make:

> I could have stayed there with them.
> Cheap, too.
> Imagine, never
> To have turned
> Wholly away from the classic
> Cold, the hill, so laid
> Out, measure by seemly measure.

Surely the phrases "classic / Cold" and "measure by seemly measure" make it clear Wright is talking about traditional poetics. Rather than remaining among the good dead poets (and writing in their formal style), Wright chooses to "take my last nourishment / Of measure from a dark blue / Ripple on swell on ripple that makes / Its own garlands." In these lines Wright echoes both Whitman, the father of American free verse, and his own dialogic poem "The Morality of Poetry" in which he decides to "let all measures die."

This play and counterplay characterizes Wright's work. Although the uncautious reader might assume from the above poem that Wright has given up rhyme and regular meter, that reader would be wrong. Donald Hall, remember, tells us that Wright was "constantly attracted to metrical verse. . . . and was always dabbling in it."[9] A little later in "New Poems," he constructs these metrical, rhymed lines in honor of Swift:

Here are some songs he lived in, kept
Secret from almost everyone
And laid away, while Stella slept,
Before he slept, and died, alone.
Gently, listen, the great shade passes,
Magnificent, who can still bear,
Beyond the range of horses' asses,
Nobilities, light, light and air.
("Written in a Copy of Swift's Poems, for Wayne Burns")

Here, Wright appears to label those who cannot appreciate Swift's (or any poet's) formal verses mere "horses' asses." Perhaps, Wright himself best explains the matter: "I do not think there is any opposition between traditional iambic verse and free verse; they're simply two different kinds of form."[10] It is as if Wright seeks only the possibility of writing in either style, without preconceived notions of the propriety of one form or another.

These books show the freedom and possibility of his *Amenities of Stone*, a volume written during the time he was learning to write effectively in free as well as formal verse. Indeed, Wright often combines these two styles, proving by example that they are not mutually exclusive. Sometimes he combines prescribed form, meter, and colloquial and formal language, as shown by the previous discussion of "Speak." Other times, he adopts the inner form, the argument of a traditional form and uses it to his ends. For example, "Love in a Warm Room in Winter" (*TC*) displays the familiar influence of Herrick's Cavalier lyrics, though Wright composes his poem in a plain, colloquial idiom:

The trouble with you is
You think all I want to do
Is get you into bed
And make love with you.

And that's not true.

I was just trying to make friends.
All I wanted to do

Was get into bed
With you and make

Love with you.

Who was that little bird we saw towering upside down
This afternoon on that pine cone, on the edge of a cliff?
In the snow? Wasn't he charming? Yes, he was, no
Now, now,
Just take it easy.
Aha!

Of course, it is the poem's inner form, its *invitation du amour* that
Wright borrows from Herrick, a poet for whom Wright admits a great
admiration. He then adapts it to his own voice and, in this way, both
accepts and subtly alters that tradition.[11]

I have established the real variety of writing styles present in
Wright's middle period. Though he may have broken with the traditions of the past in *Branch*, Wright clearly is not ready to abandon those
conventions altogether. However, few critics note this element of
constancy in Wright's work. They prefer, instead, to dwell on what
they see as his new flat voice—and to berate him for it. Much of this
critical reaction is simply vicious.[12] Responding to this backlash of criticism, Wright offers an explanation for his transition:

All this time I've been slicking into my own words
The beautiful language of my friends.
I have to use my own, now.
That's why this scattering poem sounds the way it does.
("Many of Our Waters: Variations on a Poem by a Black Child")

This angry critical response accounts, I believe, for a striking transition in the voice of the speaker in Wright's poems. Once content to
remain almost absent from the poem, the speaker now adopts an aggressive relationship with the reader. This transformation becomes
obvious if one recalls the poems of *Branch*. Repeatedly in these poems,
the speaker stays on the periphery of the poem, due, no doubt, to the

influence of Georg Trakl, whom Wright calls "the father of my sound." Here is an example of such a persona-less poem:

## IN FEAR OF HARVESTS

It has happened
Before: nearby
The nostrils of slow horses
Breathe evenly.
And the brown bees drag their high garlands,
Heavily,
Toward hives of snow.

No speaker enters the text of the poem; no personal pronoun even refers to him. Instead, what surrounds the speaker composes the poem, and the speaker's intuited sense of death and cycle permeates its images. It is precisely that intuition, conveyed in a terse series of images and culminating in a final image drawn both from the outer world of experience and the inner world of the imagination, which expresses the poem's meaning.

In Wright's evolving poetic voice, the speaker not only actively engages the movement of the poem, he also directly engages the reader—sometimes in a feisty, aggressive manner. In "Many of Our Waters: Variations on a Poem by a Black Child," the speaker interrupts the poem to address his readers:

If you do not care one way or another about
The preceding lines,
Please do not go on listening
On any account of mine. Please leave the poem.
Thank you.

One assumes that Wright does want the reader to "care about" his poem, but he chooses to confront the reader (or perhaps the critic or reviewer), as if he already envisions a segment of his audience who will read his work with disdain. "Katy Did" opens in a similar confrontational manner:

> I
> Was a good child,
> So I am
> A good man. Put that
> In your pipe.

One might easily regard the voice as belonging to a speaker with a chip on his shoulder rather than one spoken by a poet trying in good faith to say something clearly and honestly. What it does reveal, however, is the vulnerability of Wright's speaker and the extent to which the poetry of self-disclosure has resulted in a poetic posture that retains its defenses by means of a quick offense. It shows, also, a speaker open to alternatives in language and expression that might help him reach his reader. This very "All right. Try this, / Then" attitude of "Northern Pike" gives the poem its honesty and urgency, demonstrating that real communication matters more than elegance, certainty, and artifice.

Though he proves his talent for traditional poetics in various formal pieces in these volumes, Wright remarks in *Two Citizens*: "No, I ain't much. / The one tongue I can write in / Is my Ohioan" ("To the Creature of Creation"). While the statement is not entirely true, it does show Wright trying to come to terms with the language he heard and used as a boy in Martins Ferry. When he recalls that place and its figures, "Emerson Buchanan, gun on his arm. / Uncle Willy the lone, Shorty the drunk" ("Emerson Buchanan," *TC*), he realizes that he must speak of them in their own language, in what is also *his* language, for none of their names "will scan." He cannot speak of them—or like them—in formal verse alone.

Remembering a time when he told Emerson to "keep his mouth shut," Wright now mourns that he cannot "hear" his language any more, that he cannot easily make connection with it:

> I try and try to hear them, and all I get
> Is a blind dial tone.

We should not forget that Wright was a poet of two earned voices; his doctorate degree in English literature makes his academic voice as real as his colloquial one. Admittedly, there was always a marked tension between the two. But Wright once remarked on the artistic and moral value of listening to a variety of poetic voices: "I think there is something not only artistically beautiful, but very healing about the author who can step back and let other voices come out."[13] Like his master Horace, Wright was also a poor youth who made good in the adult literary world; he, too, had written of the country and the city in both formal and relaxed language. But the "healing" Wright alludes to requires his locating a voice that has roots in his Ohio past; perhaps that is the poetry of "a grown man" he seeks and finds in memorable poems such as "The Old WPA Swimming Pool in Martins Ferry, Ohio" and "October Ghosts." In these poems, Wright's idiom flows naturally from his topic: how to balance reasonably the joy and despair of this world. In these and other poems (the Jenny poems), Wright must choose either his muse Jenny, his "fat blossoming grandmother of the dead," or life on this earth in his human body. Thankfully, he chooses the latter.

### 3  "I want."

In his struggle to balance his feelings of joy and despair, Wright often invokes his lover-muse Jenny, who offers a kind of alternative to the life of the body. Wright's Eurydice, she is a presiding ethereal force who calls him to join her in the transcendent world of the dead. Such a feeling of incompleteness, expressed through his longing for Jenny, had earlier prompted Wright to admit simply: "I want" ("The Offense," *CP*).

What he "wants," though, is neither simply nor readily achieved. Rather, it is the ambitious desire "to know what it's all about"—a kind of epistemological and teleological knowledge that would allow him to reach an equilibrium between his fleeting impulse to joy and his nearly continual urge to despair. This quest for understanding surfaces initially in *Two Citizens* in an epigraph taken from Hemingway's story "The Killers":

> "Well, bright boy," Max said, looking into the mirror, "why don't you say something?"
> "What's it all about?"

"Hey, Al," Max called, "bright boy wants to know what it's all about."
"Why don't you tell him?" Al's voice came from the kitchen.
"What do you think it's all about?"
"What do you think?"

Again the verb "want" suffuses the emotional and intellectual movement of the passage. It becomes a means of self-definition, for Wright's speaker throughout *Two Citizens* is clearly Wright himself. He defines himself in terms of his wants, as if in acknowledging those he may come to self-knowledge.

Throughout these three volumes, Jenny surfaces as the consistent object of Wright's longing. Whether sexual, intellectual, or spiritual, Jenny remains the figure of his desire. She is seemingly the one thing to be sought in or out of this world. Robert Hass's essay, "James Wright," provides a catalogue of Jenny's appearances; she is: "beauty, loneliness, death, the muse, the idea of the good, a sexual shadow, a whore, the grandmother of the dead, the lecherous slit of the Ohio, an abandoner of her child, a 'savage woman with two heads . . . the one / Face broken and savage, the other, the face dead,' the name carved under a tree in childhood close to the quick, a sycamore tree, a lover, the first time he ever rose."[14]

Hass's catalogue substantiates Jenny's pervasive presence in these three volumes. What it does not provide, however, is an idea of what these references amount to, of what Jenny, as a recurrent figure, represents in Wright's poetry. To do so necessitates looking beyond those poems that refer to Jenny which Wright had allowed to be published during his lifetime.

Previously, it was believed that *Shall We Gather at the River* (1968) contained the first references to Jenny. However, since the discovery of Wright's unpublished manuscript *Amenities of Stone*, two earlier appearances have been uncovered. Written during 1961–62, Wright's unpublished "His Farewell to Old Poetry" announces Jenny as the muse of the "Old Poetry," a full six years before she appears in *Shall We Gather*. Wright identifies Jenny as the muse who "survived in trees"; in fact, he calls her "Jenny of maple leaves." More importantly, she functions as the medium through which the poets of the English classicist tradition once spoke to Wright, though now they all are silent. Once again it is helpful to recall these lines:

> Jenny, Sir Walter Ralegh and John Donne
> Brood in the trees, but they say nothing now.
> They sang delicate melodies to your voice
> When I was young.[15]

Coming as it does between the traditional work of *The Green Wall* (1957) and *Saint Judas* (1959) and the deep-image lyrics of *Branch* (1963), the poem establishes Wright's break with the past. But the poem is not joyful; it stands as yet another elegy of wanting. For Jenny has "Vanished without goodbye," and her absence has left the speaker bereft of both his muse and the poetic voice she helped him find: "Now that I cannot hear your voice, I lose / All the old echoes, Jenny, maple leaf." Finally, Jenny comes to be associated with the quick passing of time. The poem's epigraph, "*more precious . . . than the rubies*," makes reference to Sterne's *Tristam Shandy*, and Wright himself quotes the pertinent lines (without acknowledging Jenny or mentioning *Amenities* in which she appears so frequently) in an interview with Peter Stitt:

> I will not argue the matter. Time wastes too fast; every letter I trace tells me with what rapidity Life follows my pen; the days and hours of it, more precious, my dear Jenny! than the rubies about thy neck, are flying over our heads like light clouds of a windy day never to return more.[16]

The other relevant poem from *Amenities*, "Three Letters in One Evening," yields another intriguing look at Jenny. Written in the colloquial (and sometimes conversational) language with which Wright experiments in *Amenities*, the four-page, single-spaced poem concerns the speaker's response to the recent death of a woman referred to as J. . . . (whom we may safely assume is Jenny).[17] As the title implies, the poem is composed of three letters: the first to Jenny's mother, the second to the "unmarried sister," and the last to Jenny herself. (See page 204.)

The rhetoric of each letter is somewhat different from those of the others. Wright, in fact, once outlined his rhetorical plan for each section, indicating that the first letter should be "evasive, formal" and the second "direct, flat," while the third "to Jenny" ought to be "the lyric."[18] According to plan, the speaker retains distance and propriety in the first letter. He coolly remarks that he has learned in the newspaper of Jenny's death, and is, therefore, tendering his "regards / . . . . With every due respect." Of his relationship with Jenny, he says, "I knew her slightly." However, some of the remarks meant to reflect his emotional distance instead begin to expose the surface of a perilous memory:

> When I think about her face,
> I keep nothing but haze
> Falling through maples,
> October nearly gone.

Later on, the letter addressed to the "unmarried sister" indicates the speaker's true despondency at Jenny's death, "Thank you for writing me. / I can say nothing. / J. . . . is dead." Furthermore, the letter makes it apparent that the speaker and Jenny were more than "slightly" acquainted:

> Early today
> I took my stroll among some leaves left over,
> Blackened and tough almost beyond the death,
> The rot. They had gone through all that, and come
> To lie among stones. Even the winter rain
> Could not affect them now. One afternoon,
> Long past, some years ago, she rose to leave,
> Arranged her dress primly as ever, turned,
> And stirred the leaves. Without goodbye, she left.
> I sat alone thinking for a long time.
> Her face, irregular and vulnerable,
> Flamed like a maple leaf, the kind we keep
> For their quick scarlet that is almost sound,
> That falls so richly and turns gray so fast.

In effect, the poem issues a compelling if not in-depth look at Jenny's life, her marriage, and her death in "Sanduskey Falls." Jenny, whom we know mostly as a muse or a ghost from Wright's other work, here gains a personal identity. Rather than the figment of Wright's imagination that most readers have previously considered Jenny, she assumes a reality in these new poems that accounts for and gives focus to Wright's despair. What we see in the figure of Jenny, then, may not be a purely metaphorical expression of amorphous grief, but rather the expression of real and particular grief transmuted in metaphorical terms. Regardless of how one feels about the matter of authenticity, one should note that Wright later told Stitt that *Shall We Gather at the River*—the collection dedicated to Jenny—is written "about a girl I was in love with who has been dead for a long time."[19] In *Amenities of Stone*, some six years earlier than *Shall We Gather*, Wright provides this private mythos surrounding her death:

> You [the sister] were with her. Her husband had gone out
> To fetch the children.
> It was three-thirty. She had done her hair
> Up in a bun.
> She stood on a chair,
> To hold the rods still
> While you lifted up the curtains.
> You turned
> To fold a seam, she lit her cigarette.
> She squealed, then she said nothing, then you turned.
> Then the fire fell across her gently, soft
> As scarlet maple
> That is almost sound.

The muse "Jenny maple leaf" of "His Farewell to Old Poetry" meets her real or imagined death, consumed by fire like a "scarlet maple": "the dress went quickly, and the face. / J. . . .'s face. A strange darkness." As a result of her fiery death, Jenny becomes for Wright a "black leaf coiling / On the moon's left arm." A figure of human love and unfulfilled desire, Jenny now becomes an inhuman, bodiless substance doomed to inhabit an alluring blue sky or a sycamore tree, forever just beyond Wright's human reach.

The third section, Wright's letter to Jenny, establishes her profound impact on his life and art:

> This is the one thousand,
> Eighty-fifth letter I have written you,
> Since your face . . . disappeared
> Out of my life and everything that lived
> In me.

Jenny's loss symbolizes the loss to death of all things loved, the impermanence of the human condition. Her face, "One face, out of the general ruin, clear," unifies and expands the three sections of the poem. For Wright, Jenny's "disappeared" face evokes the memory of his deceased "father's face," the "many faces freed / From Continental Can at six o'clock," the face of "fine Catullus," the "old men / Of T'ang Dynasty" and the "alien Tartar faces" that rule them, and finally, the "raised" face of his "brother's" dead child.²⁰ The listing is wide-ranging and inclusive, a catalogue of the beloved dead worthy of Whitman. Wright's reverent memories of Jenny and the poems he addresses to her are his way of challenging the finality of death and of maintaining a tenuous line of communication with that other world which beckons him. Still, such a memory, necessarily fraught with a passionate yearning to join Jenny, is at once transcendental and deathly. If she cannot come back to him in the world of the living, he is sorely tempted to go to her.

Supposedly, this catharsis concludes Wright's period of brooding about death and the gravestone, what he ruefully calls his "amenities of stone": "Now my amenities of stone are done, / God damn me if I care whether or not / Anyone reads this book, now you will not." The "you" in the poem may be the dead Jenny, or it may be those readers Wright knows will not have a chance to read his *Amenities of Stone* because he had decided to suppress its publication by Wesleyan University Press. By suppressing *Amenities* Wright chooses to keep Jenny and her secret hidden, but he indicates he will do as much at the end of the second letter: "Oh, Jesus. / I think I will keep this . . . / To myself."²¹

Though Wright may have meant to retain the secrecy he first evidences in printing Jenny's name as "J. . . . ," in omitting her name from the epigraph to the unpublished "His Farewell to Old Poetry," and later in withholding publication of *Amenities*, it is clear that for one reason or another he simply could not abandon Jenny in his next three

volumes. She appears, as Hass's list demonstrates, variously and repeatedly. But beyond the act of compiling her appearances, what can
any such list reveal? What does Jenny, as a whole, amount to in
Wright's work?

Supplemented by the two new references, the list establishes Jenny
as an alluring, transcendent, and bodiless figure of desire. Whatever
the case—whether the story of Jenny's life and death is real or
apocryphal—these poems enable Wright (much like Dante seeking his
beloved Beatrice) to search for the lost Jenny and, in the process, to
question the workings of heaven and hell and the flawed world that
lies between them. In nearly every instance, Jenny appears as a deceased or inhuman form summoning Wright to join her in the world of
the dead. For Wright, she represents the pure life of the soul unsullied
by the human condition, an alternative to the life of the body. Jenny so
intrigues Wright because he makes her a figure of a Neoplatonic world
of ideals far removed from that of his limited life on earth. Of course,
as such, she proffers a beguiling choice: to join her in the life of the
soul, he must accept a release from the body that is also its death.

The yearning for and the possibility of such a release recur in
Wright's work with an astonishing frequency. Recall, for instance, the
speaker of "A Blessing" who at the moment of epiphany realizes that if
he "stepped out of" his body he would certainly "break / Into blossom."
Or the speaker of "The Jewel" who stands "upright in the wind" and
witnesses his "bones turn to dark emeralds"; and finally, the poet of
"Goodbye to the Poetry of Calcium" who wishes for release so ar-
dently that he convinces himself he is entirely gone: "Look, I am
nothing."

The choice that Jenny offers entices Wright. It is the source of much
of the tension in these collections in which Wright eventually comes to
reject the allure of a suicidal death and to accept the limited life of the
body. He confronts and resolves this dialectic most often in the Jenny
poems, where joy and despair, the earthly and the heavenly are juxta-
posed in stark and vivid contrast. In these poems, Wright frequently
adopts a poetic mode of presentation that resembles the mysterious
incantatory songs of Orpheus, enabling him to cast a spell through
which to speak again with the dead Jenny.

Six years after Wright first began to write secretly about Jenny, she appears in *Shall We Gather*. She is a reminder of the impassability of the river Styx, for she is resigned to the underworld which exists beneath the "tar and chemical strangled tomb, / The strange water, the / Ohio River, that is no tomb to / Rise from the dead / From" ("Three Sentences for a Dead Swan"). In "To the Muse," when Wright asks Jenny to reemerge from the Ohio (the modern equivalent of the Styx), he realizes she is not to be lured with falsehood. She knows what it is to live:

> I would lie to you
> If I could.
> But the only way I can get you to come up
> Out of the suckhole, the south face
> Of the Powhatan pit, is to tell you
> What you know.

Later, Wright admits with brutal clarity just what Jenny knows:

> Oh Jenny
> I wish I had made this world, this scurvy
> And disastrous place. I
> Didn't, I can't bear it
> Either, I don't blame you, sleeping down there
> Face down in the unbelievable silk of spring,
> Muse of black sand,
> Alone.

The muse of trees is now the muse of "black sand" who presents a dark alternative to painful human existence. Though Wright shows his distrust of the apparent peacefulness of death (after all, he calls the place where she resides "unbelievable"), he seems equally ready to join her if she will not come to him:

> How can I live without you?
> Come up to me, love,
> Out of the river, or I will
> Come down to you.

The tension, of course, results from Wright's juxtapositioning of "this scurvy / And disastrous place" with the more attractive, impassible resting place of the dead. In a similar fashion, the speaker of "The Idea of the Good" contemplates the release to be found in the calm of the grave, dreaming of his own death when "the black / Rock opens into ground / And closes and I die." Once in the grave, a familiar dialectic again presents itself, this time in the figures of Judas and Jenny. On one hand, the speaker's first thoughts are of Judas, the archetype of human frailty; on the other, he thinks of Jenny, the bodiless spirit that waits for him. It is altogether fitting that Judas and Jenny appear in these poems, for they represent opposite points of this intriguing dialectic. Judas is the consummate example of flawed humanity, Jenny the figure of inhuman peace and unearthly life. He is banished to hell, while she is the "soul," the "one blue wing, torn whole out of heaven" who belongs to ethereal, nonearthly existence. Judas is the embodiment of human limitation, Jenny an expression of ideal possibility.

Though "bone lonely," Wright becomes uneasy in the grave and asks Jenny, his "precious secret," to wait a while longer for him to come to her. Moreover, he makes reference to the unpublished *Amenities of Stone*, in which Jenny figures so largely, and asks for something to revivify his failing human body:

> Jenny, I gave you that unhappy
> Book that nobody knows but you
> And me, so give me
> A little life back. . . .
> Nobody else will follow
> This poem but you,
> But I don't care.
> My precious secret, how
> Could they know
> You or me?
> Patience.

And in some ways Jenny does offer a "little life," but it is a life of the spirit, not of the body, and even that life seems to issue more from Wright's songs than anything else. Orpheus, as the legend goes, played his lyre so beautifully that rocks and trees would rise from their places to follow him. Wright's lyrics to Jenny have a similar but momentary effect on her: Jenny, one can assume, is the woman "who could turn into a laurel tree / Whenever she felt like it" ("A Secret Gratitude") and is the tree who "turned into a slender woman." Thus empowered with the ability for such marvelous transformations, she amounts to the source of a tempting transcendence:

> There used to be a sycamore just
> Outside Martins Ferry,
> Where I used to go.
> I had no friends there.
> Maybe the tree was no woman,
> But when I sat there, I gathered
> That branch into my arms.
> It was the first time I ever rose.
> ("Voices between Waking and Sleeping in the Mountains")

This rising is both sexual and transcendental, and it answers Wright's recurrent prayer to "escape from my body" into a pristine world not inhabited by those who gouge strip mines and pollute rivers. However, such brief moments of transcendence exact their solemn price, for in returning to the body Wright finds it suddenly barren and inhospitable, equally victimized:

> I rose out of my body so high into
> That sycamore tree it became
> The only tree that ever loved me.
>
> And when I came back down into my own body
> Some Hanna among the angels
> Strip mined it.
> ("Son of Judas")

It is understandable, therefore, that Wright eventually comes to see what Jenny promises as antithetical to the gift of human life he may complain about but which he is not ready to give up. He recognizes the limitations of Jenny's enticing but deathly offer of "one wing," labeling it the "wing that I used to think was a poor / Blindness I had to live with with the dead" ("Voices between Waking and Sleeping in the Mountains"). Later in the same poem, Wright recovers from that "blind-ness," regains his vision, and announces to his wife Anne his willing-ness to accept this life not escape from it:

> Annie, it has taken me a long time to live.
> And to take a long time to live is to take a long time
> To understand that your life is your own life.

Thus, Wright's various "amenities of stone," begun in secret, reach a public conclusion in *Two Citizens* some twelve years later. In the haunt-ing "October Ghosts," a poem which recalls the "October nearly gone" of the earlier "Three Letters," Wright finally makes peace with "Jenny cold, Jenny darkness." At last reunited with her, he walks with Jenny "Into the gorges / Of Ohio, where the miners / Are dead with us." Each carries a "blackened crocus," a symbol of the brief and spent life of the dead. As his search for Jenny concludes, suddenly Wright sees that she is not a sycamore tree or a maple leaf, but something far different, perhaps more real:

> Jenny, fat blossoming grandmother of the dead,
> We were both young, and I nearly found you young.
> I could not find you.

Wright seems relieved to discover that Jenny—the "one wing," the "poor / Blindness," the muse of "Old Poetry," the lover who became a "black leaf coiling / On the moon's left arm," the "soul that only existed / In the Jenny sycamore"—is really the "grandmother of the dead." A Neoplatonic and bodiless presence, she has been urging an easy escape from the perils of human life, offering a suicidal release that Wright has finally and decisively refused. "October Ghosts" closes with the line:

> Now I know nothing, I can die alone.

Freed from his compulsive search for the ghostlike Jenny, Wright "can die alone"—in his own good time. When he decides, "By God, I want to live," he utters the most essential of all the "wants" Wright has expressed ("On the Liberation of Woman"); he reaches an accord with

Jenny that frees him from the pathos and self-absorption which had tempted him to "break" from his human body. Two poems from *Two Citizens* particularly express this kind of affirmation and propose a choice much different than that proffered by Jenny.

Wright demonstrably intended for the first of these, "Well, What Are You Going to Do?," to be a break from his recent work in which any sort of affirmation was difficult to come by. This poem, he insisted, would tell the truth—a truth that now entailed qualified faith as a counter to despair. One line from a draft dated 22 October 1970 boldly states Wright's best intentions for the poem, "I don't mean for this to be the usual lie."[22] In the poem the speaker recounts an incident from his youth, a time when he helped Pet, the family cow, give birth. Such a narrative could easily fall prey to sentimentality, but Wright salvages the emotional authenticity of the poem by juxtaposing the act of birth with other, less pleasing aspects of life:

> I led Marian out of her mother's belly
> Down in the cold
> Autumn thorns,
> And there was a pile of horse manure
> I couldn't evade, and so by God
> I didn't even try.
> All I could do was fall
> From time to time.

Appropriately, the first thing the calf knows of life is its "thorns." Then the boy steps in manure and is later "delicately sprayed" with the newborn's urine. Scatological humor aside, these incidents nicely balance the scene's possibilities for sentimental excess.

Finally, the poem closes with a repetition of the titular question, a question with reference to this particular incident and, by expansion, to the experience of one's entire life:

> I don't know that I belonged
> In that beautiful place. But
> What are you going to do? Be kind? Kill?
> Die?

Similarly, "The Old WPA Swimming Pool in Martins Ferry, Ohio" counters the gloom of the dead Jenny and the dying Ohio River with its simple affirmation of life garnered from the actuality of experience. It is a poem of perceived not imposed order, a poem of revelation based on the outer realm of experience in which act and deed take precedence over intellectual distance. The incident it relates, like the one discussed earlier, risks sentimentality. Wright himself seems aware of this risk, for he opens the poem by admitting, "I am almost afraid to write down / This thing."

But he does. The poem concerns the opening of a WPA swimming pool which Wright's father and uncles had helped construct. Of course, the irony is obvious: Next to the Ohio River, a natural place for swimming, the government was forced to build a cement pool because the "River is dying." Polluted beyond salvation, it was no longer safe for swimming, as Wright and his brothers had done nearly every summer day of their youth. For everyone involved the sight was shocking; Wright himself "wondered / What the hell is this?"

For once this "hole in the ground" is not a grave. Instead, it is filled with water and living bodies ready to be washed with a new kind of "holiness." It is a way for the swimmers to enter the ground and an occasion for them to surface, reborn through a strange sort of baptism. Wright's own descent below ground results in a kind of epiphany he hesitates to share with readers he assumes will be incredulous:

Oh never mind, Jesus Christ, my father
And my uncles dug a hole in the ground.
No grave for once. It is going to be hard
For you to believe: when I rose from that water,


A little girl who belonged to somebody else,
A face thin and haunted appeared
Over my left shoulder, and whispered, Take care now,
Be patient, and live.


I have loved you all this time,
And didn't even know
I am alive.

The appearance of the girl's "thin and haunted" face, perhaps a younger version of Jenny's "vanished" face, produces the kind of epiphanic moment for which Wright has been seeking throughout these three volumes. Suddenly, Wright finds fulfillment in the immediate moment; "I am alive" answers the sense of futurity and longing expressed in "I want to live." Wright's quest ends in the revelation of the moment lived to its fullest. He chooses to live his "own life" and learns to balance joy and despair, aware that the truest vision of the world can never exclude either element. If the despairing and transcendent Jenny is one wing, the other is the simple joy of living on earth.

For once, Wright has two wings. They give him the teleological understanding necessary to see the world in its paradoxical reality, as a place "Immeasurably alive and good, / Though bare as rifted paradise" ("The Quest," *CP*). This unquestioning affirmation of life characterizes the innocence of a child, the innocence lost in what Sherwood Anderson calls adulthood's "sadness of sophistication."

Moreover, the realization of this sensibility coincides with what Wright identifies in Whitman as the "spirit's emergence as a child, who is at last able to create clearly and powerfully from within his own imagination." This is the third of the three metamorphoses of the spirit Nietzsche describes in *Thus Spake Zarathustra*. It is a stage Nietzsche believes to be necessary to the full evolution of every human being:

> The child is innocence and oblivion, a new
> beginning, a play, a self-rolling wheel,
> A primal motion, an holy yea-saying.
>
> Ay, for the play of creation, my brethren,
> there needeth an holy yea-saying.[23]

Through the long struggle of these three volumes, Wright himself has come to the threshold of affirmation. He has become a "yea-sayer." It is not that Wright has found a comfortable and giddy innocence that precludes any further moments of despair, but rather having found an equilibrium between the possibility for joy and the equal possibility for grief, he leaves the hate and destruction of the second stage, reconciles the distance between himself and other humans, and offers a mature and qualified affirmation in the collections that follow.

Most importantly he comes to hear the voice of Emerson Buchanan, a voice which before had given back only a "blind dial tone." It is also the voice of those people Wright knew best and understood most: the poor, the uneducated, the forgotten. From them and from their lives Wright draws his strength as a mature poet. Even though Wright escaped the poverty of Martins Ferry, earned a doctorate in English, taught at the university level, and received a number of significant awards for his poetry—his emotional and intellectual locus remained at home in Ohio.

Though Wright never again openly refers to Jenny, he does not altogether abandon her. Along with Anne, she balances his mature work in which he finds an informed equilibrium, poised between a wing of joy and a wing of despair. Such an affirmation could only have occurred after Wright reconciled the reality of death—for which the figure of Jenny provided both mythos and memory—with the immutable order of loss that governs earthly life, and more importantly, then chose this imperfect world over that ethereal, timeless one which she had offered.

# 6 A Form Sufficiently Formless: The Rhetoric of Wright's Prose Poems

Given the blurring of distinction between poetry and prose that has occurred in American writing of recent years, it is not surprising that the Forty-Eighth International PEN Congress should have devoted a panel discussion to the crossover relationship between poetry and prose in America. It is not surprising, either, that some would choose to hail what they call this "dual enterprise," while others would instead argue, "Vive la difference."[1] After all, the prose poem—poetry not written in verse but in prose that makes ample use of poetic devices—has been the form most responsible for this blurring of genre distinctions and has been the topic of heated critical debate. It has been seen variously as a pathetic weakening of both forms, an admission of the failure of free verse, or in some cases, as a refusal of poetic responsibility.[2] None of these estimates seems altogether fair or accurate.

Recently, Michael Davidson has described the prose poem as an attempt to stretch the boundaries of genre, and he has cited two divergent tendencies among its practitioners. The first group, populated by Ron Silliman, Clark Coolidge, Michael Palmer and others, favors a broken narrative that emphasizes the "smallest elements of linguistic construction"; the second group, composed of poets such as Robert Bly, W. S. Merwin, Russell Edson, and James Wright, chooses a more contiguous narrative which parallels "some psychologically charged inner state."[3]

Of course, Davidson's second grouping interests me most, for by studying Wright's prose pieces and identifying the aesthetic pressures behind the urge to write them, one can discover the field of opportunity that the prose poem offers a poet such as Wright—and the wider alternatives it may offer poets. Largely, this amounts to the altered rhetorical stance (or the potential for several stances) available in the prose poem which was not present in the dominant modes of the fifties or sixties. For Wright, the source of this opportunity may be less what the structure or the form itself inherently offers and more what he sees it as offering: a kind of rhetorical freedom not inordinately bound either to the lucid or to the lyrical modes that Charles Altieri contends represent the continuing bifurcation of American poetics.

In such a form, perhaps because it is a kind of hybrid, Wright envisions lyrical sensitivity and narrative lucidity as coexisting on more or less equal terms, thus enabling both his intuition and intelligence to operate freely. What results is a form that can incorporate the narration of actual experience, the expression of lyrical imagination, and the artist's own self-conscious awareness of the aesthetic process. Therefore, Wright is able to move readily between an immersion in the actual experiences that go into the poem and the more artificial experience of writing them down. The form is sufficiently formless to accommodate the competing voices of the self and the varied levels of consciousness that they reflect. Before one can examine these elements at work in Wright's poems, an initial discussion of the sources and influences of the prose poem in America will be useful.

\*   \*   \*

The decision to write poetry in what appears to be a prose form, or at least in a form that is neither wholly poetry nor wholly prose, carries with it an implicit dissatisfaction with the limitations of traditional verse and even free verse. Perhaps Thomas De Quincey's passionate prose served as a starting point in the effort to link the best qualities of diverse modes. Yet, the form De Quincey had in mind is best indicated by the phrase itself, for the modifier is "passionate" and the operative noun is "prose." Baudelaire, on the other hand, sought a *poème en prose*, that is, a poetic form written deliberately in prose. Most often given

credit for originating the prose poem, Baudelaire had become dissatis-
fied with the dominant mode of French Romantic literature which had
established Victor Hugo as its leading voice.[4] Looking for a way to
incorporate the matters of daily and ordinary life within his work,
Baudelaire explores the prose poem in *Petits Poèmes en Prose*, later retitled
*Le Spleen de Paris*. Baudelaire proposes in the preface to *Le Spleen* that the
form he has come upon is not limited to classification as either "heads"
or "tails" (wholly poetry or wholly prose), but instead is a form able to
accommodate a more diverse range of impulses. He pauses to ask his
reader: "Which of us, in his ambitious moments, has not dreamed of a
poetic prose, musical, without rhyme and without rhythm, supple
enough and rugged enough to adapt itself to the lyrical impulses of the
soul, the undulations of the psyche, the prickings of consciousness?"
(Benedikt, 43)

Of course, this search for a form more responsive to the pressures
of lyric expression and the workings of human consciousness enlisted
the efforts of several key figures of French verse in addition to Baudelaire: Rimbaud, Mallarmé, Valéry, and later Reverdy and Éluard
among others. Yet, into this century no widely accepted definition of
what a prose poem amounts to has been offered. Michael Benedikt,
although admitting his reservations about defining a thing still in the
process of being discovered, proposes this generalized description: "It
is a genre of poetry, self-consciously written in prose, and characterized by the intense use of virtually all the devices of poetry, which
includes the intense use of devices of verse. The sole exception to ac-
cess to the possibilities of verse, rather than the set priorities of verse
is, we would say, the line break" (47). Benedikt's definition implies,
first, that though the prose poem may be a hybrid form, it should still
be considered a "genre of poetry"; and second, that by partaking of it,
the poet has at his or her disposal a form at once open to nearly all of
the "possibilities" of verse, yet one bearing more potential because it
avoids the "set" limitations of prescribed form. Perhaps, then, the
prose poem owes equally to the romantic insistence on possibility and
the modernist distaste of formal limitation.

It remains unclear, however, just what has tempted so many contemporary poets such as Wright to adopt this form. Russell Edson,
himself a practitioner, offers some tentative answers to that question

in his essay, "The Prose Poem in America."[5] His first answer, notwithstanding the tautology, is that poets in America have turned to the prose poem because "so many" poets here are writing them. Setting aside the tautology and acknowledging the influence of imitation, we must still account for the emergence of this rather than any other form. Edson's second response, "that something that needs expression is not being fully released by regular poetry," seems more plausible (325). That free verse itself, as much as traditional verse forms, might present inherent problems and limitations for poetic expression is not unlikely. As Stanley Plumly has argued in "Chapter and Verse," the new set of rules that govern our present free verse seem mainly to prescribe for the poet two choices in tone and manner: a rhetoric of sincerity or an emblematic use of image.[6]

Still, a more intriguing answer lies elsewhere in Edson's essay. While admitting that the prose poem has "yet to yield up a method," Edson remarks that this fact may be its greatest strength, for the writer "coming to the prose poem has no rules to keep, and just as importantly, no rules to break" (321). This remark is especially pertinent for the generation of poets who began their careers in the fold of the dominant mode which had been established by the New Critics. Certainly, the field of opportunity offered by the prose poem must have looked inviting to Wright and his generation, for in it the rhetorical gestures they had admired, practiced, and often abandoned were no longer prescribed. Implying, however, as Edson does, that writing a prose poem breaks no rules assumes that the prose poem is widely accepted which is simply not the case.

As a poetic innovator, Wright had already raised more than a few eyebrows when he decided to abandon the rhetorical distance of *The Green Wall* (1957) for the subjective images of *The Branch Will Not Break* (1963). Surely his decision to work with the prose poem, a form that the critic W. M. Spackman has called "an accident of French rhetoric . . . that the French take to be literature," could have seemed equally contumacious. To some, it must have seemed yet another breaking of the rules, not a hard-won expansion of them. Wright himself seems aware of these pressures, and he invokes Yvor Winters, one of the standard-bearers of New Critical dogma, in his defense:

I have put some prose pieces in my last couple of books and sometimes they have been called poems. They are not poems. They are
prose pieces. . . . Yvor Winters said a valuable thing in this respect. He said, poetry is written in verse whereas prose is written
in prose. That is a help because it allows us to drop the nitpicking
[over technical terms] and then go on and try to see what the
writing in question is . . . whether it is any good or not.[7]

Wright's sensitivity on this issue is, perhaps, understandable. As
much as any poet of his generation, Wright's work has been the object
of lengthy and sometimes vitriolic discussions of technique. Whether
it is his early formalist work, his experiments with the deep image, or
his more vulnerable lyrics that follow, critics have often been tempted
to concentrate on the matters of form and technique that characterize
these phases. What Wright is seeking in the above remark is a freedom
from these discussions of rules, a freedom he hopes to achieve by placing his prose works outside the domain of poetic criticism. What he
cannot deny, however, is the implicit rhetorical judgment he makes by
including these prose pieces in a collection of poetry, thereby implying—at least ostensibly—that they should be read with expectations
similar to those one brings to a poem. Although Wright may be trying
hard to argue against it, by writing prose poems—whether or not he
chooses to call them that—he has broken yet another rule in the eyes
of critics such as Spackman.

As much as Wright (and Edson) would like it to be the case, the poet
writing the prose poem cannot avoid implicitly breaking what many
consider a standard rule of poetic form, and labeling the work a hybrid
form, a poem in prose, does not effectively provide it with validity as "a
genre of poetry." Still, the fact remains that a number of poets like
Wright have chosen and continue to choose this form for their poetry.
If it is an act of rebellion, an extension of the revolt against the "square
poem" of the fifties, it is founded on the poet's need to express an
awareness of inner and outer experience that traditional and free
verse seem incapable of fully expressing. In his important book *Our
Last First Poets*, Cary Nelson postulates that the conception of history
shared by poets of Wright's generation such as Merwin and O'Hara

"informs and undermines the open forms in which they work; it leads them, eventually, to adopt open forms that very nearly destroy themselves."[8] It may be, even more so, that their awareness of the historical polarization of American poetry and its attendant emphasis on technique is the source of their urge to open forms, forms that refuse to be judged merely by their shape and meter but insist on the pressures of experience and accessible communication as judgments of value. When Nelson argues that these poets sought a form both "expansive and fractured" enough "to contain their experience," he has identified a significant issue in the movement to open forms (x). However, his language tends to be misleading, for it deemphasizes the fact that these poets had earlier reacted against a poetry which isolated them behind a wall of defensive rhetoric and, thus, were now seeking a form that would free their expression of experience rather than "contain" it. Certainly, the prose poem—a form of poetry that negates its own formal claim to poetry—offers such freedom.

By the time that James Wright published his first volume of prose poems, *Moments of the Italian Summer* (1976), he had shown an admirable willingness to investigate new forms of poetic expression. However, with the exception of Wayne Dodd's largely positive remarks in *The Ohio Review*, Wright's exploration of the prose form was not received with enthusiasm.[9] Many critics perhaps assumed that the move to prose was only the short-lived infatuation of a poet fond of experimentation. Wright, though, had a clear reason for such a move: his desire for a rhetorical stance that would integrate not divide writer and reader: "I would like to write something that would be immediately and prosaically comprehensible to a reasonably intelligent reader. That is all . . . I mean by being clear, but it is very difficult for me."[10]

In the above remark, Wright indicates a renewed regard for the rhetorical contract between writer and reader implicit in the act of writing, what Wright had earlier called "a way of arranging words to convey a vision and evoke a true response in the feelings of readers." But Wright can be even more blunt in his assessment of the need for personal and aesthetic courage in such a transformation: "It is only after the most devoted labor that a poet can strip his language of everything except what he sees and feels. Purification of one's language is purification of the heart. It demands courage. It requires the character which must exist and stand forth once the rhetoric is taken away."[11] Concerned that his "attempt to be clear has failed" in the early formalist work and in the subjective images of his middle phase, Wright assumes the altered rhetorical stance of the prose poem in an effort to establish a more vigorous relationship with his subject and a strengthened relationship with his reader:[12] "There's something about the sudden rejection of poetry (or maybe it's a rejection of a certain kind of rhetoric) which in itself can suddenly reach over into some kind of rhythm, some closeness. . . . Maybe that is real poetry. It's a paradox."[13]

For the most part, Wright's prose pieces may indeed reject the rhetoric of detached wit or irony, but they do not ignore poetic devices. Wright knows, as well as any poet, that it is not the length of a line that really matters but what one does within that line. In the prose poem, Wright discovers a more responsive form, the source of which Stanley Plumly has described in this way: "The intersection of the flexibility of free verse rhythm with the strategy of storytelling has produced a kind of prose lyric: a form corrupt enough to speak flat out in sentences yet pure enough to sustain the intensity, if not the integrity of the line."[14] Moreover, the poetic aspects of Wright's prose are obvious, especially if one differentiates between an inner and an outer form. The outer form is surely that of prose, but the inner form, the mode of expression and manner of development of the piece, is mostly poetic. Wright may neglect (or refuse) poetic outer form, but he does not neglect the use of simile, assonance, consonance, metaphor, rhythm, repetition, and a kind of leaping movement between images in his prose pieces.

In Wright's prose poems, though, the form and these devices draw less attention than the poet's thinking and feeling, less attention than the experience conveyed. Perhaps Wright sees the prose form as the most open of all forms, one not attended by centuries of technical discussion and not limited by prescriptive advice. Then, too, the accessibility of the prose form provides an avenue for communication that is "consecutive and clear," a direct route from the poet to his or her audience of readers.

More so than his other work, his prose pieces effectively combine intellect and imagination, colloquial and elevated language, and humor and seriousness within a kind of integrated lyric. "The Flying Eagles of Troop 62," a fine example of such an integrated piece published in *To a Blossoming Pear Tree* (1977), is dedicated to Ralph Neal, Wright's scoutmaster in Martins Ferry, Ohio. Neal was a man of compassion and understanding, for he knew the boys and their "slime hole of a river valley" and knew equally that most of them were bound for the valley's factories and steel and glass mills, and even some for jail. "Ralph Neal loved us," Wright says, "mostly for his knowledge of what would probably become of us."

The piece employs various tonal shifts, from the humor of the boys' "mocking and parodying the Scout Law" to the painful seriousness of a sexual awakening felt in the "aching stones of our twelve-year-old groins." But perhaps the most startling tonal balance is that achieved by the poet's intellect and imagination. On the one hand, Wright is able to think rationally, to make deft literary allusions such as the following:

> The Vedantas illustrate the most sublime of ethical ideals by describing a saint who, having endured through a thousand lifetimes of every half-assed mistake and unendurable suffering possible to humanity from birth to death, refused at the last moment to enter Nirvana because he realized that his scruffy dog, suppurating at the nostrils and half mad with rabies, could not accompany him into perfect peace.[15]

In such a passage, Wright encourages his readers to participate intellectually, to join in considering the moral and ethical implications of the story that he has just related. And, at least in the beginning, it is more of a *story* than a poem, a tactic which enables Wright to reverse the expectations of readers who may have been anticipating (and who may feel constrained by) the traditional rhetoric of poetry and, perhaps, to convince them to read on. If one function of the prose poem is to enable the poet to envision and work within a form not bound by the traditional constraints of poetic form, a corollary purpose is to allow the reader to encounter and engage a piece equally free of preconceived matters of rhetoric and structure.

In effect, the prose poem inverts the process of reading that Stanley

Fish describes in *Is There a Text in This Class.*[16] In his experiment, Fish told a group of students that a list of six names written on a chalkboard was a poem, when in actuality these names were simply the remainder of his lecture notes for another course. Because the class responded with an exhaustive and imaginative exegesis of the list-poem, Fish postulates that in reading poetry the act of recognition (in this case, his telling the class that the list of names composed a poem) always triggers the identification of formal characteristics which produce a poem. In this line of thinking, the actual reading of the text and the noting of its formal devices does not distinguish it as a poem, but rather the preliminary and publicly shared recognition of the object as a poem before one reads it causes a reader to note later the distinguishing features of a poem. On the contrary, the very shape or form of the prose poem inverts this process by frustrating or delaying the recognition of the object, mainly because it is not at present widely regarded as a poem. Readers must first read the piece, assess the nature of its content, and identify its formal characteristics (simile, metaphor, image, assonance, consonance, and so on) before those readers can recognize it as a poem. The process, in essence, frees readers, helping them to step outside of many of the cultural and aesthetic prescriptions they have inherited regarding the way a poem is to be approached, identified, and read. Assuming that Fish's theory accurately represents the way a poem is read and thereby constituted by its readers, the prose poem would, for the moment at least, offer those readers an object for which they have no institutionally or culturally derived frame of reference to direct their act of recognition. This freedom, however, might be short-lived. When—or if—the prose poem is institutionalized as a genre of poetry, readers may come to it, prepared by an expanded cultural and aesthetic knowledge, perfectly able to recognize it immediately as a poetic form.

The story that begins "The Flying Eagles of Troop 62," of course, equates Ralph Neal with the unnamed saint, but its manner more than its meaning warrants further attention. First, it is a kind of thinking person's remark, a literary allusion. The story, though, is told in one long and rather breathless sentence, abounding with adjectives and adverbs in a fashion that Wright rarely shows. Wright chooses adjectives and adverbs that are both elevated ("suppurating," "unendurable") and colloquial ("scruffy," "half-assed"), yet the passage displays a careful musical rhythm that modulates between the two. Although the piece shows a lively vocabulary, Wright's playfulness and erudition are not self-serving; he has his reader in mind, too. Even if that "reasonably intelligent reader" does not know the definition of "suppurating," she or he can infer from "scruffy" the general state of the dog.

Later, Wright shows the capacity to think not only rationally, but also imaginatively when he remembers Neal; here, thinking is balanced by an equal dose of feeling:

> When I think of Ralph Neal's name, I feel some kind of ice breaking open in me. I feel a garfish escaping into a hill spring where the crawdads burrow down to the pure bottom in hot weather to get the cool.

What Wright achieves here is a thoughtful balance of intelligence and emotion. He frees himself—perhaps aided by the rhetorical license granted him in the prose poem—to accept these opposite impulses and to unify them within a single piece. He is not limited, therefore, to an expression dominated either by its lucidity or its lyricism, and in this fashion he shows that intelligence and intuitive feeling are not mutually repellent in the contemporary poem, that they can and do exist simultaneously within the competing voices or layers of the self. Thus, when Robert Pinsky asserts that Wright makes a "mess" of the above passage by "not thinking enough," Pinsky is trying to impose his own standards for discursiveness on Wright's work.[17] Pinsky, an intelligent poet and critic, would rather have Wright thinking more than feeling in his poems, but Wright himself is more concerned with integrating the two within a single work, often within these competing voices.

Wright's success at creating a poem more accessible to his reader is apparent in the above passage. His poetry, of course, was not always so "immediately comprehensible," and the nature of this transition becomes more startling if one compares this passage to work characteristic of his own (and his generation's) earlier modes. A look at an early version of Wright's "At the Executed Murderer's Grave" reveals the florid rhetorical style common in the fifties and a dense, almost impenetrable surface of images:

> Bewildering calm, you tangle blade and bone
> Fang, fist, and skull that huddle down alone.
> Sparrows above him, gay as young police,
> Line up the lawn, the hedge, the fearful trees.
> The fierce blood of the dead lies smitten dumb
> Under the vengeance of a lily's bloom . . .[18]

Even though Wright and many of his generation reacted against this mode, what resulted—a poetry founded on associational leaps—was not always more accessible. Often these lyrics asked the reader to make leaps of intuition between seemingly disparate images, to imagine how "the moon walks, / Hunting for hidden dolphins / Behind the darkening combers / Of the ground" ("By a Lake in Minnesota"). Many academic readers in the 1960s were unprepared to deal with, and therefore, to accept these lyrics influenced by the work of Neruda, Lorca, and Trakl; they often remarked, according to Bly, "I hear you gentlemen have rejected the intellect."[19]

As a reaction to this sort of critical tunnel vision, Wright may have turned to the prose poem and the opportunities it presented. It would appear that the prose poem offers fertile ground for the self-conscious poet, one made fully aware of himself in the act of writing. Perhaps the hybrid form itself enables the poet to draw upon the competing voices of the self and the levels of consciousness that they represent. Then again, especially for Wright, this new form seems to provide an attractive means to integrate the impulses that had dominated each of his previous modes.

Another prose piece from *Blossoming Pear*, "The Secret of Light," demonstrates the altered rhetorical stance that issues from such self-consciousness on the part of the poet. While watching an Italian park scene, the speaker notices a "startling woman" and unleashes his imagination in an effort to describe her lovely hair:

> Directly in front of me, perhaps thirty yards away from me, there is a startling woman. Her hair is as black as the inmost secret of light in a perfectly cut diamond, a perilous black, a secret light that must have been studied for many years before the anxious and disciplined hand could achieve the necessary balance between

courage and skill to stroke the strange stone and take the one chance he would ever have to bring that secret to light.

Of course, the entire section is centered by the lyricism of its diamond metaphor; however, Wright, clearly the speaker, refuses to remain falsely in such ecstasy. He admits into the poem the actuality of experience and interjects it in a self-consciously narrative manner:

> While I was trying to compose the preceding sentence, the woman rose from her park bench and walked away. I am afraid her secret might never come to light in my lifetime. But my lifetime is not the only one.

In such a move, Wright addresses himself, his poem, and his audience directly, assuming the rhetorical stance of the self-conscious poet in the process of creating. If only for a brief moment, he acknowledges the poetic act he has initiated and its difficulties. Unlike the rhetorically detached poet characteristic of the metaphysical poems of the fifties, and unlike the poet of rhetorical subjectivity dominant in the sixties, Wright admits the limitations of his art. He openly claims his disappointment that he can no longer work his way toward the mysterious light he has begun to envision. Still, he rejects this voice of despair, for in a manner reminiscent of "Mutterings over the Crib of a Deaf Child," a competing voice counters it. In a lesser (perhaps less integrated) lyric, such despondency would prevail; it might become the self-centered end of discovery, not the means to further revelation that it becomes. This incident and the thought and feeling it has evoked lead him to epiphany: "It is all right with me that my life is only one life. I feel like the light of the river Adige." The lyrical resolution, therefore, directs him not to bathos but to an emotionally charged intellectual acceptance; he comes "to know" and to accept both limitation and possibility.

Published in *This Journey*, one final prose poem warrants attention, for "May Morning" illustrates Wright's own awareness of the rules he supposedly breaks by writing in that form and his desire to undermine what Donald Hall has referred to as "the eternal American tic of thinking about art in terms of its techniques."[20] As Michael Heffernan notes, "May Morning"—ostensibly a prose poem—is actually a hybrid sonnet not broken into lines.[21] It combines Shakespearean and Petrarchan rhyme within a new pattern (*a b b a, c d d c, e f b e f b*). Indeed, the form is so subtly disguised that Wright is able to embed an obvious feminine rhyme such as boulder/shoulder without calling undue attention to it.[22] What follows is the prose poem as it appears in *This Journey*, with slash marks to indicate the line breaks as they occur in the sonnet version:

> Deep into spring, winter is hanging on. / Bitter and skillful in his hopelessness, / he stays alive in every shady place, / starving along the Mediterranean: / angry to see the glittering sea-pale boulder / alive with lizards green as Judas leaves. / Winter is hanging on. He still believes. / He tries to catch a lizard by the shoulder. / One olive tree below Grottaglie / welcomes the winter into noontime shade, / and he talks softly as Pythagoras. / Be still, be patient, I can hear him say, / cradling in his arms the wounded head, / letting the sunlight touch the savage face.[23]

By experimenting with these forms (and disguising them), Wright further blurs the less essential distinctions between them; he again achieves the freedom, inventiveness, and playfulness of his unpublished collection, *Amenities of Stone* (1961–62). Although some may be tempted to narrow Wright's purpose for disguising the sonnet to a somewhat spiteful urge to fool his friend Bly (one of the final readers of the posthumous *This Journey* and a staunch advocate of free verse), it is more sensible to imagine that Wright had larger goals in mind. Through the disguised form of "May Morning," Wright subverts the American tendency to dwell on a poem's technique, emphasizes, instead, the equally important matter of what the poet thinks and feels within that poem (whatever the form), and encourages his readers to decide on other than "nitpicking" terms "whether the writing is any good or not." He implicitly undercuts the mere critic of technique, one version of which might argue against the "technical atrophy" of the prose poem form, while another might complain of the stultifying influence of fixed form. What Wright seeks is a poetry of possibility in which form, as Robert Creeley has said, is "never more than an extension of content."

\* \* \*

Although it may be critically untenable to infer from a discussion of Wright's prose poems the particular characteristics of all others writing in that mode, it is possible from such a discussion to delineate the special qualities that drew Wright to the prose poem. First, the form offers a means for the poet to address self-consciously himself, the aesthetic process of writing, and his audience of readers (who themselves are freed from their preconceptions of poetic form and rhetoric). The freedom of this rhetorical stance, a freedom not present in the modes that had dominated earlier decades, enables the poet to move readily between perceived outer experience (or narrative) and interior experience (intellectual or imaginative activity). This quality, I believe, accounts for the parallel Davidson notes between the prose poem's narrative and the poet's "psychologically charged inner state." The poet, thus, is empowered with the capability to immerse himself both in the actual experiences that compose the poem and in the more artificial (because aesthetic) experience of writing, or thinking about writing.

Second, the form proffers a mode in which lucidity and lyricism interact on equal terms, without one bearing the weight of prescription. What results is a form in which intelligence, intuition, humor, and seriousness intermingle in a series of abrupt rhetorical and tonal shifts, creating unity out of variety. Third, the mode of the prose poem allows the poet to work within a form sufficiently formless to accommodate the shifting levels of consciousness and the competing voices that speak for the self or selves.

Finally, and perhaps most importantly, if the prose poem is the logical end result of the rebellion against the square poem of the fifties, it is not so much that prescribed form is passé (witness Wright's "May Morning"). Rather the prose form permits Wright to step outside the rules that have governed traditional and even free verse and, in the process, to discover in a field of opportunity not previously available to him an alternative to the poetics of polarization.

# 7 "The Poetry of a Grown Man": Affirmation and Integration in

*To a Blossoming Pear Tree*

and *This Journey*

In *To a Blossoming Pear Tree* (1977) and *This Journey* (1982), James Wright, much like his former teacher Theodore Roethke, moves from despair to joy, from an anguished vulnerability to the patient acceptance of a Nietzschean "yea-sayer."[1] Such a move is representative of Wright's mature work, in which the nagging doubt and depression that characterize his early writing disappear in a poetry of affirmation and integration. Wright comes to know the loveliness and wonder of a spiritual light—a personal and wholly revivifying acceptance of the dual realities of human possibility and human limitation. Although already conversant with the enticing beauty of an earthly darkness, he learns to appreciate its dialectic opposite, the light of the sun, for:

> Any creature would be a fool to take the sun
>     lightly
> The indifferent god of brief life, the
> Small mercy.[2]
> ("Among Sunflowers," *TJ*)

The tenor of optimism in this transition is reminiscent of his *The Branch Will Not Break*, in which he discovers the "abounding delight of the body."[3] But more importantly, this "delight" does not issue merely from his being at home within his own body but from his feeling equally at home within the natural world and with the complement of beings that compose the physical universe. Wright, the homeless traveler, the quester for a more perfect place, discovers that the world which surrounds him is itself "abounding" with a spiritual presence which, on occasion, he can see and feel as tangibly as he can those creatures that embody it. He comes to resolve the most pressing and continual of his thematic (and religious) concerns: the separation of humans beings from one another, from the natural world and its inhabitants, and from the spiritual or godlike presence of the universe.

\* \* \*

Throughout Wright's career, the speaker of his poems undergoes a number of striking alterations in voice and language, in the way the persona speaks the poem. Wright's movement to a more integrated mode of rhetoric, however, can best be seen in the manner in which he regards the poem he is speaking and the audience he is addressing. In the early poems, say, "A Fit against the Country," Wright distances himself from both the poem as artifact and the audience as listener, using a "ferociously perfect form" to protect himself from both. Later, even his poems that celebrate unity and transcendence, such as "In Fear of Harvests," sometimes leave the distance between speaker and reader (and speaker and poem) curiously unresolved. Finally, the aggressive speaker of Wright's "New Poems" frequently antagonizes his reader, asking him or her to "please leave the poem" if that reader does not care for the preceding lines.

Each of the previous modes betrays an unsettling relationship between the writer and the reader, as if Wright's conception of the rhetoric of poetry somehow disavows the pact between its necessary participants. However, his venture into the integrational mode of the prose poem may be seen fairly as an extension of the redefined poetics of *Amenities of Stone,* in which Wright first begins to mute the distinction between art and life, word and experience. In such a way of thinking, the art of poetry and the art of living become mysteriously conjoined until poetry itself both expresses and constitutes life. This is not to say that the self becomes the solipsistic center of the poem, for the self in Wright's poems is no more important than the contents and workings of the larger universe that surrounds it. The speaker, while decentered as the object of the poem's concern, is not, however, absent or protectively distanced, but remains both witness and participant in the larger pageantry of the experiential world.

Such a view insists that both writer and reader share this role of witness-participant, that art itself—rather than a formulaic and after-the-fact recitation of experience—amounts to a lively interchange between lively individuals. This attitude is behind Wright's tendency in his late work to acknowledge the reader (and his or her role) in the midst of his poems. Addressed directly to his "reader," Wright's 23 September 1975 prose journal entry clarifies the matter and issues a compelling look at his conception of the rhetorical contract:

### To the Reader

Look, I don't know who you are. I wish I did. But I happen to feel like telling you something. One of my numerous critics . . . remarks that I have an annoying habit of addressing you directly. . . . it took me a long time to figure out what he was trying to say. I'm still not sure, but I think he means that my verses offend you. They offend you because you think there is something called art, like poetry, and that art is something that gives us a chance to deny, with sublime skill, that you are alive and that I am alive.[4]

The draft, heavily marked with corrections, goes on to include a nasty tirade against the imagined reader whom Wright, according to the unnamed critic, has "annoyed." Clearly troubled by the remarks of the critic and pained by the supposed failure of his own rhetorical strategy, Wright at first reacts defensively. He skewers both his reader and the collective human race, condemning them to a lonely and loveless death if they cannot appreciate the fundamental beauty of life found in a simple "dragon fly" resting upon his window. Later, though, Wright reconsidered what he had written and apparently found it unacceptable and untruthful. He crossed out nearly all of his lengthy diatribe against the reader and replaced it with eleven short words that affirm the integrity of the relationship between writer and reader: "What in hell am I going to do without you? Nothing."

In the above entry, attentiveness to experience—and to the value of life itself—becomes a measure of poetic sensibility and worth. Wright implicitly asserts that art is not a freeze-dried moment of life, but rather its living embodiment. Requiring both attention and action, the act of composing a poem results in an entity that contributes to and not merely reflects the living universe.

More importantly, Wright refuses to deny the validity and vitality of the poet-reader relationship. It is just this sort of profound awareness of the rhetorical contract that permeates *To a Blossoming Pear Tree* and *This Journey*. When he addresses his reader as "you," he now embraces rather than shuns that reader, effectively ending his isolation from both audience and poem.

"Redwings," the initial poem of *To a Blossoming Pear Tree*, shows the speaker's redefined need to embrace his reader and his new regard for clarity. It is not a simple poem by any measure; its elliptic structure and parallel images remind one of the emotionally and imagistically complex poems of *Branch*. But now Wright makes certain that an "intelligent person of good will" can follow him through the poem's various layers of reality, its compression of time, and its equation of the human and the natural. The poem opens with remarks concerning the "scientific" eradication of a redwing blackbird population along the Kokosing River. For the speaker, an aerial view of the river conjures up unsettling associations:

> It turns out
> You can kill them.
> It turns out
> You can make the earth absolutely clean.
>
> My nephew has given my younger brother
> A scientific report while they both flew
> In my older brother's small airplane
> Over the Kokosing River, that looks
>
> Secret, it looks like the open
> Scar turning gray on the small
> Of your spine.
>
> Can you hear me?[5]

In the face of "scientific" man whose goal is to "make the earth absolutely clean," Wright feels vulnerable and, in fact, wounded; the thought of an earth "absolutely clean" of life is not a comforting one. Still, the "open scar" he envisions is on "your spine," and the pronoun thus includes both speaker and reader in this pain. When the speaker intuits this connection between the victimized redwings and all of humanity threatened by nuclear destruction, he pauses to make certain that his readers understand his associational leap. He asks, "Can you hear me?"

Of course, the question is double-edged. On one hand, it queries, "Are you capable of understanding?" On the other, it wonders, "Am I making this clear; do you follow me; am I speaking so you can 'hear' my point?" The latter implication carries more import, I believe, for it demonstrates a marked alteration in the speaker's attitude toward his reader. Rather than dismissing his readers from the poem, Wright now wishes them to follow him through the intricate series of emotional and intellectual leaps which will follow. He pauses in midpoem not to chastise his readers but to secure a bond with them. Having done so, he then presents two intuitively related memories of significance:

> It was only in the evening I saw a few redwings
> Come out and dip their brilliant yellow
> Bills in their scarlet shoulders.
> Ohio was already going to hell.
> But sometimes they would sit down on the creosote
> Soaked pasture fence posts.
> They used to be few, they used to be willowy
> and thin.
>
> One afternoon, along the Ohio, where the sewer
> Poured out, I found a nest,
> The way they build their nests in the reeds,
> So beautiful,
> Redwings and solitaries.
> The skinny girl I fell in love with down home
> In late autumn married

A strip miner in late autumn.
Her five children are still alive,
Floating near the river.

As a child, in the midst of an Ohio that "was already going to hell,"
near a sewer pipe along the damaged river, Wright was still able to find
a last vestige of beauty: the "willowy and thin" redwings who nest
there. This recollection of beauty further compresses time; it causes
him to recall a past lover who, like the birds, was rather "skinny." Because the associational leap is private and is Wright's own, he asks the
reader to understand how the dead lover (only her children "are still
alive") and the redwings that "used to be" both amount to a kind of
beauty destroyed by the harsh and unforgiving world. In closing the
poem, Wright establishes an expansive connection between his own
fate and that of the dead lover, the imperiled birds, and the rest of
humanity:

Somebody is on the wing, somebody
Is wondering right at this moment
How to get rid of us, while we sleep.

Together among the dead gorges
Of highway construction, we flare
Across the highways and drive
Motorists crazy, we fly
Down home to the river.

There, one summer evening, a dirty man
Gave me a nickel and a potato
And fell asleep by a fire.

Wright was well aware of the poem's risks, not only its emotional
but also its aesthetic vulnerabilities. In fact, after it was first published,
he scribbled some revisions on a photocopy of the poem as it originally
appeared in *The Nation*, the most important of which were meant to
lessen the inaccessibility of its memories, and in effect, to let the reader
in on his precious secret. Significantly, Wright added the two words
"down home" to indicate where he fell in love with the "skinny girl";

then after a few minor changes, he crossed out his name at the bottom of the photocopied page and wrote out these closing lines, all of which he eventually put a pencil line through:

I don't know how they're going to get
Rid of me.

You are dead, Jenny. God, damn the murderers
Who shot us down.

Oh Jenny,
We
They are dead.[6]

Wright did not retain the references to Jenny in any published version of "Redwings." It would seem, then, that his own reticence contributed largely to the elliptic quality of the poem, in which a single image or word thrusts the poem forward to another recollection, another intuition. The speaker leads his reader on an elegiac journey of the imagination. Along the way, the reader meets things of beauty—the birds, the lover Jenny, the Ohio River, the collective human race—whose beauty has been broken nearly beyond repair. However, it is significant that the speaker embraces both prey and predator, for remember, those who seek to kill the redwings are the speaker's brothers and nephew. In the end, though, the meager gift of the "dirty man" effectively counters this sense of predation, isolation, and vulnerability. The figure of the hobo, in fact, gains a kind of heroic stature in Wright's late work, for one solution to the ugliness of separation which he bemoans is achieved by the agency of love.

\* \* \*

In "Redwings" Wright does not so much see different things as learn to see differently. The experiential world does not bring forth a gallery of new wonders; instead, Wright himself becomes able to see familiar things in a new light. One of those things is other human beings, with whom he sets out to reestablish a meaningful communion. When Wright had earlier remarked in "A Secret Gratitude" that we humans "are capable of anything," he had in mind primarily our potential for destructiveness, our ability to destroy our own bodies and the larger body of the natural world. Such malevolence shows up considerably less often in Wright's late work, and in place of it we find instances of "utmost sweetness" much like that of "The Silent Angel":

> As I sat down by the bus window in Verona, I looked over my left shoulder. A man was standing there in one of the pink marble arches at the base of the great Roman Arena. He smiled at me, a gesture of the utmost sweetness, such as a human face can rarely manage to shine with, even a beloved face that loves you in return.

This gesture of fundamental human sympathy is—like the kindness of the hobo—gifted to Wright, not paid or even asked for. And it is a moment that the despairing Wright could easily have overlooked; most often it is a pony or a sycamore tree that, by some mysterious movement of its own, closes the gap between two lonely beings. Here, it is another human being:

> He raised his hand at the last moment to wave me out of Verona as kindly as he could. . . . Even after he had vanished back into the archway, I could see his hand.

Hands become an important image in Wright's later work; they become agents of reconciliation. Here, a man's hand, not clenched into a fist or cupped around a gun, but a hand raised in tribute lingers in Wright's memory long after both the man and Verona are gone from his sight. Certainly, few would question the capacious quality of Wright's memory; in fact, he was thought to have a photographic memory and was capable of reciting long passages from the work of writers he admired.[7] Still, it is not the capacity but the *selectivity* of that memory which most strikes one about the way that Wright uses it in his poetry. For every lovely pastoral image of Ohio, there are easily twice as many that recall its desecration at the hands of the Hanna Coal Company and its great river polluted by industrial greed and carelessness. What Wright chooses to remember is rarely the most comforting of incidents. In his last two books, however, Wright calls from that prodigious memory a litany of a more balanced sort, images that often counter the earlier despairing visions.

In "Hook," the central incident occurred several years ago when the speaker was "only a young man." While waiting for a bus in the midst of a cruel Minneapolis winter, Wright meets and identifies with a Sioux whose battles with life remind Wright of his own, for the Sioux's "scars / Were just my age." Like the two previous men, this Sioux offers Wright a gift—some money "to get home on":

> Did you ever feel a man hold
> Sixty-five cents
> In a hook,
> And place it
> Gently
> In your freezing hand?
>
> I took it.
> It wasn't the money I needed.
> But I took it.

Though he may lack a human hand, the Sioux does not lack human gentleness or compassion. He, too, is a hero, having faced the worst of life and survived with apparently some human kindness intact. Further, the distance from the emotional darkness of *Shall We Gather at the River* to the spiritual light of *Blossoming Pear* can be measured in the figure of this one Sioux. Earlier, in "I Am a Sioux Brave, He Said in Minneapolis," the "just plain drunk" Indian who is the subject of the poem merely reminds Wright of "how lonely the dead must be." In this instance, however, Wright's need for a sign of human love is answered by the Sioux; though he may not have "needed" the money, he did need a brief respite from his feelings of isolation and loneliness.

Wright's interest in hands as a means to human reconciliation and communication is found in several poems of *Blossoming Pear*. Appropriately, one of the book's two epigraphs is from Sherwood Anderson, whose *Winesburg, Ohio* examines the various perils and rewards of humans "touching" each other with their hands. In fact, hands eventually become a medium of communication far more efficacious than words.

In silence and through only touching hands, George Willard and Helen White come to know what makes the "mature life of men and women in the modern world possible." Touching hands reduces their existential loneliness and brings them to the considerable human understanding that "I have come to this lonely place and here is this other."[8]

This "lonely place," of course, is home—a locale from which there is no release that is not also death. As Peter Stitt contends, Wright's protagonist continually encounters the dual and conflicting elements of his individual "quest": the desire to "escape into a paradisal existence" while, on the other hand—knowing full well that no escape is imminently forthcoming—the will to tough it out here as bravely as he can.[9] In his late work, however, Wright wants less to travel to see a new and perfect place than to stay in the same place and see it in a fresh way. Given that he cannot secure a spot in paradise without first abandoning this world, Wright learns to control his yearning, intent not upon remaking the world into paradise but upon facing the world as it is and seeing what good can be found here.

That Wright achieves such a feat can be demonstrated by looking at "Beautiful Ohio," the final poem of *Blossoming Pear*, and comparing it to "Redwings," the initial poem of the collection. Wright always assented to Frost's notion of the necessity for unity in a collection of poems.[10] If the book itself contained twenty-five poems, Frost had argued, the twenty-sixth poem was the book as a whole, as a unit. It is not surprising, therefore, to find that in "Beautiful Ohio" Wright sits above the same sewer pipe that appears in "Redwings." But now the rank flow from the pipe shines with "the speed of light," revealing, in its very motion, a world of flux that shows beauty in the most unexpected of places:

> And the light caught there
> The solid speed of their lives
> In the instant of that waterfall.
> I know what we call it
> Most of the time.
> But I have my own song for it,
> And sometimes, even today,
> I call it beauty.

Relieved of his loneliness by the actions of the "silent angel" and the Sioux, Wright can see in the brevity of human life—even in the refuse of it—a compelling light and beauty.

\* \* \*

The decision to live within this limited world, of course, requires that Wright reassess his relationship not only with other humans but also with the beings of nature. Throughout his career he has sought a way to reconcile the separation of the human from the natural. When he finds momentary relief in his interaction with an Indian pony or a dog or a simple pod of milkweed, he reassures himself that Emerson was right in his romantic treatise, *Nature*, that, indeed, "nature is the symbol of spirit." From a close attention to natural facts, Wright seeks to derive spiritual facts. With varying degrees of success, he does so, discovering intimations of order, meaning, and value in natural things.[11]

These last two books are no exception. Wright is just as anxious to encounter numinous experience as he was in *Branch*. Now, however, he is a bit more cautious in this endeavor, and perhaps, more honest with his reader about the results. He learns to modulate between intuitive immersion and intellectual distance, and in a poem such as "In Exile," Wright refuses the easy closure of a trumped-up epiphany:

> I kneel above the single rail of the Baltimore and Ohio track. The little green snake lies there blazing on the steel. It is almost perfect noon. He has no shadow to cast anywhere. But even if it were twilight, he would have slight shade to cast. What can I do to join him? His face seems turned toward the fireweed along the track. I too turn my face and gaze at the fireweed along the track. The roots must be healthy. . . .

Tempted "to join" the snake, that is, wanting essentially to partake of a pure natural order, Wright assumes its posture and gazes at the fireweed. Instead of transcendence, he discovers that the beauty of the flowers shows only that their "roots must be healthy." The humor and honesty announce a break from lyrical absorption, and they mark a poet willing to risk transcendence, but one truthful enough with himself and his readers to admit when he does not find it.

In fact, what Wright learns from being an attentive, Emersonian observer of the natural world is not always an intimation of unity with it; just as often, such attention delineates the qualities of consciousness that isolate the human from the natural. A couple of poems from these last two volumes serve quite well to illustrate the divergent attitudes that characterize the poles of this dialogue: "To a Blossoming Pear Tree" and "A Reply to Matthew Arnold on My Fifth Day in Fano."

In "To a Blossoming Pear Tree" the speaker admires the "pure" natural splendor of the blooming tree and realizes it is "perfect, beyond my reach." Furthermore, he comes to "envy" the tree not only because it cannot "listen" to the story of "something human" that he wishes to tell it, but also because it cannot *feel* human loneliness, cannot feel "ashamed," or "hopeless" as can the man of Wright's "human" story. When this "old man" approached the speaker:

> He paused on a street in Minneapolis
> And stroked my face.
> Give it to me, he begged.
> I'll pay you anything.

Moved by the need "to take / Any love he could get," the old man desperately struggled for some way to get out "of the cold."

It is just this kind of desolation of the spirit that separates the human and the natural. The pear tree could not "possibly / Worry or bother or care" about the equally "terrified" feelings of the speaker and the old man because it is incapable of experiencing these human emotions. Humanity and nature are not brothers, and the poem tells us so:

> Young tree, unburdened
> By anything but your natural blossoms
> And dew, the dark
> Blood in my body drags me
> Down with my brother.

The halting rhythm, the mournful repetition of "b" and "d" consonant sounds, and the abrupt line breaks combine in a kind of musical descent in this last stanza. Wright sides, and with good reason, with his fellows, for whom this one old man evokes and signifies the beauty and the terror of being "something human." One can hear echoes of Ransom's "I am shaken; but not as a leaf."

Yet, to read only "To a Blossoming Pear Tree" and not also, say "A Blessing" or "Milkweed," or especially "A Reply to Matthew Arnold" would distort one's understanding of Wright's view of the natural world. These are moments in his work in which the disparity between the human and the natural appears less consequential. Too, there are moments like that of "A Reply to Matthew Arnold" where nature and humanity appear ultimately in brief accord.

Not only does "A Reply to Matthew Arnold" serve as a foil to Wright's "To a Blossoming Pear Tree," but it also shows the manner in which Wright juxtaposes the competing voices of the self within a single dialogic poem in much the same manner as his earlier poems "Mutterings over the Crib of a Deaf Child" and "The Morality of Poetry" employed this format. Written as a response to Arnold's "In Harmony with Nature," the poem appropriately opens with an epigraph from that poem: "In harmony with Nature? Restless fool . . . Nature and man can never be fast friends." Wright then proceeds to dispute Arnold's contention that humankind must "pass" nature or "rest her slave":

> It is idle to speak of five mere days in Fano, or five long days, or five years. As I prepare to leave, I seem to have just arrived. To carefully split yet another infinitive, I seem to have been here forever or longer, longer than the sea's lifetime and the lifetimes of all the creatures of the sea, than all the new churches among the hill pastures and all the old shells wandering about bodiless just off the clear shore. Briefly in harmony with nature before I die, I welcome the old curse:
>
> a restless fool and a fast friend to Fano, I have brought this wild chive flower down from a hill pasture. I offer it to the Adriatic. I am not about to claim that the sea does not care. It has its own way of receiving seeds, and today the sea may as well have a flowering one, with a poppy to float above it, and the Venetian navy underneath. Goodbye to the living place, and all I ask it to do is stay alive.

While one voice within the poet pejoratively labels his felt unity with nature simply an "old curse," the other voice readily accepts this immersion. The interaction of dissonant voices displays the poet's rational awareness of the emotional state he is entering. In fact, the intellect plays a large part in the first stanza, so much so that the speaker calls attention to how "carefully" he is breaking the rules of grammar by splitting infinitives. It is a way of indicating, of course, that the speaker realizes he is about to break other "rules" of rational conduct, as well. He is not limited, therefore, to an expression either wholly lucid or purely lyrical.

Admitting the intellect as well as the imagination, Wright's integrated lyric proves that a poet need not perish on either side of the wall critics assert must separate the "paleface" from the "redskin." In a manner not too distant from Whitman (whom D. H. Lawrence called "the first white aboriginal"), Wright shows that intelligence and intuitive feeling are not mutually repellent, that, indeed, they can and do exist simultaneously. Poets and critics would do well to note the alternative Wright's poetry offers to the present-day aesthetics of polarization, for in "A Reply to Matthew Arnold," Wright creates a poem more responsive to the competing tensions of contemporary existence.

"A Reply to Matthew Arnold" is a poem of great humility. Faced with the complexity of the natural world, Wright does not arrogantly dismiss it as disorderly or attempt to order it according to his human predispositions. He shows the quality of mind that he admires in the work of Thomas Hardy: Hardy's knowledge that "the most commonplace creatures are not to be approached with condescension" but rather with an affection made powerful by "his awe in the presence of his own ignorance of them."[12] In an afterword to the novel *Far from the Madding Crowd*, Wright praises Hardy's attention to the natural world—a thing Wright calls "a strangeness in which" we all "have a share." When he quotes from D. H. Lawrence on the quality that makes Hardy's work equal to that of the "great writers," he clarifies his own regard for the workings of nature and his idea of our "share" in it:

> D. H. Lawrence writes of a 'quality which Hardy shares with the great writers . . . this setting behind the small action of his protagonists the terrific action of unfathomed nature; setting a small system of morality, the one grasped and formulated by the human

consciousness within the vast, uncomprehended and incomprehensible morality of nature or life itself' (30).

Branding himself a "restless fool" and a "fast friend" to nature, Wright acknowledges the paradoxical reality of natural cycle. He accepts both the sea's ability to populate, to spread the various "seeds" of life, and its opposite capability to destroy life, as evidenced by the "Venetian navy underneath" it. In spite of this, Wright is "not about to claim that the sea does not care." This final statement counters an earlier poem, "At the Slackening of the Tide," where Wright listens for a similar mourning on the part of the sea, but instead hears the sea (like Pilate) merely "Washing its hands."

Although Wright did not know he was critically ill with cancer at the time he wrote "A Reply to Matthew Arnold," his acceptance of "the living place" is also his way of saying "goodbye" to it. This is his way of saying, finally, that its paradox is its beauty. Though Wright is familiar with both elements of the dialectic, he chooses here to affirm the real possibility that humanity and nature can live "briefly in harmony." Asking nothing for himself, he asks only that the "living place" he loves "stay alive" after he is gone—no small desire in an age seemingly on the brink of nuclear destruction.[13]

These moments of sympathy between the human and the natural filter through the poems of *This Journey* like sunlight through green leaves. They color the book with hues of green light. Perhaps the best example of Wright's new accord with nature and his integrated prose style is "The Turtle Overnight" (*TJ*), in which language, form, and theme work together in Horatian unity.

The poem represents another example of what Richard Hugo regarded as the value of risking sentimentality in poetry. In it the poet risks the type of identification with natural things and the natural world that Hyatt Waggoner contends is characteristic of the American "visionary" poet, one who refuses to see himself as a "homeless" traveler or a passive observer but rather as a participant in natural processes. In fact, Wright's description of Gabriel Oak, his favorite character in Hardy's *Far from the Madding Crowd*, fairly well describes his own role in "The Turtle Overnight": "He is . . . surrounded by things which fill him with inexorable affection, and with which, at last, he becomes miraculously identified" ("*Far from the Madding Crowd*: An Afterword," 27).

The finely crafted first section displays the best of Wright's later work. Its invocation of wonder at natural things—once present in *Branch*—simply overpowers any human sense of loss and isolation and shows the influence of Roethke's nature poetry. Also, it reaches over into what Wright calls "some kind of rhythm, some closeness of life" through its repetitions and lilting prose rhythm. Finally, it shows Wright's sense of humor, a presiding force in his later work.

> I remember him last night in his comeliness. When it began to rain, he appeared in his accustomed place and emerged from his accustomed place and emerged from his shell as far as he could reach—feet, legs, tail, head. He seemed to enjoy the rain, the sweet-tasting rain that blew all the way across lake water to him from the mountains, the Alto Adige. It was as near as I've ever come to seeing a turtle take a pleasant bath in his natural altogether. All the legendary faces of broken old age disappeared from my mind, the thickened muscles under the chin, the nostrils brutal with hatred, the murdering eyes. He filled my mind with a sweet-tasting mountain rain, his youthfulness, his modesty as he washed himself all alone, his religious face.

The turtle takes on a "religious" shape larger than itself. Described in his "comeliness," in delicate and archaic language, the turtle bathes in his humorous "natural altogether," innocently and modestly giving himself over to the rain. His ritualized emergence banishes from the speaker's mind "the faces of broken old age," the "hatred," the "murdering eyes" of death and cycle and replaces them with "sweet-tasting mountain rain." The turtle's appearance enables Wright to do as Roethke sought to do in "The Longing": to "unlearn the lingo of exasperation, all the distortions of malice and hatred."

The piece continues with the turtle's reappearance on the following morning. In this harmonious setting of mutual "trust," a watchdog sleeps on as the turtle raises his face to the "green sunlight":

> For a long time now this morning, I have been sitting at this window and watching the grass below me. A moment ago there was

no one there. But now his brindle shell sighs slowly up and down in the midst of the green sunlight. A black watchdog snuffles asleep just behind him, but I trust that neither is afraid of the other. I see him lifting his face. It is a raising of eyebrows toward the light, an almost imperceptible turning of the chin, an ancient pleasure, an eagerness.

The turtle shows an "eagerness" to receive the sunlight, a "lifting" and a "raising" that amount to ascension. Wright admires this kind of rising, for when his speaker rises (as he does into the sycamore in *Two Citizens*), he finds comfort and release.

Later, the final two stanzas show that Wright can intricately maneuver parallel images in prose as well as he did earlier in the deep-image lyric "Miners," one of the best examples of this technique in *The Branch Will Not Break*. Here, his mind jumps from camomila, to the turtle's neck and "understanding" face, to a boyhood memory of another face in Ohio:

> Along his throat there are small folds, dark yellow as pollen shaken across a field of camomila. The lines on his face suggest only a relaxation, a delicacy in the understanding of the grass, like the careful tenderness I saw once on the face of a hobo in Ohio as he waved greeting to an empty wheat field from the flatcar of a freight train.

> But now the train is gone, and the turtle has left his circle of empty grass. I look a long time where he was, and I can't find a footprint in the empty grass. So much air left, so much sunlight, and still he is gone.

A seemingly omnipresent figure in Wright's work, the hobo, by virtue of his condition, remains homeless, caught up in a restless search for a place that might convince him to stop wandering. In much of Wright's work, he is an apt symbol of Wright himself, whose quest, as Peter Stitt has argued, is largely a quest for home. In these final two collections, however, Wright reconciles himself to the imperfect world and its constant state of flux. He begins to see things that remind him of home not the lack of one; his is a kind of pastoralism with eyes open beyond the physical world.

Wright recognizes that the source of this pastoral peace is actually inner and spiritual, that it resides in a specific locale only as much as one learns to see there inklings of one's own inner spiritual universe. Now, this turtle serves as a better symbol of Wright's redefined attitude toward his place in the world, for wherever it wanders in its "brindle shell," even in death, this turtle always carries its home with it.

In flawless, attentive prose, the piece presents a numinous experience that lessens Wright's fear of "broken old age" and his own eventual death. Whereas Roethke in "The Far Field" had "come upon warblers in early May" and found a means "to forget time and death," here Wright does nearly the same thing by being attentive to a simple turtle. Moreover, this harmony with nature is important not because it amounts to a statement of admiration for natural beauty. Rather, it is significant as a figure for Wright's acceptance of the larger constraints of death and change that govern all living beings. It offers his acknowledgment of factors over which we have no control—factors, however, which control our lives. In this poem, Wright accepts what the despairing poet of *The Green Wall* and *Saint Judas* was unable to accept.

If Wright had found understanding in the "good darkness" of many of the poems in *Branch*, in *This Journey* he discovers it in the "green sunlight." To know Wright's work is to realize, finally, that such a paradox is entirely in keeping with the manner of his thinking and feeling.

\* \* \*

Thus illuminated by the poetry of the present moment, Wright comes to "feel a kinship" with natural things that is visionary and religious in basis ("Small Wild Crabs Delighting on Black Sand," *TJ*). He follows the advice given in Roethke's essay "Open Letter" and hunts for a "clue to existence from the sub-human."[14] Moreover, the sense of questing that directs Roethke's *The Far Field* is also apparent in Wright's *This Journey*. Even a quick glance at *The Far Field* will reveal the repetition of the word "journey" and the pervasiveness of "light," of things that "shine" or "shimmer." Wright, also, finds comfort and an instant of transcendence in the bright sunlight, showing a nearly heliotropic response to its beckoning:

> I am going home with the lizard,
> Wherever home is,
> And lie beside him unguarded
> In the clear sunlight.
> We will lift our faces even if it rains.
> We will both turn green.
> ("Wherever Home Is," *TJ*)

Wright's inclusive speaker links himself and the lizard in a new community of things. Together they become the transformed "we" of the poem's final lines, partaking of a transcendent and spiritual rising to a "home" in the clear light to which they "lift" their faces.

Hank Lazer asserts that the image of light amounts to a spiritual element in Wright's work, that when Wright nears the light he is nearing God, though "God's presence is implied or inferred, never directly stated" in his poetry.[15] On occasion, however, he does more than merely gain proximity to this spiritual presence; sometimes he is infused with it, shining with an inner light as perceptible as the glow of a lightning bug:

> I think I am going to leave them folded
> And sleeping in their slight gray wings.
> I think I am going to climb back down
> And open my eyes and shine
> ("Lightning Bugs Asleep in the Afternoon," *TJ*)

The location of this spiritual presence is not accidental; its light, once internalized, evokes the purity and power of the spirit made flesh. Discovered within the body and the mind only after considerable struggle, this light reveals itself as love: a thing worthy of our full human faith, but sadly, often the subject of skeptical derision. A version of a prose poem included in Wright's unpublished papers, "Epistle to Roland Flint," addresses the reality of an inner spiritual life:

> We are advised by a poet even more ancient than Dante and Hor-
> ace that a certain God, who lives far off at a great distance deeply
> within us, has an absorbing interest in our human lives, and (the
> poet in question said many such sinister and strange things) that
> this distant God is love; and that he is not mocked.[16]

Such an awareness of a spiritual presence within nature and the human self does not restrict its benefits to the rewards of a supposed
hereafter, and indeed, is not dependent on that. It offers its best rewards right here on earth. During his long journey from darkness to
light, Wright has become whole again through the kind of attentiveness to nature and faith in the self from which an instant of numinous
experience might issue. This sort of moment occurs in "The Secret of
Light," where Wright balances his most fundamental notion of human
limitation with an equal notion of possibility:

> It is all right with me to know that my life is only one life. I feel like
> the light of the river Adige.

Wright's "The Journey" further describes this discovery and explains the "inmost secret of light" (or life) he finds in the figure of a
"slender and fastidious" spider, who is able to keep herself "poised"
and controlled "while ruins crumbled on every side of her":

> Many men
> Have searched all over Tuscany and never found
> What I found there, the heart of the light
> Itself shelled and leaved, balancing
> On filaments themselves falling. The secret
> Of this journey is to let the wind
> Blow its dust all over your body,
> To let it go on blowing, to step lightly, lightly
> All the way through your ruins, and not to lose
> Any sleep over the dead, who surely
> Will bury their own, don't worry.

The secret, Wright tells us, is to come to grips with the evanescence of
the physical world that surrounds us and with our own transience—
with the very dust that we shall eventually become. We can then "step

lightly, lightly" through the "ruins" we must inhabit and occasionally must create to live, and which, finally, will surely do us in, "don't worry."

It is significant that Wright's final collection does not end with the resolution of "The Journey," as the poem appears less than halfway into the volume. Instead, the collection ends less with an acceptance of death than with an invocation of religious transcendence, a kind of ascension to the sunlight for which the turtle shows such an "eagerness" and longing. As confidently (and cautiously) as he can, Wright resolves the haunting sense of separation due to original sin that permeates his early work.

Wright, enthralled by a moment of beauty and spiritual transformation, experiences an unfamiliar inversion in "A Winter Daybreak above Vence":

> I turn and somehow
> Impossibly hovering in the air over everything,
> The Mediterranean, nearer to the moon
> Than this mountain is,
> Shines. A voice clearly
> Tells me to snap out of it. . . .
>
> Look, the sea has not fallen and broken
> Our heads. How can I feel so warm
> Here in the dead center of January. I can
> Scarcely believe it, and yet I have to, this is
> The only life I have. I get up from the stone.
> My body mumbles something unseemly
> And follows me. Now we are all sitting here
>     strangely
> On top of the sunlight.

Ending in affirmation and possibility, the poem makes use of the familiar dialogic format that Wright has been fond of since his earliest collections. Wright is told by the voice of his rational self "to snap out of it," to realize that such ascension is impossible, but he, nevertheless, manages to conclude the poem sitting on "top of the sunlight." Joining his body and his spirit at the close of the poem—and at the end of the collection—he is again whole, and neither of the competing voices within the self has been altogether silenced in the process. Moreover, the poem's close surely answers Wright's perpetual yearning "to be lifted up" into a sort of ontological and transcendental awareness of the human self.

Though the journey was not without its moments of darkness and despair, not without the need to backtrack and reevaluate his course, in *This Journey* Wright succeeds in affirming the clearest hope of *The Green Wall*: that he might resolve the distance separating him from other humans, from the natural world, and from the earth "where we belong." He achieves an awareness of spiritual life, a presence that infuses him with the shining light of affirmation, acceptance, and patience. In this final stage of his career, Wright becomes Nietzsche's "yea-sayer," discovering and evoking the child's "innocence and oblivion . . . an holy yea-saying" that refuses an easy and self-centered despair.[17] As Stitt reminds us, Wright's introduction to Hy Sobiloff's *Breathing of First Things* is titled "The Quest for the Child Within."[18] Though he is ostensibly speaking of Sobiloff's coming to maturity as a poet, Wright's remarks about Sobiloff clearly reflect his "struggle" to "learn . . . how to be true to his own self." That struggle, Wright says, "involves a good deal more than the rediscovery of a childlike radiance and joy, though that rediscovery may lie at the end of the journey." And for Wright it did.

In "A Fit against the Country" Wright had asked us to "be glad" of our eviction from Paradise and cautioned us to hold ourselves carefully away from the "tempting" but deadly enticements of the physical world. However, in "The Journey" he tells us that such a world is all we have—that its enticements, in fact, amount to a physical as well as spiritual bounty ready (and meant) for our taking. Because Wright is a religious poet, one who has discovered at last a reason for celebration and a means to celebrate, his final poems read like epistles which, though perhaps not designed for that purpose, instruct as much as delight us. Although our own journey may be fraught with peril, it is attended equally with beauty: For every wing intent upon descending to despair, there exists another in equipose, resolute and persistent in its urge to rise.

# Conclusion

James Wright's career—in its constancies and transitions, its moments of intense joy and abject despair, its fullness and its brevity—offers fertile ground for literary study. But more than a simple literary history, his work amounts to the history of a life lived, an honest human effort to front the experiential world and take on what it gives him—whether good or bad, angel or serpent. In fact, Wright always held in high regard the attitude of Theodor Storm, who dismissed the benefits of literary success to return "home" and serve not as lyric poet but as district magistrate for his town. In Storm's actions Wright identified two ideas that helped to shape his own attitude toward the role of a poet; he praised Storm for his understanding that the "main thing" for an artist to accomplish was "not to get on in the world but to get home," and for his awareness that an artist's goal "was not to make a successful career, but to live one's life."[1]

One of the most striking things about Wright's professional career is the manner in which his personal life, especially his disposition to the natural world and its inhabitants, becomes so inextricably bound up within his aesthetic ideas of form, rhetoric, and voice. He owes most clearly to the Emersonian tradition that considers a struggle with language to be a struggle with the self—a locating of the self within a world of "natural facts." The foremost goal of Emerson's "Seer" is to be attentive enough to natural facts that they become "spiritual facts" capable of informing and, moreover, defining the self. Language, then, becomes a means of self-definition, and to be frivolous or irresponsible with language becomes a negation of the self and the world it inhabits.

As a nature poet, Wright was not always convinced of Emerson's pronouncement that "nature is the symbol of spirit." His attention was often rewarded, occasionally disappointed. But he looked anyway. In an age of flash and glitz, it is neither popular nor sophisticated to say that one finds solace in an attentiveness to natural things. Wright, however, was more concerned with discovering a means of restoring the powers of the individual self than with meeting trendy standards:

> It comforts me more and more to realize and to observe and to feel the great self-restoring power that the creatures of nature have while we human beings are making such a mess of things. . . . Roethke said a beautiful thing once when he talked to a class about the poetry of nature. He said that we ought to remember that there is an inner nature, and I think he was suggesting . . . that, perhaps, poetry could remind us of the need for restoration through the inner nature.[2]

Again, Wright links an inner and an outer nature, joins an individual self with the larger self of the physical universe. And again such a conjoining issues its Emersonian result: a revivification of the inner life.

The act of attentive seeing is so important to Wright that he can wholly define the value of being human in terms of how good one is at doing it: "Simply to *be* a man (instead of one more variety of automaton, of which we have some tens of thousands) means to keep one's eyes open."[3] Such an attitude possesses a moral and aesthetic urgency, for the duty to keep one's eyes open assumes that there is a preexistent order within the natural world that the attentive person may identify and perhaps learn from. It accounts for the personal and aesthetic transition which occurred within the pages of Wright's *Amenities of Stone*, the volume in which he first questions and eventually rejects a poetry that *imposes* order on experience in favor of a poetry that *perceives* order.

Because Wright associates the act of language with the act of selfhood, it is not surprising that the mode and manner of his work would alter as the self redefines its values and goals, its very identity. In a

1958 review of Robert Penn Warren's *Promises*, Wright chides the kind of poet he thought was prevalent in the day for lacking the aesthetic and personal courage that enabled Warren to explore a new, less protective mode of writing poems. He calls the output of the group—his own work included—merely the "ten thousand safe and competent versifyings produced by our current crop of punks in America. . . . we all know who we are . . . us safe boys."[4] Wright, as the permutations and explorations of his career illustrate, did not long remain one of the "safe boys," but rather dropped the armor of perfect form and risked a vulnerability in his poetry that opened him to both personal and aesthetic attacks. As Dave Smith has indicated, one can see the inklings of Wright's yearning for a more responsive poetry in this review of Warren; though he is ostensibly describing the kind of individual character that stands behind Warren's new work, one can sense in the passion of Wright's words his effort to convince himself to make the same kind of leap:

> In effect, a major writer at the height of his fame has chosen, not to write his own good poems over again, but to break his own rules, to shatter his words and try to recreate them, to fight through and beyond his own craftsmanship in order to revitalize his language.[5]

The transitions which characterize Wright's own career are largely efforts to increase the clarity and precision of his language, the struggle to discover in that language a means to speak directly with a reader and to convey his ideas and feelings in a way that re-creates them in the reader's mind. If the line between his life and his art gradually becomes more muted, it is because Wright recognizes, as Emerson had before him, that words themselves are modes of action capable of sustaining or violating the purity of a writer's relationship with his world. A writer fond of showy or self-aggrandizing rhetoric is guilty of dissembling, profoundly deceiving not only his reader but also himself. For Wright, words can both express life and constitute it. Late in his career, he became so convinced of the fundamental relationship between poetry and life that he occasionally used the terms interchangeably, most notably in an unpublished fragment appropriately titled "Didactic Poem":

> Life's final enemy is rhetoric.
> The enemy of poetry is death.[6]

Wright's conception of rhetoric is classical; it owes to Horace's *Ars Poetica*, a significant piece by perhaps the most significant of Wright's numerous literary mentors. From Horace, Wright learns the importance of a unified field of composition, one drawing equally from the intellect and the imagination and one not bound inordinately to nitpicking rules of technique. Following the advice of Horace and the example of Warren, he breaks both the rules that he had learned from others and those that he had set for himself in a concerted effort to say something clearly and meaningfully. The well-wrought poems of high formal rhetoric, the poems of the deep image, the spare "bone lonely" lyrics, and the delicate prose of his prose poems matter less when viewed as individual examples of disparate styles than they do when viewed as a unified whole: the expressions of a poet speaking to his reader in the best way he could imagine.

The stages that I have identified in Wright's career and the labels of containment, vulnerability, and integration I have given them also matter less as separate ideas than they do as parts of the broad map of Wright's professional life, as individual roads traveled on a long artistic journey. It is perhaps marginally surprising that one should discover there paths of constancy nearly overlooked among the major turns in direction that are the sustaining gift of his work. Wright believed that being a poet carries with it a two-fold responsibility: to know the forms and manners of the past and to contribute to those something new of one's own. In fact, his admiration for Whitman can be traced to Whitman's insistence on the necessity of poetic innovation. At one time Wright, embroiled in an aesthetic redefinition replete with professional and personal consequences, considered invoking the support of Whitman for the suppressed collection *Amenities of Stone* and its successor *New Poems*. On a title page dated 10 August 1961, Wright crossed out *Amenities of Stone*, replaced it with *New Poems*, and scribbled beneath the new title: "I note Whitman on the defense of the past: 'If he does not provide new forms, he is not what is wanted.' "[7] Wright clearly is a poet who could imagine no greater failure for a writer than to remain static, to do—as Fitzgerald accused Hemingway of doing—the aesthetic injustice of finding a good thing and never leaving it.

Above all else, Wright valued an aesthetic that forever sought to reshape itself for the better; it amounted to his most compelling artistic goal: "The kind of poetry I want to write is / The poetry of a grown man." He knew that this proposition had much to do with an Horatian "pity / For the pure clear word," and he seemed to realize that its attainment was still ahead of him and involved a great deal of work:

> I know something about the pure clear word,
> Though I am not yet a grown man.

A little later in the same poem, Wright identified the salient characteristic of a poet who wished to write the poetry of a grown man:

> He grows.

The evolution of Wright's poetry throughout his career is mostly an expression of this ethic, what he calls elsewhere the poet's absolute devotion to a "furious and unceasing growth."[8] To do less is to betray one's language—and one's self.

What Wright had in mind by asking that a writer grow is certainly more than mere aesthetic refinement, or for that matter intellectual, spiritual, or emotional deepening. Rather, it is a broadening of the self that encompasses all of these, melding equal parts into a collective (and strengthened) whole. While making some final revisions to the text of *To a Blossoming Pear Tree* in November 1976, Wright seemed to have come upon the perfect epigraph to express such an attitude toward personal growth. Though he eventually chose to delete this epigraph from the book, the words of his old master Ben Jonson could well have been his own: "It is not growing, like a tree / In bulk, doth make man better bee."[9]

Moreover, Wright's conception of the "poetry of a grown man" asks most clearly that he establish an Emersonian "original relation to the universe." His view of the "universe" is perhaps broader than that of most nature poets, for it is composed by a physical reality and its accompanying spiritual presence—and by the words of those who have paid attention to it. The "continuity" that William Matthews alludes to in Wright's work, I believe, derives from what Matthews calls the need "to forge a personal relationship to literary tradition."[10] Such a conception enables Wright to feel equally comfortable reading and learning from Chaddiock Tichbourne or Emerson or Donne or Roethke. It means that Wright must "get home": accept his personal past—the blessing and curse of family, friends, and place—and incorporate those elements within the literary history he inherits.

Franz Wright recently described the kind of intimate relationship with literary history that he believes his father achieved:

> In his presence the great poets, living and dead, ceased to be the remote and inaccessible monuments they often appear to be; they became real in his person, a visionary but very human company, the embodiment of a great hope or desire in yourself and in everyone, something that you may dare to explore if you could come to see that poetry is not a form of ambition or even self-expression, but as Char so beautifully put it, a contribution of the creature to creation.[11]

Wright was a profoundly traditional poet, one fond of saying that the great figures of the literary past were most assuredly "on our side." This literary tradition was not a burden to Wright, or even a source of tension, once he was able to discern how he might avoid merely being shaped by it and instead offer his own contributions to it. Wright openly proclaimed himself a "traditionalist," asserting that "whatever we have in our lives that matters has to do with our discovering our true relation to the past."[12] In the body of his work, James Wright shares with his readers the elaborate and often arduous process of such a discovery.

# Select Bibliography

## PRIMARY SOURCES

Wright, James. *The Branch Will Not Break*. Middletown, Conn.: Wesleyan Univ. Press, 1963.
———. *Collected Poems*. Middletown, Conn.: Wesleyan Univ. Press, 1971.
———. *Collected Prose*. Edited by Anne Wright. Ann Arbor: Univ. of Michigan Press, 1983.
———. *The Green Wall*. New Haven, Conn.: Yale Univ. Press; London: Oxford Univ. Press, 1957.
———. *Leave It to the Sunlight*. Durango, Colo.: Logbridge-Rhodes, 1981.
———. *Moments of the Italian Summer*. Takoma Park, Md.: Dryad Press, 1976.
———. *A Reply to Matthew Arnold*. Durango, Colo.: Logbridge-Rhodes, 1981.
———. *Saint Judas*. Middletown, Conn.: Wesleyan Univ. Press, 1959.
———. *A Secret Field*. Edited by Anne Wright. Durango, Colo.: Logbridge-Rhodes, 1985.
———. *Shall We Gather at the River*. Middletown, Conn.: Wesleyan Univ. Press, 1968.
———. *The Summers of James and Anne Wright*. New York: Sheep Meadow Press, 1981.
———. *This Journey*. New York: Vintage Books, 1982.
———. *To a Blossoming Pear Tree*. New York: Farrar, Straus, and Giroux, 1977.
———. *Two Citizens*. New York: Farrar, Straus, and Giroux, 1973.
Wright, James, Robert Bly, and William Duffy. *The Lion's Tail and Eyes*. Madison, Minn.: Sixties Press, 1962.

## TRANSLATIONS

Char, René. *Hypnos Waking*. Selected and translated by Jackson Matthews with the collaboration of Barbara Howes, W. S. Merwin, William Jay Smith, Richard Wilbur, William Carlos Williams, and James A. Wright. New York: Random House, 1956.
Guillen, Jorge. *Cantico: A Selection*. Edited by Norman Thomas di Giovanni and translated by J. A. Wright. Boston: Little, Brown and Company, 1965.

Hesse, Herman. *Poems*. Selected and translated James Wright. New York: Farrar, Straus, and Giroux, 1970.

―――. *Wanderings: Notes and Sketches*. Translated by James Wright. New York: Farrar, Straus, and Giroux, 1973; London: Cape, 1972.

Neruda, Pablo. *Twenty Poems*. Translated by James Wright and Robert Bly. Madison, Minn.: Sixties Press; London: Rapp and Whiting, 1968.

Neruda, Pablo, and Cesar Vallejo. *Selected Poems*. Edited by Robert Bly and translated by John Knoepfle, Robert Bly, and James Wright. Boston: Beacon Press, 1971.

Storm, Theodor. *The Rider on the White Horse*. Translated by James Wright. New York: Signet, 1964.

Trakl, George. *Twenty Poems of Georg Trakl*. Translated by James Wright, John Knoepfle, and Robert Bly. Madison, Minn.: Sixties Press, 1961.

Vallejo, Cesar. *Twenty Poems of Cesar Vallejo*. Translated by John Knoepfle, James Wright, and Robert Bly. Madison, Minn.: Sixties Press, 1962.

## SECONDARY SOURCES

Altieri, Charles. *Enlarging the Temple: New Directions in American Poetry in the 1960's*. Lewisburg, Pa.: Bucknell Univ. Press, 1979.

―――. "Objective Image and Art of Mind in Modern Poetry." *PMLA* 91 (1976): 101–14.

―――. *Self and Sensibility in Contemporary American Poetry*. Cambridge: Cambridge Univ. Press, 1984.

Andre, Michael. "An Interview with James Wright." *Unmuzzled Ox* 1 (n.d.): 3–18.

―――. "Levertov, Creeley, Wright, Auden, Ginsberg, Corso, Dickey: Essays and Interviews with Contemporary American Poets." Diss., Columbia Univ., 1974.

Atlas, James. "Yelping and Hooting: Some Developments in Contemporary American Poetry." *London Magazine*, April 1974, pp. 15–32.

Auden, W. H. Foreword to *The Green Wall*, by James Wright. New Haven, Conn.: Yale Univ. Press, 1957.

Barnstone, Willis. "The Impact of Poetry in Spanish on Recent, American Poetry." In *Spanish Writers of 1936: Crisis and Commitment in the Poetry of the Thirties and Forties*. Edited by Jamie Ferran and Daniel P. Testa. London: Tamesis, 1973, pp. 137–41.

Benedict, Estelle. *Library Journal*, 15 Sept. 1968, p. 3145.

Berg, Stephen, and Robert Mezey, eds. *Naked Poetry*. Indianapolis: Bobbs-Merrill, 1969.

Berke, Roberta. *Bounds Outs of Bounds: A Compass for Recent American and British Poetry*. New York: Oxford Univ. Press, 1981.

"Beside the Styx." *Times* [London] *Literary Supplement*, 17 Oct. 1968, p. 1172.

Birkerts, Sven. "James Wright's 'Hammock': A Sounding." *Agni Review* 21 (Spring 1985): 121–35.

Blakely, Roger. "Form and Meaning in the Poetry of James Wright." *South Dakota Review* 25, no. 2 (Summer 1987): 20–30.

Bloom, Harold. "The Dialectic of Romantic Poetry in America." *The Southern Review* 7 (1971): 140–75.

Bly, Carol. "James Wright's Visits to Odin House." *Ironwood* 10 (1977): 33–37.

Bly, Robert. "American Poetry: On the Way to the Hermetic." *Books Abroad* 46 (1972): 17–24.

———. "James Wright." *Café Solo* 2 (1970): 6–9.

———. "A Note on James Wright." *Ironwood* 10 (1977): 64–65.

———. *Talking All Morning.* Ann Arbor: Univ. of Michigan Press, 1980.

———. "The Work of James Wright." *The Sixties* 8 (Spring 1966): 57–78. (Listed under "Crunk," pseudonym of Robert Bly.)

———. "A Wrong-Turning in American Poetry." *Choice* 3 (1963): 33–47.

———. ed. *Leaping Poetry: An Idea with Poems and Translations.*1972. Boston: Beacon Press, 1975.

Breslin, James E. "James Wright's *The Branch Will Not Break.*" *American Poetry Review* 11, no. 2 (March–April 1982): 139–46.

Brooks, Cleanth. "Poetry since the Wasteland." *The Southern Review* 1 (Summer 1965): 487–500.

Brooks, Van Wyck. *America's Coming of Age.* New York: B. W. Huebsch, 1915. Rpt. in *Van Wyck Brooks: The Early Years.* Edited by Claire Sprague. New York: Harper, 1968.

Browne, Michael Dennis. "Drawing a Bead on Louis Gallo from Minneapolis, Minnesota." *Carleton Miscellany* 17 (Winter 1977): 33–37.

Bugeja, Michael. "James Wright: The Mastery of Personification in *This Journey.*" *Mid-American Review* 4, no. 2 (Fall 1984): 106–15.

———. "The Mathematics of Morality in James Wright's 'Hammock' Poem." *Indiana Review* 9, no. 1 (Winter 1986): 68–73.

Butscher, Edward. "The Rise and Fall of James Wright." *Georgia Review* 28 (Spring 1974): 257–68.

Cambon, Glauco. *The Inclusive Flame: Studies in American Poetry.* Bloomington: Indiana Univ. Press, 1965.

———. *Recent American Poetry.* Minneapolis: Univ. of Minnesota Press, 1962.

Carroll, Paul. *The Poem in Its Skin.* Chicago: Follett Publishing Company, 1968.

Coles, Robert. "James Wright: One of Those Messengers." *American Poetry Review* 2, no. 4 (1973): 36–37.

Conquest, Robert. "Mistah Eliot—He Dead?" *Audit* 1, no. 2 (1960): 12–17.

Costello, Bonnie. "James Wright: Returning to the Heartland." *New Boston Review* 5 (Aug.-Sept. 1980): 12–14.

Davis, William V. " 'A Grave in Blossom': A Note on James Wright." *Contemporary Poetry: A Journal of Criticism* [Bryn Mawr] 4, no. 3 (1982): 1–3.

DeFrees, Madeline. "James Wright's Early Poems: A Study in 'Convulsive' Form." *Modern Poetry Studies* 2 (1979): 241–51.

———. "That Vacant Paradise." *Ironwood* 10 (1977): 13–20.

Dickey, James. *Babel to Byzantium: Poets and Poetry Now.* New York: Farrar, Straus, and Giroux, 1967.

_____. "In the Presence of Anthologies." *Sewanee Review* 66 (Spring 1958): 294–314.

_____. *Spinning the Crystal Ball: Some Guesses at the Future of American Poetry.* Washington, D.C.: Library of Congress, 1967.

_____. *The Suspect in Poetry.* Madison, Minn.: Sixties Press, 1964.

Ditsky, John. "James Wright Collected: Alterations on the Monument." *Modern Poetry Studies* 2 (1972): 252–59.

Dougherty, David C. "James Wright: The Murderer's Grave in the New Northwest." *The Old Northwest: A Journal of Regional Life and Letters* 2 (1976): 45–54.

_____. "The Skeptical Poetry of James Wright." *Contemporary Poetry: A Journal of Criticism* 2, no. 2 (1977): 4–10.

_____. "Themes in Jeffers and James Wright." *Robinson Jeffers Newsletter* 30 (1972): 6.

Edson, Russell. "The Prose Poem in America." *Parnassus* 5, no. 1 (Fall/Winter 1976), 321–325.

Elkins, Polk Andrew. "The Continuity and Development of James Wright's Poetry." Diss., Northwestern Univ., 1980.

Elliot, David Lindsay. "The Deep Image: Radical Subjectivity in the Poetry of Robert Bly, James Wright, Galway Kinnell, James Dickey, and W. S. Merwin." Diss., Syracuse Univ., 1978.

Elliot, William D. "Poets of the Moving Frontier: Bly, Whittemore, Wright, Berryman, McGrath, and Minnesota North Country Poetry." *Midamerica: Yearbook of the Society for the Study of Midwestern Literature* 3 (1976): 17–38.

Engel, Bernard F. "From Here We Speak." *The Old Northwest: A Journal of Regional Life and Letters* 2 (1976): 37–44.

_____. "The Universality of James Wright." *Society for the Study of Midwestern Literature Newsletter* 10, no. 3 (1980): 26–28.

Faas, Egbert. *Towards a New American Poetics: Essays and Interviews: Olson, Snyder, Duncan, Creeley, Bly, Ginsberg.* Santa Barbara, Calif.: Black Sparrow Press, 1978.

Fiedler, Leslie A. "A Kind of Solution: The Situation of Poetry Now." *Kenyon Review* 26 (1964): 5479.

Foster, Richard. "Debauched by Craft: Problems of the Younger Poets." *Perspective* 12 (1960): 3–17.

Friedman, Norman. "The Wesleyan Poets III: The Experimental Poets." *Chicago Review* 19, no. 2 (1966): 52–73.

"From Literature to Life." *Times* [London] *Literary Supplement,* 28 Nov. 1963, p. 995.

Fussell, Edwin. *Lucifer in Harness: American Meter, Metaphor, and Diction.* Princeton, N.J.: Princeton Univ. Press, 1973.

Gallo, Louis. "Thoughts on Recent American Poetry." *Carleton Miscellany* 17 (Winter 1977): 12–27.

Garrett, George. "Against the Grain: Poets Writing Today." In *American Poetry.* Edited by Irvin Enrenpreis. Stratford-Upon-Avon Studies 7. London: Edward Arnold, 1965, pp. 221–39.

Gattuccio, Nicholas. "Now My Amenities of Stone Are Done: Some Notes on the Style of James Wright." *Concerning Poetry* 15, no. 1 (1983): 61–76.

Gerke, Robert S. "Ritual, Myth, and Poetic Language in the Poetry of James Wright." *The Bulletin of the West Virginia Association of College English Teachers* 7 (Spring 1982): 17-23.

Graves, Michael. "Crisis in the Career of James Wright." *The Hollins Critic* 22, no. 5 (Dec. 1985): 1-9.

———. "James Wright's 'Written in a Copy of Swift's Poems, for Wayne Burns.' " *The Scriblerian and the Kit Cats: A Newsjournal Devoted to Pope, Swift, and Their Circle* 15, no. 1 (1982): 71-72.

———. "A Look at the Ceremonial Range of James Wright." *Concerning Poetry* 16, no. 2 (1983): 43-54.

Hall, Donald, ed. Introduction to *Contemporary American Poetry*. Baltimore: Penguin, 1962.

Hamod, Sam. "Floating in a Hammock: James Wright." *Contemporary Poetry* 2, no. 2 (1977): 62-65.

———. "Moving inside the Poetry of James Wright." Diss., Univ. of Iowa, 1973.

Harris, Victoria. "James Wright's Odyssey: A Journey from Dualism to Incorporation." *Contemporary Poetry: A Journal of Criticism* 3, no. 3 (1978): 56-74.

———. "Relationship and Change: Text and Context of James Wright's 'Blue Teal's Mother' and Robert Bly's 'With Pale Women in Maryland' " *American Poetry* 3, no. 1 (Fall 1985): 43-55.

Haskell, Dennis. "The Modern American Poetry of Deep Image." *Southern Review: Literary and Interdisciplinary Essays* (Adelaide, Australia). 12 (1979): 137-66.

Hass, Robert. "James Wright." *Ironwood* 10 (1977): 74-96.

Henriksen, Bruce. "Poetry Must Think." *New Orleans Review* 6, no. 3 (1979): 201-07.

———. "Wright's 'Lying in a Hammock at William Duffy's Farm in Pine Island, Minnesota.' " *Explicator* 21 (Jan. 1974): item 40.

Heyen, William, ed. *American Poets in 1976*. Indianapolis: Bobbs-Merrill Company, 1976.

Heyen, William, and Jerome Mazzaro. "Something to Be Said for the Light: A Conversation with James Wright." Edited by Joseph R. McElrath, Jr. *Southern Humanities Review* 6 (1972): 134-53.

Holden, Jonathan. *The Rhetoric of the Contemporary Lyric*. Bloomington: Indiana Univ. Press, 1980.

Howard, Richard. *Alone with America: Essays on the Art of Poetry in the United States since 1950*. New York: Atheneum, 1969.

———. "James Wright's Transformations." *New York Arts Journal*, Feb.-March 1978, pp. 22-23.

———. "My Home, My Native Country: James Wright." *Ironwood* 10 (1977): 101-10.

Ignatow, David. "What I Feel at the Moment Is Always True." *Ironwood* 10 (1977): 45-46.

Jackson, Richard. "The Time of the Other: James Wright's Poetry of Attachments." *Chowder Review* 10-11 (1978): 126-44.

Janssens, G. A. M. "The Present State of American Poetry: Robert Bly and James Wright." *English Studies* 51 (April 1970): 112-37.

Jauss, David. "Wright's 'Lying in a Hammock at William Duffy's Farm in Pine Island, Minnesota.' " *Explicator* 41, no. 1 (1982): 54-55.

Kalaidjian, Walter. "Many of Our Waters: The Poetry of James Wright." *Boundary 2: A Journal of Postmodern Literature* 9, no. 2 (1981): 101-21.

Kameen, Paul. "Madness and Magic: Postmodernist Poetics and the Dream." *Criticism: A Quarterly for Literature and the Arts* 24, no. 1 (1982): 36-47.

Kazin, Alfred. "James Wright: The Gift of Feeling." *New York Times Book Review*, 20 July 1980, p. 13, 25.

Kinnell, Galway. "Poetry, Personality, and Death." *Field* 4 (Spring 1971).

Kostelanetz, Richard. "Reactions and Alternatives: Post-World War II American Poetry." *Chelsea* 26 (1969): 7-34.

Krauth, Leland. " 'Beauty Breaking through the Husks of Life': Sherwood Anderson and James Wright." *Midamerica: The Yearbook of the Society for the Study of Midwestern Literature* 10 (1983): 124-38.

Lawrence, D. H. *Studies in Classic American Literature*. Rev. ed. New York: Viking, 1964.

Lense, Edward. " 'This Is What I Wanted': James Wright and the Other World." *Modern Poetry Studies* 11, no. 1-2 (1982): 19-32.

Lensing, George S., and Ronald Moran. *Four Poets of the Emotive Imagination: Robert Bly, James Wright, Louis Simpson, and William Stafford*. Baton Rouge: Louisiana State Univ. Press, 1976.

Levine, Ellen Sue. "From Water to Land: The Poetry of Sylvia Plath, James Wright, and W. S. Merwin." Diss., Univ. of Washington, 1974.

Lewis, R. W. B. *The American Adam*. Chicago: Univ. of Chicago Press, 1955.

Lieberman, Laurence. *Unassigned Frequencies: American Poetry in Review, 1964-77*. Urbana: Univ. of Illinois Press, 1977, pp. 182-189.

Logan, John. "The Prose of James Wright." *Ironwood* 10 (1977): 154-55.

Malkoff, Karl. *Escape from the Self: A Study of Contemporary American Poetry and Poetics*. New York: Columbia Univ. Press, 1977.

Martin, Philip. "A Dungeon with the Door Open." *Carleton Miscellany* 17 (Winter 1977): 30-33.

Martone, John. " 'I Would Break into Blossom': Neediness and Transformation in the Poetry of James Wright." *Publications of the Arkansas Philogical Association* 9, no. 1 (1983): 64-75.

Martz, William. *The Distinctive Voice*. Glenview, Ill.: Scott Forsman and Co., 1966.

Matthews, William. "The Continuity of James Wright's Poems." *The Ohio Review* 18, no. 2 (1977): 44-57.

––––––. "Entering the World." *Shenandoah* 20 (1969): 80-93.

Mazzaro, Jerome. "Dark Water: James Wright's Early Poetry." *The Centennial Review* 27, no. 2 (1983): 135-55.

McDonald, Walter. "Blossoms of Fire: James Wright's Epiphany of Joy." *Conference of the College Teachers of English Proceedings* 46 (Sept. 1981): 22-28.

McElrath, James. "Something to Be Said for the Light: A Conversation with James Wright." *Southern Humanities Review* 6 (1972): 134-53.

McKenzie, James J. "A New American Nature Poetry: Theodore Roethke, James Dickey, and James Wright." Diss., Univ. of Notre Dame, 1971.

McMaster, Belle M. "James Arlington Wright: A Checklist." *Bulletin of Bibliography* 31 (1974): 71–82, 88.

McPherson, Sandra. "You Can Say That Again. (Or Can You?)" *Iowa Review* 3 (1972): 70-75.

Meredith, Everett Bernard. "The Autobiographical Image in the Poetry of James Wright." Diss., West Virginia Univ., 1979.

Mills, Ralph J., Jr. *Contemporary American Poetry*. New York: Random House, 1965.

———. *Creation's Very Self*. Fort Worth: Texas Christian Univ. Press, 1969.

———. *Cry of the Human: Essays on Contemporary American Poetry*. Urbana. Univ. of Illinois Press, 1975.

Molesworth, Charles. *The Fierce Embrace*. Columbia: Univ. of Missouri Press, 1979.

———. "James Wright and the Dissolving Self." In *Contemporary Poetry in America: Essays and Interviews*. Edited by Robert Boyers. New York: Schocken Books, 1974, pp. 267–78.

Moore, James. "American Poetry in and out of the Cave": Part I, "The Yenan Complex." *Lamp in the Spine*, no. 3 (Winter 1972): 12–27.

Moran, Robert, and George Lensing. "The Emotive Imagination: A New Departure in American Poetry." *The Southern Review* 3, no. 1 (Jan. 1967): 51–67.

Nathan, Leonard. "The Private 'I' in Contemporary Poetry." *Shenandoah* 22 (Summer 1971): 80–99.

———. "The Traditional James Wright." *Ironwood* 10 (1977): 131–37.

———. "The Tradition of Sadness and the American Metaphysic: An Interpretation of the Poetry of James Wright." In *The Pure Clear Word: Essays on the Poetry of James Wright*. Edited by Dave Smith. Urbana: Univ. of Illinois Press, 1982, pp. 159–74.

Orlen, Steven. "The Green Wall." *Ironwood* 10 (1977): 5–12.

Pearce, Roy Harvey. "The Burden of Romanticism: Toward the New Poetry." *Iowa Review* 2 (Spring 1971): 109–28.

———. *The Continuity of American Poetry*. Rev. ed. Princeton: Princeton Univ. Press, 1965.

Perloff, Marjorie G. "Poetry Chronicle: 1970–71." *Contemporary Literature* 14, no. 1 (Winter 1973): 97–131.

Piccione, Anthony. "Robert Bly and the Deep Image." Diss., Ohio Univ., 1969.

Pinsky, Robert. *The Situation of Poetry: Contemporary Poetry and Its Traditions*. Princeton, N.J.: Princeton Univ. Press, 1976.

Plumly, Stanley. "Chapter and Verse." *American Poetry Review* 7 (Jan.-Feb. 1978): 21–35; (May–June 1978): 21–32.

———. "Sentimental Forms." *Antaeus* 30–31 (1978): 321–28.

Poulin, A., Jr. "Contemporary American Poetry: The Radical Tradition." In *Contemporary American Poetry*. 1st ed. Edited by A. Poulin, Jr. Boston: Houghton-Mifflin, 1971, pp. 387–400.

Rahv, Philip. *Image and Idea*. Rev. ed. New York: New Directions, 1957.

Rexroth, Kenneth. *American Poetry in the Twentieth Century*. New York: Herder and Herder, 1971.

Robinett, Emma Jane. " 'No Place to Go but Home': The Poetry of James Arlington Wright." Diss., Univ. of Notre Dame, 1976.

_____. "Two Poems and Two Poets." *Ironwood* 10 (1977): 38–44.

Rosenthal, M. L. *The New Modern Poetry.* New York: Oxford Univ. Press, 1967.

_____. *The New Poets.* New York: Oxford Univ. Press, 1967.

Saunders, William S. "Indignation Born of Love: James Wright's Ohio Poems." *The Old Northwest: A Journal of Regional Life and Letters* 4 (1978): 353–69.

_____. *James Wright: An Introduction.* Columbus: State Library of Ohio, 1979.

Scott, Shirley Clay. "Surrendering the Shadow." *Ironwood* 10 (1977): 46–63.

Seay, James. "A World Immeasurably Alive and Good: A Look at James Wright's *Collected Poems.*" *Georgia Review* 27 (Spring 1973): 71–81.

Serchunk, Peter. "On the Poet, James Wright." *Modern Poetry Studies* 10, no. 2–3 (1981): 85–90.

Seyffert, Henriette. "Three Contemporary Translator Poets: W. S. Merwin, Willis Barnstone, and James Wright." Diss., Indiana Univ., 1970.

Smith, Dave. "Chopping the Distance on James Wright." *Back Door,* nos. 7 and 8 (Spring 1975), pp. 89–95.

_____. "James Wright: The Pure Clear Word, An Interview." *American Poetry Review* 9, no. 3 (1980): 19–30. Rpt. in *The Pure Clear Word: Essays on the Poetry of James Wright.* Edited by Dave Smith. Urbana: Univ. of Illinois Press, 1982, pp. 3–42.

_____. "That Halting, Stammering, Movement." *Ironwood* 10 (1977): 111–30.

_____. ed. *The Pure Clear Word: Essays on the Poetry of James Wright.* Urbana: Univ. of Illinois Press, 1982.

Spendal, R. J. "Wright's 'Lying in a Hammock at William Duffy's Farm in Pine Island, Minnesota.' " *Explicator* 34 (1976): item 64.

Stein, Kevin. "James Wright's 'A Blessing': Revising the Perfect Poem." *Indiana Review* 8, no. 1 (Winter 1985): 63–68.

_____. "A Redefinition of the Poetic Self: James Wright's *Amenities of Stone.*" *The Ohio Review* 33 (1984): 9–28.

_____. "The Rhetoric of Containment, Vulnerability, and Integration in the Work of James Wright." *Concerning Poetry* 20 (1987): 117–27.

Stepanchev, Stephen. *American Poetry since 1945: A Critical Survey.* New York: Harper and Row, 1965.

Stiffler, Randall. "The Reconciled Vision of James Wright." *Literary Review* 28, no. 1 (1984): 77–92.

Stilwell, Robert. "Samples." *Michigan Quarterly Review* 7 (Fall 1969); 278–82.

Stitt, Peter. "The Art of Poetry XIX: James Wright." *Paris Review* 16 (Summer 1975): 34–61.

_____. "The Garden and the Grime." *Kenyon Review* 6, no. 2 (1984): 76–91.

_____. "James Wright and Robert Bly." *Hawaii Review* 2 (Spring 1975): 89–94.

_____. "The Poetry of James Wright." *Minnesota Review* 2 (1972): 13–32.

_____. "The Quest Motif in *The Branch Will Not Break.*" In *The Pure Clear Word: Essays on the*

*Poetry of James Wright*. Edited by Dave Smith, Urbana: Univ. of Illinois Press, 1982, pp. 65–77.

———. *The World's Heiroglyphic Beauty*. Athens: Univ. of Georgia Press, 1985.

Stryk, Lucien. "Zen Buddhism and Modern American Poetry." *Yearbook of Comparative and General Literature* 15 (1966): 186–91.

Sutton, Walter. *American Free Verse: The Modern Revolution in Poetry*. New York: New Directions Books, 1973.

———. "Criticism and Poetry." In *American Poetry*. Edited by Irvin Ehrenpreis. Stratford-Upon-Avon Studies 7. London: Edward Arnold, 1965, pp. 175–95.

Taylor, Henry. "Eight Poets." *Michigan Quarterly Review* 14 (Winter 1975): 92–100.

———. "In the Mode of Robinson and Frost." In *The Pure Clear Word: Essays on the Poetry of James Wright*. Edited by Dave Smith. Urbana: Univ. of Illinois Press, 1982, pp. 49–64.

Taylor, Richard Lawrence. "Roots and Wings: The Poetry of James Wright." Diss., Univ. of Kentucky, 1974.

Thompson, Phyllis Hoge. "James Wright: His Kindliness." *Ironwood* 10 (1977): 97–100.

Tisdale, Bob. "Blood Relations." *Carleton Miscellany* 17 (Winter 1977): 12–27.

Toole, William B., III. "Wright's 'At the Slackening of the Tide.' " *Explicator* 22 (1963): item 29.

Van den Heuvel, Cor. "The Poetry of James Wright." *Mosaic* 7 (Spring 1974): 163–70.

Waggoner, Hyatt. *American Visionary Poetry*. Baton Rouge: Louisiana State Univ. Press, 1982.

Wallace-Crabbe, Chris. "Mendeleef, Grass Roots, and the Wombat Mandala." *Carleton Miscellany* 17 (Winter 1977): 37–40.

Whittemore, Reed. *From Zero to the Absolute*. New York: Crown, 1967.

———. "Silence, Surrealism, and Allegory." *Kayak* 40 (1974): 57–67.

Wilkes, John E., III. "Aeolian Visitations and the Harp Defrauded: Essays on Donne, Blake, Wordsworth, Keats, Flaubert, Heine, and James Wright." Diss., Univ. of California, Santa Cruz, 1973.

Williams, Miller. "James Wright, His Poems: A Kind of Overview, In Appreciation." In *The Pure Clear Word: Essays on the Poetry of James Wright*. Edited by Dave Smith. Urbana: Univ. of Illinois Press, 1982, pp. 234–46.

Williamson, Alan. "History Has to Live with What Was Here." *Shenandoah* 25 (Winter 1974): 85–91.

———. *Introspection and Contemporary Poetry*. Cambridge: Harvard Univ. Press, 1984.

———. "Language against Itself: The Middle Generation of Contemporary Poets." In *American Poetry since 1960: Some Critical Perspectives*. Edited by Robert B. Shaw. Cheadle, England: Carcanet Press, 1973.

Wright, Anne. "A Horse Grazes in My Long Shadow: A Short Biography of James Wright." *Envoy*, (Spring–Summer 1981), pp. 1–5.

Wright, Franz. "Some Thoughts on My Father." *Poets and Writers Magazine* 15, no. 1 (1987): 20–21.

Yenser, Stephen. "Open Secret." *Parnassus* 6 (1978): 125–42.

## REVIEWS

### The Green Wall

Booth, Phillip. "World Redeemed." Review of *The Green Wall*, by James Wright. *Saturday Review*, 20 July 1957, p. 18.

Fitts, Dudley. "Five Young Poets." Review of *The Green Wall*, by James Wright. *Poetry* 94 (Aug. 1959): 333-39.

Mazzaro, Jerome. Review of *The Green Wall*, by James Wright. *Poetry Broadside* 1, no. 3 (Winter 1957): 6, 10.

Nathan, Leonard. Review of *The Green Wall*, by James Wright. *Voices* 165 (Jan.–April 1958): 51-53.

Nemerov, Howard. "Younger Poets: The Lyric Difficulty." Review of *The Green Wall*, by James Wright. *Kenyon Review* 20 (1958): 25-37.

Palmer, J. E. "The Poetry of James Wright: A First Collection." Review of *The Green Wall*, by James Wright. *Sewanee Review* 65 (1957): 687-93.

Simon, John. Review of *The Green Wall*, by James Wright. *Audience* 5, no. 2 (1958): 98-102.

Simpson, Louis. "Poets in Isolation." Review of *The Green Wall*, by James Wright. *Hudson Review* 10 (1957): 458-64.

Whittemore, Reed. Review of *The Green Wall*, by James Wright. *New Orleans Poetry Journal* 4, no. 2 (1958): 38-43.

### Saint Judas

Booth, Phillip. "Four Modern Poets." Review of *Saint Judas*, by James Wright. *New York Times Book Review*, 27 Sept. 1959, p. 22.

Deutsch, Babette. Review of *Saint Judas*, by James Wright. *New York Herald Tribune Book Review*, 15 Nov. 1959, p. 8.

Galler, David. "Three Poets." Review of *Saint Judas*, by James Wright. *Poetry* 96 (June 1960): 185.

Gunn, Thom. "Excellence and Variety." Review of *Saint Judas*, by James Wright. *Yale Review* 49 (1959): 295-305.

Hall, Donald. Review of *Saint Judas*, by James Wright. *Encounter* 15, nos. 1-3 (1960): 83.

Hecht, Anthony. "The Anguish of the Spirit and the Letter." Review of *Saint Judas*, by James Wright. *Hudson Review* 12 (1959-60): 593-603.

Hoffman, Daniel G. "Between New Voice and Old Master." Review of *Saint Judas*, by James Wright. *Sewanee Review* 68 (Autumn 1960): 674-80.

Langland, J. Review of *Saint Judas*, by James Wright. *Northwest Review* 3, no. 2 (Spring 1960): 73-9.

Robie, B. A. Review of *Saint Judas*, by James Wright. *Library Journal*, 15 Sept. 1959, p. 2645.

Scott, W. T. "Four New Voices in Verse." Review of *Saint Judas*, by James Wright. *Saturday Review*, 21 May 1960, pp. 39-40.

Stange, R. Review of *Saint Judas*, by James Wright. *Carleton Miscellany* 1, no. 3 (Summer 1960): 101-8.

## The Branch Will Not Break

Baro, Gene. "Curiosity and Illumination." Review of *The Branch Will Not Break*, by James Wright. *New York Times Book Review*, 1 Sept. 1963, p. 5.

Gunn, Thom. "Modes of Control." Review of *The Branch Will Not Break*, by James Wright. *Yale Review* 53 (Spring 1964): 447–58.

Hartman, Geoffrey. "Beyond the Middle Style." Review of *The Branch Will Not Break*, by James Wright. *Kenyon Review* 25 (Autumn 1963): 751–57.

Jerome, Judson. "For Summer, A Wave of New Verse." Review of *The Branch Will Not Break*, by James Wright. *Saturday Review*, 6 July 1963, pp. 30–32.

Logan, John. "Poetry Shelf." Review of *The Branch Will Not Break*, by James Wright. *Critic* 22 (August 1963): 85–6.

Nemerov, Howard. Review of *The Branch Will Not Break*, by James Wright. *The New Leader*, 13 May 1963, p. 20.

Rubin, L. D. "Revelations of What Is Present." Review of *The Branch Will Not Break*, by James Wright. *The Nation*, 13 July 1963, pp. 38–39.

Smith, Hal. Review of *The Branch Will Not Break*, by James Wright. *Epoch* 12, no. 4 (Spring 1963), 257.

Smith, Ray. Review of *The Branch Will Not Break*, by James Wright. *Library Journal*, 1 June 1963, p. 2259.

Strickhausen, Harry. "In the Open." Review of *The Branch Will Not Break*, by James Wright. *Poetry* 102 (Sept. 1963): 391–392.

Weeks, R. "The Nature of the 'Academic.' " Review of *The Branch Will Not Break*, by James Wright. *Chicago Review* 16, no. 3 (1963): 138–44.

## Shall We Gather at the River

Benedict, Estelle. Review of *Shall We Gather at the River*, by James Wright. *Library Journal*, 15 Sept. 1968, p. 3145.

Brownjohn, Alan. "Dark Forces." Review of *Shall We Gather at the River*, by James Wright. *New Statesman*, 12 Sept. 1969, pp. 346–47.

Dickey, William. "A Place in the Country." Review of *Shall We Gather at the River*, by James Wright. *Hudson Review* 22 (1969): 347–68.

French, Robert. "Shall We Gather at the River." Review of *Shall We Gather at the River*, by James Wright. *Minnesota Review* 8 (Fall 1968): 382–83.

Ignatow, David. "Shall We Gather at the River." Review of *Shall We Gather at the River*, by James Wright. *New York Times Book Review*, 9 March 1969, p. 31.

Kessler, Jascha. "The Caged Sybil." Review of *Shall We Gather at the River*, by James Wright. *Saturday Review*, 14 Dec. 1968, p. 35.

Lieberman, Laurence. "A Confluence of Poets." Review of *Shall We Gather at the River*, by James Wright. *Poetry* 114 (April 1969): 40–41.

Matthews, William. "Entering the World." Review of *Shall We Gather at the River*, by James Wright. *Shenandoah* 20 (Summer 1969): 80–93.

Meyers, Bert. "Our Inner Life." Review of *Shall We Gather at the River*, by James Wright. *Kayak* 18 (1969): 71–74.

Moss, Stanley. "Joy out of Terror." Review of *Shall We Gather at the River*, by James Wright. *New Republic*, 29 March 1969, pp. 30–32.

Review of *Shall We Gather at the River*, by James Wright. *New York Review of Books*, 7 May 1970, p. 35.

Stepanchev, Stephen. Review of *Shall We Gather at the River*, by James Wright. *The New Leader* [New York], 2 Dec. 1968, p. 18.

Zweig, Paul. "Pieces of a Broken Mirror." Review of *Shall We Gather at the River*, by James Wright. *The Nation*, 7 July 1969, pp. 20–22.

## Collected Poems

Carruth, Hayden. "Here Today: Poetry Chronicle." Review of *Collected Poems*, by James Wright. *Hudson Review* 24 (Summer 1971): 320–36.

Cushman, Jerome. Review of *Collected Poems*, by James Wright. *Library Journal*, 15 Feb. 1971, p. 642.

Davidson, Peter. "Three Visionary Poets." Review of *Collected Poems*, by James Wright. *Atlantic Monthly*, Feb. 1972, pp. 106–7.

Deutsch, Babette. "A Fashionable Poet?" Review of *Collected Poems*, by James Wright. *New Republic*, 17 July 1971, p. 27.

Ditsky, John M. "James Wright Collected: Alterations on the Monument." Review of *Collected Poems*, by James Wright. *Modern Poetry Studies* 2 (1973): 252–59.

Goldstein, Laurence. Review of *Collected Poems*, by James Wright. *Michigan Quarterly Review* 40 (1972): 214–17.

Hecht, Roger. "Poems from a Dark Century." Review of *Collected Poems*, by James Wright. *The Nation*, 2 Aug. 1971, p. 88.

Hughes, J. W. "Humanism and the Orphic Voice." Review of *Collected Poems*, by James Wright. *Saturday Review*, 22 May 1971, p. 31.

Seay, James. "A World Immeasurably Alive and Good: A Look at James Wright's *Collected Poems*." Review of *Collected Poems*, by James Wright. *Georgia Review* 27 (1973): 71–81.

Spender, Stephen. "The Last Ditch." Review of *Collected Poems*, by James Wright. *New York Review of Books*, 22 July 1971, pp. 3–4.

Stitt, Peter A. "James Wright Knows Something about the Pure Clear Word." Review of *Collected Poems*, by James Wright. *New York Times Book Review*, 16 May 1971, p. 7.

Williamson, Alan. "Pity for the Clear Word." Review of *Collected Poems*, by James Wright. *Poetry* 119 (1972): 296–300.

Zweig, Paul. "Making and Unmaking." Review of *Collected Poems*, by James Wright. *Partisan Review* 40, no. 2 (1973): 269–79.

## Two Citizens

Bedient, Calvin. "Two Citizens." Review of *Two Citizens*, by James Wright. *New York Times Book Review*, 11 August 1974, p. 6.

Cooney, Seamus. Review of *Two Citizens*, by James Wright. *Library Journal*, 15 April 1973, p. 1291.

Deutsch, Babette. "Chiefly Ironists." Review of *Two Citizens*, by James Wright. *New Republic*, 28 April 1973, p. 25.

Engelberg, Edward. "Discovering America and Asia: The Poetry of Wright and Merwin." Review of *Two Citizens*, by James Wright. *Southern Review* 11 (1975): 440–43.

Henry, Gerrit. "Starting from Scratch." Review of *Two Citizens*, by James Wright. *Poetry* 124 (1974): 292–95.

Lieberman, Laurence. "The Shocks of Normality." Review of *Two Citizens*, by James Wright. *Yale Review* 63 (March 1974): 453–73.

Perloff, Marjorie G. "The Corn-Pone Lyric: Poetry 1972–73." Review of *Two Citizens*, by James Wright. *Contemporary Literature* 16 (1975): 84–125.

Pritchard, William. Review of *Two Citizens*, by James Wright. *Hudson Review* 26, no. 3 (Autumn 1973): 581.

Ramsey, Paul. "American Poetry in 1973." Review of *Two Citizens*, by James Wright. *Sewanee Review* 82 (Spring 1974): 393–406.

## Moments of the Italian Summer

Dodd, Wayne. "That Same Bodily Curve of the Spirit." Review of *Moments of the Italian Summer*, by James Wright. *The Ohio Review*, 18, no. 2 (1977): 59–62.

## To a Blossoming Pear Tree

Carruth, Hayden. Review of *To a Blossoming Pear Tree*, by James Wright. *Harper's* 256 (June 1978): 86–89.

Kenner, Hugh. Review of *To a Blossoming Pear Tree*, by James Wright. *New York Times Book Review*, 12 Feb. 1978, p. 12.

Kinzie, Mary. "Through the Looking Glass." Review of *To a Blossoming Pear Tree*, by James Wright. *Ploughshares* 5, no. 1 (1979): 202–40.

Pastan, Linda. Review of *To a Blossoming Pear Tree*, by James Wright. *Library Journal*, 15 Dec. 1977, p. 2503.

Pinsky, Robert. "Light, Motion, Life." Review of *To a Blossoming Pear Tree*, by James Wright. *Saturday Review*, 21 Jan. 1978, pp. 47–49.

Serchunk, Peter. "James Wright: The Art of Survival." Review of *To a Blossoming Pear Tree*, by James Wright. *Hudson Review* 31 (1978): 548–50.

Stitt, Peter. "Poetry Chronicle." Review of *To a Blossoming Pear Tree*, by James Wright. *Georgia Review* 32 (1978): 691–99.

## This Journey

Callaway, Kathy. "The Very Rich Hours of the Duke of Fano." Review of *This Journey*, by James Wright. *Parnassus* 11, no. 1 (Fall–Winter 1983): 58–72.

Garrison, Joseph. Review of *This Journey*, by James Wright. *Library Journal*, 15 March 1982, p. 640.

Heffernan, Michael. " 'To Catch a Lizard by the Shoulder': James Wright as Crypto-Sonneteer." *Poet and Critic* 18, no. 1 (Fall 1986): 50–53.

Hirsch, Edward. "Stepping through the Ruins." Review of *This Journey*, by James Wright. *New York Times Book Review*, 18 April 1982, pp. 15, 37.

Lazer, Hank. "The Heart of the Light." *Virginia Quarterly Review* 59 (1983): 711–24.

Shaw, R. B. Review of *This Journey*, by James Wright. *The Nation*, 7 Aug. 1982, p. 118.

Torrens, James. Review of *This Journey*, by James Wright. *America*, 10 July 1982, p. 36.

Weigl, Bruce. "How Lovely a Music We Make: James Wright's *This Journey*." Review of *This Journey*, by James Wright. *Poet Lore* 78, no. 2 (Summer 1983): 103–114.

## Collected Prose

Carruth, Hayden. Review of *Collected Prose*, by James Wright, edited by Anne Wright. *American Book Review* 6, no. 1 (Nov.–Dec. 1983): 2.

# Notes

## CHAPTER 1

1  Van Wyck Brooks, *America's Coming of Age* (1915), rpt. in *Van Wyck Brooks: The Early Years*, ed. Claire Sprague (New York: Harper, 1968), pp. 82, 86, 128. In Brooks's view, we "chiefly lack" in our literature three things: "intimate feelings, intimate intellectual contact, even humor" (127).

2  Philip Rahv, *Image and Idea* (New York: New Directions, 1957), p. 1.

3  Roy Harvey Pearce, *The Continuity of American Poetry*, rev. ed. (Princeton: Princeton Univ. Press, 1965); D. H. Lawrence, *Studies in Classic American Literature*, rev. ed. (New York: Viking, 1964). Stephen Gould Axelrod quotes extensively from Emerson and cites a number of these sources, adding Santayana's distinction between "genteel" and "barbaric" American writers, in his *Robert Lowell: Life and Art* (Princeton: Princeton Univ. Press, 1978). Axelrod argues that the divergent manner in which American writers react to "myths of experience" allows for a tangible division in our literature "between writers who experience primarily with the head and those who experience with the blood" (10–11).

4  R. W. B. Lewis, *The American Adam* (Chicago: Univ. of Chicago Press, 1955), p. 7.

5  Pearce, p. 433.

6  Charles Altieri, *Self and Sensibility in Contemporary American Poetry* (Cambridge: Cambridge Univ. Press, 1984). Altieri provides a provocative and intelligent assessment of the poetics of the seventies, following on the heels of his earlier discussion of the aesthetics of the sixties, *Enlarging the Temple* (Lewisburg, Pa.: Bucknell Univ. Press, 1979).

7  John Gould Fletcher, "Two Elements in Poetry," *Saturday Review of Literature*, 27 Aug. 1927, p. 65.

8  Walter Sutton, *American Free Verse: The Modern Revolution in Poetry* (New York: New Directions, 1973), p. 152.

9  Karl Shapiro, *Essay on Rime* (New York: Random House, 1945), p. 60.

10  Richard Hugo, *The Triggering Town* (New York: Norton and Company, 1979), p. 32.

11   W. H. Auden, *The Dyer's Hand* (New York: Vintage Books, 1968), p. 27. A bit earlier on the same page, Auden makes a similar pronouncement emphasizing the limited capability of art to reduce earthly despair, "Poetry is not magic."

12   James Wright, "A Plain Brave Music," *Chelsea* 12 (Sept. 1962): 136–37; rpt. in *Collected Prose*, ed. Anne Wright (Ann Arbor: Univ. of Michigan Press, 1983), p. 285.

13   Robert Bly, "Looking for Dragon Smoke," in *Leaping Poetry: An Idea with Poems and Translations*, ed. Robert Bly (Boston: Beacon Press, 1975), p. 1.

14   Louis D. Rubin, *The Nation*, 13 July 1963, p. 39.

15   Robert Pinsky, *The Situation of Poetry* (Princeton: Princeton Univ. Press, 1976), p. 117. Pinsky's most recent collection of poems, *History of My Heart* (New York: Ecco, 1984) shows he has welcomed imagination and emotion to the discursive poem and shows, too, the remarkable results that can be achieved by doing so.

16   Altieri, *Self and Sensibility in Contemporary American Poetry*, p. 18, 19. In calling for an aesthetics based on "self-consciousness and the duplicity of rhetoric," Altieri offers a renewed lucidity as a solution to our poetic problems. On the other hand, Jonathan Holden and Stanley Plumly cite the lyrical qualities present in the work of William Stafford, Galway Kinnell, Charles Wright, David Wagoner, James Wright, and others as evidence of the value of lyricism in contemporary poetry. Altieri, of course, devotes a good deal of time to refuting their arguments for the new poetry, and thus, a version of R. W. B. Lewis's "lively dialogue" is once again active. See Jonathan Holden, *The Rhetoric of the Contemporary Lyric* (Bloomington: Indiana Univ. Press, 1980); and Stanley Plumly, "Chapter and Verse," *American Poetry Review* 7 (Jan.-Feb. 1978): 21–35; 7 (May–June 1978): 21–32.

17   Wright, "A Plain Brave Music," p. 285.

18   I am indebted to R. G. Collingwood's *The Idea of Nature* (Oxford: Oxford Univ. Press, 1945) for his lucid discussion of the evolving theories of nature. Collingwood states that where Berkeley or Kant would regard nature as "alien to mind, mind's other or opposite," Whitehead does not. Collingwood argues that Whitehead refuses "to regard mind as something utterly disparate from nature" and instead insists "that mind as we know it in man is something that has come to be what it is by developing functions belonging to life in general" (173–74).

19   Hyatt Waggoner, *American Visionary Poetry* (Baton Rouge: Louisiana State Univ. Press, 1982), p. 7.

20   Wright, "One Voice and Many—A Poet's Debt to Prose," *New York Times Book Review*, 18 March 1984, p. 14.

21   Alan Williamson, *Introspection in Contemporary Poetry* (Cambridge: Harvard Univ. Press, 1984), p. 197.

22   Warner Berthoff, *A Literature without Qualities* (Berkeley and Los Angeles: Univ. of California Press, 1979), p. 17.

## CHAPTER 2

1   Louis Simpson, "Poets in Isolation," review of *The Green Wall*, by James Wright, *Hudson Review* 10 (1957): 461.

2   Richard Wilbur, in *Poets on Poetry*, ed. Howard Nemerov (New York: Basic Books, 1966), p. 143.

3   Gerald Graff, *Literature against Itself* (Chicago: Univ. of Chicago Press, 1979), p. 139.

4   James Wright, interview with Peter Stitt, "The Art of Poetry XIX: James Wright," *Paris Review* 16, no. 62 (Summer 1975): 48. Wright was not unaware, however, of the potential limitations inherent in these formalist strategies. Such formal perfection, he feared, might become an end instead of a means, or worse, an impediment to the aesthetic process by separating the poet from the experiential world. In "The Stiff Smile of Mr. Warren," a review of Robert Penn Warren's *Promises*, Wright admits these misgivings: "One of the innumerable ironies which hound writers, I suppose, is the fact that the very competence which a man may struggle for years to master can suddenly and treacherously stiffen into mere *armor against experience* instead of an instrument for contending with that experience" (*Kenyon Review* 20, no. 4 [Autumn 1958]: 645–655; rpt. in *Collected Prose*, ed. Anne Wright [Ann Arbor: Univ. of Michigan Press, 1982], 240–41).

5   Adrienne Rich, "When We Dead Awaken: Writing as Re-Vision," in *American Poets in 1976*, ed. William Heyen (Indianapolis: Bobbs-Merrill, 1976), p. 283.

6   Allen Tate, "Poetry Modern and Unmodern," in *Essays of Four Decades* (Chicago: Swallow Press, 1959), p. 228.

7   John Gould Fletcher, "Two Elements in Poetry," *Saturday Review of Literature*, 27 Aug. 1927, p. 66.

8   John Crowe Ransom, "T. S. Eliot, Historical Critic," in *The New Criticism* (Norfolk, Conn.: New Directions, 1941), p. 175.

9   Dave Smith, Introduction to *The Pure Clear Word: Essays on the Poetry of James Wright*, ed. Dave Smith (Urbana: Univ. of Illinois Press, 1982), p. xiv.

10  James Wright, *The Green Wall*, Yale Series of Younger Poets no. 53 (New Haven, Conn.: Yale Univ. Press, 1957). Further references to the text are to this edition; references to *Saint Judas* are to the following edition: Middletown, Conn.: Wesleyan Univ. Press, 1959.

11  George Williamson, "Donne and the Poetry of Today," in *A Garland for John Donne*, ed. Theodore Spencer (Gloucester, Mass.: Peter Smith, 1958), pp. 153–54.

12  Richard Hugo, *The Triggering Town* (New York: Norton, 1979), pp. 27–8.

13  Miller Williams, "James Wright, His Early Poems: A Kind of Overview, in Appreciation," in *The Pure Clear Word*, p. 242; William Matthews, "The Continuity of James Wright's Poetry," *The Ohio Review* 18 (Spring/Summer 1977), 44–57; rpt. in *The Pure Clear Word*, p. 101.

14  Theodore Roethke. "How to Write Like Somebody Else," *Yale Review* 48 (March 1959): 336–43; rpt. in *On The Poet and His Craft*, ed. Ralph Mills (Seattle: Univ. of Washington Press, 1965), p. 69.

15  Jurij Lotman, *The Structure of the Artistic Text*, trans. R. Vroon (Ann Arbor: Univ. of Michigan Press, 1977), p. 9. Lotman argues that "it is not uncommon to find the same individual acting as both addresser and addressee of a message. . . . Here information is not transmitted in space, but in time, and serves as a means of the auto-organization of the individual" (9). For a wider, theory-based discussion of the

importance of the dialogic text, see M. M. Bakhtin, *The Dialogic Imagination*, ed. Michael Holquist, trans. Caryl Emerson and Michael Holquist (Austin: Univ. of Texas Press, 1981). Bakhtin's theory of language operates on the assumption of "heteroglossia": that meaning is determined in any utterance primarily by its context rather than its text, that is, that an utterance is made fundamentally different from others—even the same utterance spoken at another time—by the social, historical, and physiological conditions that surround it at that moment. "Dialogism," therefore implies, as Holquist explains, that "everything means, is understood, as part of a greater whole—there is a constant interaction between meanings, all of which have the potential of conditioning others" (426). Such an attitude, of course, more or less ensures that no spoken word can exist without grounding within this dialogism, or as Holquist puts it, that "there can be no actual monologues." Although this specific theory of language makes the act of language a fundamentally argumentative process in a way much more complex and far-reaching than I mean here, I believe it provides a general framework for examining the process of dialogization within Wright's poems. Certainly, Wright realizes that the word "poetry" itself—and each word that a poet speaks—is subject to the pressures of heteroglossia and dialogism.

16  Wright's use of the word "lucidity," of course, brings to mind Altieri's recent discussion of the conflicting pressures of "lucidity and lyricism" discussed earlier; see *Self and Sensibility in Contemporary American Poetry* (Cambridge: Cambridge Univ. Press, 1984).

17  Victoria Harris, "James Wright's Odyssey: A Journey from Dualism to Incorporation," *Contemporary Poetry* 3, no. 3 (1978): 65.

18  David Antin, "Modernism and Post-Modernism: Approaching the Present in American Poetry," *Boundary 2* (Fall 1972): 118. Calling the equation of morality and metrics "clumsy and pretentious," Antin asserts that such an attitude accounts for the fear of experience in the work of Eliot, Allen Tate, and Robert Lowell: "The taste for the ironic moral poem is a taste for a kind of pornography which offers neither intellectual or emotional experience but a fantasy of controlled intensity. . . . The idea of metrics as a 'moral' or 'ideal' traditional order against which the 'emotional' human impulses of a poet continually struggle in the form of his real speech is a transparently trivial paradigm worthy of a play by Racine and always yields the same small set of cheap musical thrills" (120).

19  Steve Orlen, "The Green Wall," *Ironwood* 10 (1977): 6.

20  Although M. M. Bakhtin believes this sort of dialogization is best suited to the novel, he acknowledges its existence within certain twentieth-century poems in which there is a "prosification" of the lyric. Wright's poem seems an especially good example of a kind of dialogue Bakhtin describes in which the statements of the second speaker are omitted but still retain their influence: "The second speaker is present invisibly, his words are not there, but deep traces left by these words have a determining influence on all the present and visible words of the first speaker. We sense that there is a conversation, although there is only one person speaking . . . for each present, uttered word responds and reacts with its every fiber to the

invisible speaker." See M. M. Bakhtin, *Problems of Dostoevsky's Poetics*, ed. and trans. Caryl Emerson, Theory and History of Literature, vol. 8 (Minneapolis: Univ. of Minnesota Press, 1984), pp. 200, 197.

21  Madeline DeFrees, "James Wright's Early Poems: A Study in 'Convulsive' Form," *Modern Poetry Studies* 2, no. 6 (1972): 247.

22  T. S. Eliot, "Donne and Our Time," in *A Garland for John Donne*, p. 12.

23  James Seay, "A World Immeasurably Alive and Good: A Look at James Wright's *Collected Poems*," *Georgia Review* 27 (1973), 71–81; rpt. in *The Pure Clear Word*, p. 114.

24  Wright, "The Stiff Smile of Mr. Warren," review of *Promises*, by Robert Penn Warren, *Kenyon Review*, rpt. in *Collected Prose*, p. 246.

25  "Reading a Newspaper on a Beach" appears to have remained unpublished after Wright suppressed the publication of *Amenities of Stone*. The quoted material is taken directly from the typescript of the book, dated 5 March 1961, which Anne Wright was kind enough to offer for study. See the James Wright Papers, file 3.2.4, Kenyon College Libraries.

26  For an intelligent discussion of the differences between the *Saint Judas* version and the *Poetry* version of "At the Executed Murderer's Grave," see Jane Robinett, "Two Poems and Two Poets," *Ironwood* 10 (1977): 38–44. A third version of the poem was printed in *Botteghe Oscure* (Italy) 23 (1959): 244. Wright discusses with Dave Smith these three versions, James Dickey's hand in revising the poem, and the various reactions to the two Doty poems in "James Wright: The Pure Clear Word, An Interview," *American Poetry Review* 9, no. 3 (1980), pp. 19–30; rpt. in *The Pure Clear Word*, pp. 3–42. For example, Wright calls the earlier version of the poem which appeared in *Poetry* (92 [1958]: 277) "very, very overblown and rhetorical."

27  Wright did not include "I Regret I Am Unable to Attend" in any of his published collections; the poem appeared in *Minnesota Review* 1 (Winter 1961): 149.

28  Allen Tate, "A Note on Donne," in *Essays of Four Decades*, p. 244.


# CHAPTER 3

1  For helpful critical discussions detailing the evolution of Wright's work between *Saint Judas* and *The Branch Will Not Break*, see James Seay, "A World Immeasurably Alive and Good: A Look at James Wright's *Collected Poems*," *Georgia Review* 27 (1973): 71–81; Robert Bly [Crunk, pseud.], "The Work of James Wright," *The Sixties* 8 (Spring 1966): 57–78; George Lensing and Ronald Moran, *Four Poets of the Emotive Imagination: Robert Bly, James Wright, Louis Simpson and William Stafford* (Baton Rouge: Louisiana State Univ. Press, 1976). William Matthews, "The Continuity of James Wright's Poems," *The Ohio Review* 18, no. 2 (1977): 44. Matthews argues that Wright is a profoundly traditional poet and that his originality owes to the ability to "forge a personal relationship to tradition." His "openness" in *Branch*, Matthews contends, results from a "spiritual quality" Wright learned to express only after much effort.

2  Robert Bly [Crunk, pseud.], "The Work of James Wright," pp. 57–58.

3   Dickey's mostly accurate but rather nasty review, titled "In the Presence of An-
    thologies," appears in *Sewanee Review* 66 (Spring 1958): 294–314.
4   Richard Foster, "Debauched by Craft: Problems of the Younger Poets," *Perspective* 12
    (Spring Summer) 1960: 3–17.
5   Nicholas Gattuccio, "Now My Amenities of Stone Are Done: Some Notes on the
    Style of James Wright," *Scape* 1 (1981): 38; rpt. in *Concerning Poetry* 15, no. 1 (1983):
    61–76. Gattuccio's carefully researched article provides a timetable for Wright's
    work with these separate manuscripts. Here is a brief summary: In 1960, Wright
    proposed first, *Now I Am Awakened* (unpublished). Second came a reduction of *Awak-
    ened* that Wesleyan accepted in early 1960, though the manuscript was still untitled.
    The third draft of Wright's book to succeed *Saint Judas* was the 5 March 1961 version
    of *Amenities of Stone*, the topic of this essay. Wright withdrew *Amenities* and submitted
    *New Poems* (not to be confused with the "New Poems" section of *Collected Poems*) which
    seems a further reduction of *Amenities*. After withdrawing *New Poems*, Wright sub-
    mitted *The Blessing* to Wesleyan in December 1961. Finally, in August of 1962, the
    final version of the manuscript, this one titled *The Branch Will Not Break*, arrived at
    Wesleyan, a collection of forty-five poems (twenty-eight of which were included in
    *Amenities*).
6   Wright's titling a section of *Amenities* "Academic Poems" can be regarded as both
    defiant and ironic. After the publication of *New Poets of England and America*, those
    poets included in the anthology—as was Wright—were universally labeled "aca-
    demic poets." It became the current term for dismissal, as "confessional poet"
    would become later. Wright was painfully aware of the disparity between his "aca-
    demic" poems and his "explorations." In a 20 March 1960 draft of a table of contents
    for *Now I Am Awakened*, Wright drew a broad line across the middle of the page
    dividing the poems at the top, labeled "New Style," from those on the bottom writ-
    ten in what he called his "Old Style." (Wright Papers, file 3.1.4, Kenyon College
    Libraries).
7   These two poems are "The Thieves" and "President Harding's Tomb." Other
    poems from *Amenities* which appear in *Branch* are "As I Step over a Puddle at the End
    of Winter, I Think of an Ancient Chinese Governor," "In Fear of Harvests," "Three
    Stanzas from Goethe," "Lying in a Hammock at William Duffy's Farm in Pine Is-
    land, Minnesota," "In the Face of Hatred," "Fear is What Quickens Me," "A Mes-
    sage Hidden in an Empty Wine Bottle That I Threw into a Gully of Maples One
    Night at an Indecent Hour," "How My Fever Left," "Miners" (revised), "Two Poems
    about President Harding" (revised and made into two poems), "The Undermining
    of the Defense Economy," "Twilights," "Two Hangovers" (revised into two
    poems), "Depressed by a Book of Bad Poetry, I Walk toward an Unused Pasture and
    Invite the Insects to Join Me," "Two Horses Playing in the Orchard" (formerly "The
    Thieves"), "By a Lake in Minnesota," "From a Bus Window in Central Ohio, Just
    before a Thunder Shower," "March" (revised), "Spring Images," "Snowstorm in
    the Midwest," "Having Lost My Sons, I Confront the Wreckage of the Moon:

Christmas, 1960," "American Wedding," "Rain," "Today I Was Happy, So I Made This Poem," "I Was Afraid of Dying," and "A Blessing" (revised).

8   Donald Hall, Introduction to *Contemporary American Poetry*, ed. Donald Hall (Baltimore: Penguin, 1962), pp. 17, 24.

9   James Wright, interview with Dave Smith, "James Wright: The Pure Clear Word, An Interview"; rpt. in *The Pure Clear Word: Essays on the Poetry of James Wright*, ed. Dave Smith (Urbana: Univ. of Illinois Press, 1982), p. 18.

10  This citation and all subsequent references to the book refer to the 5 March 1961 typescript of *Amenities of Stone*. I am indebted to Mrs. James Wright for her permission and frequent help in the study of *Amenities*. This typescript is now collected with the James Wright Papers, file 3.2.4, Kenyon College Libraries.

11  All of the preceding quotations appear on various versions of "The Thieves," gathered with the working drafts of poems to be included in Wright's *New Poems*. See Wright Papers, file 3.1.4, Kenyon College Libraries.

12  Wright, *The Branch Will Not Break* (Middletown, Conn.: Wesleyan Univ. Press, 1963), p. 32.

13  Wright, interview with Peter Stitt, "The Art of Poetry XIX: James Wright," *Paris Review* 16, no. 62 (Summer 1975): 38.

14  Wright, interview with Stitt, "The Art of Poetry XIX," p. 48.

15  Dated 6 March 1962, Wright's handwritten note on the text of "Two Images of One Place" can be found in file 3.1.6 of his Papers.

16  Wright, interview with Stitt, "The Art of Poetry XIX," p. 49.

17  Robert Kelly, "Notes on the Poetry of Deep Image," *Trobar* 2 (1961): 15.

18  W. H. Auden, *The Dyer's Hand and Other Essays* (New York: Vintage Books, 1968), p. 22.

19  Bly, p. 67.

20  Wright Papers, file 3.2.2. In addition, the title to another draft of the poem gives evidence of the invocational tone of Wright's poem—and the object of his invocation: "He Prays to the Muse for a Place among Honest Men Who Are Forgotten."

21  Madeline DeFrees, "That Vacant Paradise," *Ironwood* 10 (1977): 18.

22  Wright, *Two Citizens* (New York: Farrar, Straus and Giroux, 1973), p. 55. Chief among critics asserting that *Two Citizens* represents the fullest expression of Wright's common language poetry are: Robert Hass, "James Wright," *Ironwood* 10 (1977): 74–100; Peter Stitt, "James Wright—Poetry of the Present," *Ironwood* 10 (1977): 140–53; and Dave Smith, "That Halting, Stammering Movement," *Ironwood* 10 (1979): 11–30.

23  Donald Hall, interview with author, 13 September 1982.

24  Hall, interview with author, 13 September 1982.

25  Wright, interview with Smith, "James Wright: The Pure Clear Word, An Interview," p. 18.

26  "Holding a Pearl in My Hand, April 1962," Wright Papers, file 3.3.

27  Wright, *The Fifties* 2 (1959): 56.

28 Wright, interview with Smith, "James Wright: The Pure Clear Word, An Interview," p. 18.

## CHAPTER 4

1 Hall, Introduction, *Contemporary American Poetry*, ed. Donald Hall (Baltimore: Penguin, 1962), p. 17.

2 Wright attributes his own alteration in styles to the realization that "it is fatally easy to write in an almost automatic way. After you master certain gimmicks, whether it is in formal verse or in rhyme or in so-called free verse, then it is pretty easy to repeat them. . . . For a while during the fifties most writers were tending to write in too facile, too glib a way in regular meters and rhyme. Some of us turned away to free verse. Since then I think that whenever one opens a magazine nearly all the poems one sees will be in free verse. More and more they strike me as being just as facile and automatic in their way as the earlier poems had been in other ways. That is, it isn't a solution to one's artistic problems just to stop rhyming." See Dave Smith, "James Wright: The Pure Clear Word, an Interview," in *The Pure Clear Word: Essays on the Poetry of James Wright*, ed. Dave Smith (Urbana: Univ. of Illinois Press, 1982), pp. 16–17.

3 As the preceding chapter attests, Wright's yearning to free himself from the constraints of rhetoric did not produce immediate results. The compressed, elliptical quality of some of the poems in *Branch* owes, at least partly, to his fear of the adornments of rhetoric; still, for a poet trained to admire the forms and manners of a highly rhetorical poetics, distinguishing the rhetorical features he should abandon from the elements of imagination he should retain was a difficult process in itself. His comments at the bottom of a draft for the poem "A Small Elegy at Night in the Country" display both his willingness to change and the troublesome questions such a decision presented: "I would reduce the typescript above to 1 single line, if such would let the poem emerge. But that's just it, that's as far as I've been able to struggle so far; I am not afraid to abandon rhetoric, but I still can't judge which is rhetoric and which is true imagination!" This draft is dated 2 March 1962. See the Wright Papers, file 3.1.6, Kenyon College Libraries.

4 In addition to those mentioned in note 1 of chapter 3, several other critics provide an assessment of Wright's alteration: Leonard Nathan judges this alteration—and Wright's poetry in general—to derive its force from the tradition of the American Metaphysical poem in "The Tradition of Sadness and the American Metaphysic," *The Pure Clear Word*, pp. 159–74. Edward Butscher identifies the change as the beginning of the general decline in Wright's poetic powers in "The Rise and Fall of James Wright," *Georgia Review* 28 (1974): 257–68; rpt. in *The Pure Clear Word*, pp. 124–35. Finally, Victoria Harris examines this alteration as a movement from isolation to unity with natural forces in "James Wright's Odyssey: A Journey from Dualism to Incorporation," *Contemporary Poetry* 3, no. 3 (1978): 56–74.

5  John Crowe Ransom, "Wanted: An Ontological Critic," *Beating the Bushes* (New York: New Directions, 1972), p. 43.

6  Ransom, "Thoughts on the Poetic Discontent," *The Fugitive* 4, no. 2 (June 1925): 64; Cleanth Brooks, "The Language of Paradox," *The Well-Wrought Urn* (London: Dennis Dobson, 1949), p. 3.

7  Ransom, "Poetry: A Note on Ontology," *The World's Body* (New York: Scribner's, 1938); rpt. in *Modern Criticism*, eds. Walter Sutton and Richard Foster (New York: Odyssey Press, 1963), p. 230.

8  Karl Shapiro, *Essay on Rime*, (New York: Random House, 1945), p. 65.

9  Robert Bly, "Looking for Dragon Smoke," in *Naked Poetry*, eds. Stephen Berg and Robert Mezey (Indianapolis: Bobbs-Merrill Company, 1969), p. 12. Bly's essay is dated 1967 and differs greatly—specifically in his attack on the New Critics—from an essay of the same title which appears in *Leaping Poetry*, ed. Robert Bly (1972; Boston: Beacon Press, 1975), pp. 1–6.

10  Wright, "A Note on Trakl," in *Collected Prose*, ed. Anne Wright (Ann Arbor: Univ. of Michigan Press, 1983), p. 82.

11  Wright, "A Note on Trakl," p. 83.

12  Wright's translation of Trakl's "Lamentation" is housed with the James Wright Papers, file 3.2.8, Kenyon College Libraries.

13  Trakl, *Twenty Poems*, trans. James Wright, John Knoepfle, and Robert Bly (Madison, Minn.: Sixties Press, 1961), p. 23. In an interview with the author (13 September 1982), Donald Hall indicated that it was Wright who first "introduced" much of Trakl's poetry to Robert Bly.

14  Wright, *The Branch Will Not Break* (Middletown, Conn.: Wesleyan Univ. Press, 1963), p. 52. All further references to this collection are to this edition.

15  Wright, "A Note on Cesar Vallejo," *Twenty Poems of Cesar Vallejo*, trans. John Knoepfle, James Wright, and Robert Bly (Madison, Minn.: Sixties Press, 1962); rpt. in *Collected Prose*, p. 86.

16  Vallejo, *Twenty Poems of Cesar Vallejo*, p. 45. Vallejo's poem first appeared in *Los Heraldos Negros* (1918). An August 20, 1960, draft of Wright's translation reveals a third stanza even closer to Wright's poem "The Jewel": "There is this cave / in the air behind my body / that nobody is going to touch: / this small room of silences / that spoke to a flower of fire." See Wright Papers, file 3.2.12.

17  Matthews, "The Continuity of James Wright's Poetry," in *The Pure Clear Word: Essays on the Poetry of James Wright*, ed. Dave Smith (Urbana: Univ. of Illinois Press, 1982), p. 107.

18  Though Karl Malkoff, in *Crowell's Handbook of Contemporary American Poetry* (New York: Crowell, 1973), p. 39, also refers to this use of image as the "deep image," Bly himself prefers calling this approach simply "the image poem." Stephen Stepanchev labels this method "the subjective image" in *American Poetry since 1945: A Critical Survey* (New York: Harper and Row, 1965), p. 175.

19  Kelly, "Notes on the Poetry of the Deep Image," *Trobar* 2 (1961): 16.

20 Bly, "A Wrong-Turning in American Poetry," *Choice* 3 (1963): 33–47. Bly's essay asserts that American poetry of the twentieth century has turned away, rather destructively, from the imagination and intuition to more rational concerns with wit and sophistication. He distinguishes between the move "inward" of Neruda, Lorca, and Vallejo, for example, and the move "outward" best represented, he believes, by the poetry of Ransom and Tate. In making this familiar distinction between poetry issuing from unconscious impulses and, on the contrary, poetry derived from conscious ruminations, Bly argues that one paradoxical result of the emphasis on conscious modes of expression is that "there have been almost no poems touching on political subjects, although such concerns have been present daily" (38). Politics, Bly reasons, is a subject too intense and too intimate for poets wishing to retain rhetorical detachment from their work.

21 Wright Papers, file 3.2.16.

22 Wright, interview with Bruce Henricksen, "Poetry Must Think," *New Orleans Review* 6, no. 3, (1978): 201–07; rpt. in *Collected Prose*, p. 181.

23 Wright Papers, file 3.2.11.

24 Wright Papers, file 3.2.10. As late as August 31, 1961, "Eisenhower's Visit to Franco, 1959" was combined with another political piece in *Branch*, "In Memory of a Spanish Poet," to compose a much longer poem. It is not surprising, then, that one can still see evidence of their common origin: both poems equate darkness with natural goodness, and light with political evil, and they appear back to back in the collection. On the above date, Wright recognized the obvious difficulty— notwithstanding the similarity of theme—of including the figures of Miguel Hernandez, Franco, and Eisenhower all in one poem: "Perhaps the problem is that there are 2 poems here: 1. "In Memory of Miguel Hernandez," 2. "Eisenhower's Visit to Franco, 1959." See file 3.2.7. The combined poem's first stanza, incidentally, at one time contained a reference to "the good darkness / of women's hands that touch loaves," lines which surface in *Branch* in the poem "Trying to Pray." Certainly it is not unusual for a poet to try the same lines in several different poems until they find a home, but note the stark contrasts that Wright establishes in the (now) three poems: the military versus the agricultural, the weapons of war versus the waters of spiritual life, and the silos which house missiles for destruction versus the silos which store grain for bread.

25 Wright, in "An Interview with Michael Andre," *Unmuzzled Ox* 1, no. 2 (February 1972): 3–18; rpt. in *Collected Prose*, pp. 145, 142.

26 Wright, in "Poetry Must Think," by Bruce Henricksen, p. 184.

27 Altieri, *Enlarging the Temple: New Directions in American Poetry in the 1960's* (Lewisburg, Pa.: Bucknell Univ. Press, 1979). Although I have Altieri's work specifically in mind, others have contributed to this discussion. See, for example, Roy Harvey Pearce, "The Burden of Romanticism: Toward the New Poetry," *Iowa Review* 2 (Spring 1971): 109–28.

28 Peter Stitt, breaking from the all too common critical preoccupation with Wright's style, focuses on the thematic concerns and strategies of *Branch*. Stitt defines

Wright's strategy as a "quest": "In his search for happiness, for comfort, for consolation, and for sustenance, the poet turns from the city to the country, from society
to nature, from human beings to animals, and from fear of the finality of death to a
trust in immortality." See "The Quest Motif in *The Branch Will Not Break*," in *The Pure
Clear Word*, pp. 65–77.

29 The two sections of "Two Hangovers" were once included in a four-part sequence
of poems titled, "Poems Written upon Several Occasions When I Was Drunk." The
first section was titled "Hung Over"; it is the first section (as it now stands) of "Two
Hangovers." The second section was the poem "A Message Hidden in an Empty
Wine Bottle That I Threw into a Gully of Maple Trees One Night at an Indecent
Hour"; this section is identical to the poem of the same title which appears in *Branch*.
In this section of the poem, the speaker acknowledges, "I am dying, / I am growing
old." The third section was titled, "Having Been Drunk Last Night, I Try to Waken
and Greet the World Once Again"; except for its title, this is identical to the second
section of "Two Hangovers." Here the speaker finds reassurance in the figure of
the blue jay abandoning itself to "entire delight." The final section was the poem,
"Today I Was Happy, So I Made This Poem," which again is identical to the poem
of the same name that appears in *Branch*. Thus, the sequence ends with the speaker's revelation that "it is impossible to die," a stunning assertion for a speaker who
began the sequence in a kind of deathbed and who had resigned himself and all
living things to a similar fate. The poem establishes the revivifying qualities inherent in natural things. Included in the unpublished *Amenities of Stone* in the above
order, these poems never appeared in print in that form.

30 Friedman, "The Wesleyan Poets III: The Experimental Poets," *Chicago Review* 19, no.
2 (1966): 73.

31 Again, I offer thanks to Anne Wright for her permission to study "Just off the
Highway to Rochester, Minnesota." See the 5 March 1961 draft of *Amenities of Stone*,
Wright Papers, file 3.2.4.

32 Wright, "Meditations on René Char," *René Char's Poetry* (Rome: Deluca, 1959); rpt. in
*Collected Prose*, p. 65.

33 Butscher, "The Rise and Fall of James Wright," in *The Pure Clear Word*, pp. 129, 125.

34 "The Blessing" was published in *Poetry* 97 (1960–61): 343.

## CHAPTER 5

1 Peter Stitt, "James Wright Knows Something about the Pure Clear Word," review
of *Collected Poems*, by James Wright, *New York Times Book Review*, 16 May 1971, p. 7.

2 For a helpful and intelligent discussion of Wright's post-*Branch* work, see Dave
Smith, "That Halting, Stammering Movement," in *The Pure Clear Word: Essays on the
Poetry of James Wright*, ed. Dave Smith (Urbana: Univ. of Illinois Press, 1982), pp.
175–95. Randall Stiffler, "The Reconciled Vision of James Wright," *Literary Review*
28, no. 1 (1984): 77–92, proposes a generalized argument for Wright's affirmative

stance in the later volumes. Curiously, though he quotes occasionally from poems that refer to Jenny, Stiffler makes no reference to the figure of Jenny in Wright's work and makes no attempt to explain her significant role in Wright's transition to a poetry which balances joy and despair. Elsewhere, Michael Graves argues that Wright experiences "a crisis in which the self is felt and perceived to be totally unacceptable and totally unchangeable." Graves asserts that the work of Kierke-gaard, Ortega y Gasset, and Juan Ramon Jimenez enabled Wright to "endure and dramatize" this emotional and spiritual despair in which the muse Jenny plays such an integral role; see "Crisis in the Career of James Wright," *The Hollins Critic* 22, no. 5 (December 1985): 1–9.

3 James Wright, *Two Citizens* (New York: Farrar, Straus, and Giroux, 1973), p. 23. Further references to the text are to this edition, hereafter referred to as *TC*.

4 James Wright, "The Delicacy of Walt Whitman," in *Collected Prose*, ed. Anne Wright (Ann Arbor: Univ. of Michigan Press, 1983), p. 10.

5 Wright, *Shall We Gather at the River* (Middletown, Conn.: Wesleyan Univ. Press, 1968), p. 14. Further references to the text are to this edition, hereafter referred to as *SW*.

6 The poem was to appear in the "Explorations" section of *Amenities*, a spot reserved for poems Wright considered a break from his formal past. Although it appears in *SW* in exactly the same form as it appears in *Amenities*, the *Now I Am Awakened* (there-fore earlier) version of "Late November in a Field" is prefaced by the two lines quoted above. See the James Wright Papers, files 3.2.4 and 3.2.11, Kenyon College Libraries.

7 Wright, *Collected Poems* (Middletown, Conn.: Wesleyan Univ. Press, 1971), p. 208. Further references to the text are to this edition, hereafter referred to as *CP*. The "New Poems" section of *CP* contains thirty-one new poems; two additional new poems are printed on the flyleaf of the book.

8 Smith, "That Halting, Stammering Movement," p. 177. Smith's instructive essay discusses the connection between emotion and Wright's new language; he argues, also, that *Two Citizens* represents a movement to "possibility" in Wright's poetry.

9 Donald Hall, interview with author, 13 September 1982.

10 Wright, interview with Bruce Henricksen, "Poetry Must Think," in *Collected Prose*, p. 174.

11 Wright was never shy about admitting his love for Herrick's work, and his class-room presentations often included lengthy discussions of Herrick's poetry. His young students, however, were not always convinced; a 25 February 1974 note from Wright's papers offers his brief account of such an instance: "This afternoon, after I had lectured for an hour or so, a girl came up and exclaimed, 'I feel so shaken! How can you go on and on so passionately about the poems of Robert Herrick? I think he's too—too pretty. I don't think I like him' " (Wright Papers, file 5.2.5).

12 The critical response varies from Paul Zweig's mild rebuff: "He [Wright] has given us a scattering of fine poems, but no sustained work in which the governing vision and the artistic achievement are adequate to each other" ("Making and Unmaking,"

*Partisan Review* 40, no. 2 [1973]: 269–73) to much more virulent attacks. William Pritchard nastily states: "As far as the music of poetry goes, to say nothing of the presence of interesting ideas about love and death, Wright's poetry indeed ain't much" ("Poetry Matters," *Hudson Review* 26, no. 3 [Autumn 1973]: 581). Not to be outdone, Edward Butscher coldly assesses *Two Citizens* as a betrayal: "He has betrayed us and betrayed himself by refusing to accept the implications of his own gift, by insisting upon filtering all experience through the wringer of drunken emotions, regardless of their irrational narrowness" ("The Rise and Fall of James Wright," in *The Pure Clear Word*, p. 133).

13 Wright, "One Voice and Many—A Poet's Debt to Prose," *New York Times Book Review*, 18 March 1984, p. 15.

14 Robert Hass, "James Wright," in *The Pure Clear Word*, pp. 218–19.

15 Both "His Farewell to Old Poetry" (several drafts of which Wright indicates were written "in Bly's chickenhouse") and "Three Letters in One Evening" were to be included in *Amenities of Stone*, though Wright's various tables of contents make it uncertain in which section they were to appear. Wright chose to keep both poems unpublished. As always, I thank Anne Wright for her help in studying these poems. See the Wright Papers, specifically files 3.2.4 and 3.2.10, though drafts of both poems reappear frequently in various files. Of particular interest is a draft of "His Farewell to Old Poetry," this one using the slightly altered title "His Farewell to Poetry," in which "Jenny" is replaced with a name that nearly rhymes with it: "She is dead. / She loved the measure that I write in now. / . . . Nancy is dead, and so am I" (Wright Papers, file 5.3.1).

16 Wright, interview with Peter Stitt, "The Art of Poetry XIX: James Wright," *Paris Review* 16, no. 62 (Summer 1975): 43.

17 One draft of "Three Letters in One Evening," dated 5 February 1961, removes all doubt that "J. . . ." refers to Jenny. Above each spot in the typescript where "J. . . ." appears, Wright has filled in the four empty spaces, those indicated by the ellipsis, with the handwritten letters "e n n y" (Wright Papers, file 3.2.10).

18 Wright Papers, file 3.2.10.

19 Wright, interview with Stitt, "The Art of Poetry XIX: James Wright," p. 52. An immensely shy man, Wright shares the secret of Jenny with Stitt. Wright describes what he had in mind for *Shall We Gather at the River*, his book for Jenny: "I was trying to move from death to resurrection and death again, and challenge death finally. Well, if I must tell you, I was trying to write about a girl I was in love with who has been dead for a long time. I tried to sing with her in that book. Not to recreate her; you can't recreate anybody, at least I can't. But I thought maybe I could come to terms with that feeling which has hung on in my heart for so long."

20 Wright's early poem "The Accusation" (*Saint Judas*) raises an interesting question about Jenny's face: Was her face a crimson color because it was birthmarked? In the above poem the speaker calls the birthmark on his lover's face a "slash / Of fire" that reveals the "truth" about human limitation. He ends the poem, much like "October Ghosts," in futile search for his dead lover: "Now you are dead, and I grow

old . . . / How can I ever love another? / You had no right to banish me / From that scarred truth of wretchedness, / Your face, that I shall never see / Again, though I search every place."

21 The tension between such an insistence on secrecy and Wright's yearning to claim his lover-muse Jenny, whatever her real or apocryphal identity, is evident in one version of the dedicatory page for the unpublished collection, *Now I am Awakened*. At one time Wright considered—and partially crossed-out—the following dedication: "To _____ , / ~~who won't read it, at least not here~~ / who won't even read it, for all I know." He later reconsidered, asserting, "No! This page must remain absolutely independent, inviolate, sanctified, an embodiment of deepest faith. . . ." Several years later, of course, the dedicatory page of *Shall We Gather at the River* carried the simple inscription, "Jenny." See the Wright Papers, file 3.2.10.

22 Wright Papers, file 5.1.3.

23 Friedrich W. Nietzsche, *Thus Spake Zarathustra*, trans. A. Tille, rev. M. M. Bozman (London: J. M. Dent and Sons, 1958), p. 20.

## CHAPTER 6

1 In discussing the great similarity of narrative in poetry and short fiction, Raymond Carver described the venture as a "dual enterprise." On the other hand, Kirkpatrick Sale execrated the idea of mixing genres as destructive of both, and he closed his remarks by urging, "Vive la difference." Other panelists included: Joyce Carol Oates, Cynthia Macdonald, Mark Strand, and Allen Ginsberg. These remarks are quoted from Darlyn Brewer, "The 48th International PEN Congress," *Coda* [*Poets and Writers Magazine*] 13, no. 4 (April/May 1986): 11.

2 W. M. Spackman, for one, refuses to acknowledge the validity of the prose poem form, denouncing it as "one of those accidents of French rhetoric . . . which the French take to be literature" ("Au Fil du Moi," *Parnassus* 4, no. 1, [Fall/Winter 1975]: 190). His disregard for the form is based mainly on the technical sloppiness that he discerns among its practitioners, as if they believed "the way to write is not learn how" (193). Therefore, he considers the form not a movement toward possibility but a retreat from responsibility. However, when Kirkpatrick Sale inveighs against the prose poem, it is as if he is bemoaning the general decline of western culture: "Prose poetry is a bastard-child. It is like thinking you could have a symphony sculpture or ballet poetry. If the lines between poetry and fiction have grown fuzzy, it is the dismantling of standards or the very idea of standards, and a loss of genuine authenticity within this world, a loss of artistic expression" (as quoted in Darlyn Brewer, "The 48th International PEN Congress," p. 11).

3 Michael Davidson, "Writing at the Boundaries," *New York Times Book Review*, 24 February 1985, pp. 1, 28. Davidson contends that writers "who work at the boundaries may appear to be thumbing their noses at traditional literary values, but they are also trying to understand those values and the world view they support. . . . The

boundary to what is possible in writing is a fiction created by and within writing. Only when the boundary is recognized as movable can it become a generative element in art rather than an obstacle to its growth."

4   Michael Benedikt, Introduction to *The Prose Poem: An International Anthology*, ed. Michael Benedikt (New York: Dell, 1976), p. 44.

5   Edson, "The Prose Poem in America," *Parnassus* 5, no. 1 (Fall/Winter 1976), 321–325.

6   Stanley Plumly discusses the emergence of the "prose lyric," its sources, influences, and general qualities in "Chapter and Verse," *American Poetry Review* 7 (Jan.–Feb. 1978): 21–35; (May–June 1978): 21–32.

7   Wright, in Dave Smith, "James Wright: The Pure Clear Word, An Interview" *The Pure Clear Word: Essays on the Poetry of James Wright*, ed. Dave Smith (Urbana: Univ. of Illinois Press, 1982), p. 19. Wright goes on elsewhere to say: "We should try to avoid yet another discussion about the difference between poetry and prose. That discussion is physically depressing, like a stupid joke which everyone present has known and loathed for years. I should like to record my gratitude to Mr. Yvor Winters for his beautifully impatient statement that poetry is written in verse while prose is written in prose. The statement may not have solved any problems of aesthetics, but it made the actual reading of books a little easier, and as such, *Mr. Winter's words clear my mind and lighten my heart, as though an ancient burden had been lifted from my back*" [emphasis added]. See Wright, *"Far From the Madding Crowd*: An Afterword," in *Collected Prose*, ed. Anne Wright (Ann Arbor: Univ. of Michigan Press, 1982), p. 25.

8   Cary Nelson, *Our Last First Poets* (Urbana: Univ. of Illinois Press, 1981), p. x.

9   See Wayne Dodd's review of *Moments of the Italian Summer* in *The Ohio Review* 18, no. 2 (Spring/Summer 1977): 59–62.

10  Wright, in Smith, "James Wright: The Pure Clear Word, An Interview" p. 24.

11  Wright, "A Plain Brave Music," *Chelsea* 12 (September 1962), rpt. in *Collected Prose*, pp. 285, 286.

12  Wright, interview with Peter Stitt, "The Art of Poetry XIX: James Wright," *Paris Review* 16, no. 62 (Summer 1975): 51.

13  Wright, "One Voice and Many—A Poet's Debt to Prose," *New York Times Book Review*, 18 March 1984, p. 14. According to the *New York Times Book Review*, the essay is "an edited version of a talk Wright gave on March 30, 1977 in a series of 'Conversations' sponsored by the Academy of American Poets." In it Wright reveals that many prose writers were "sort of like secret friends" to him; he mentions, among others, Twain, Mencken, Tolstoy, and Forster.

14  Plumly, "Chapter and Verse," 7 *American Poetry Review* (Jan.-Feb. 1978): 27.

15  Wright, *To a Blossoming Pear Tree* (New York: Farrar, Straus and Giroux, 1977), p. 38.

16  Stanley Fish, *Is There a Text in This Class: The Authority of Interpretative Communities* (Cambridge: Harvard Univ. Press, 1980), p. 326. Fish contends that "shared ways of seeing" exist within an interpretative community. According to Fish, this accounts for the way that poems (and other objects) are "constituted in unison" by the group's individual members, and accounts for how the following list of names came to be interpreted as a poem by his class: "Jacobs-Rosenbaum / Levin / Thorne /

Hayes / Ohman (?)" (323). As a result of this experience, he argues that "acts of recognition, rather than being triggered by formal characteristics, are their source" (326).

17 Robert Pinsky, "Light, Motion, Life," *Saturday Review*, 21 January 1978, p. 49.

18 This version of the poem appeared in *Poetry* 92 (August 1958): 277.

19 Robert Bly, in Michael Clifton, "An Interview with Robert Bly," *Solitude and Silence* (Boston: Beacon Press, 1980), p. 96. Elsewhere, Bly asserts that "the prose poem appears whenever poetry gets too abstract. The prose poem helps bring the poet back to the physical world. . . . In the prose poem we see the world is actually made up of one leaf at a time, one Lutheran at a time, one apartment door at a time" (*Talking All Morning* [Ann Arbor: Univ. of Michigan Press, 1980], pp. 115, 116).

20 Donald Hall, Introduction to *Contemporary American Poetry*, ed. Donald Hall (Baltimore: Penguin, 1962), p. 23.

21 Michael Heffernan, *Poet and Critic* 18, no. 1 (Fall 1986): 50–53.

22 F. W. J. Hemmings reminds us that among the first prose poems which Baudelaire published were versions altogether identical to poems he had written earlier in verse. So, we have identical versions of "L'Invitation au voyage" and "Le Chevelure," the one written in verse and the other in prose. See Hennings, *Baudelaire the Damned* (New York: Scribner's, 1982), p. 188.

23 Wright, *This Journey* (New York: Vintage Books, 1982), p. 23.


## CHAPTER 7

1 Friedrich W. Nietzsche, *Thus Spake Zarathustra*, trans. A. Tille, rev. M. M. Bozman (London: J. M. Dent and Sons, 1958), p. 20.

2 Wright, *This Journey* (New York: Vintage, 1982), p. 76. Further references to the text are to this edition.

3 Wright, interview with Peter Stitt, "The Art of Poetry XIX: James Wright," *Paris Review* 16, no. 62 (Summer 1975): 49.

4 Wright's typescript of "To the Reader," marked with numerous handwritten corrections and insertions, can be found in the James Wright Papers, file 5.3.1, Kenyon College Libraries.

5 Wright, *To a Blossoming Pear Tree* (New York: Farrar, Straus, and Giroux, 1977), p. 3. Further references to the text are to this edition.

6 Wright Papers, file 5.3.2.

7 Through their interviews with Wright, both Dave Smith and Peter Stitt were convinced of the remarkable quality of his memory. Stitt, in fact, admits to spending several needless "hours in the library looking up and checking" the extended passages of prose and poetry that Wright quoted during their sessions, for Wright's versions were "always accurate" ("The Art of Poetry XIX," p. 36). Confronted with similar exhibitions of Wright's near total recall, Smith remembers "clearly the sense" that the books filling the shelves in Wright's apartment "were virtually

husks because Wright held all that was alive in them within his own mind." (Smith's remarks appear in his brief preface to the text of "The Pure Clear Word: An Interview," in *Collected Prose*, ed. Anne Wright [Ann Arbor: Univ. of Michigan Press, 1983], 191.)

8   Sherwood Anderson, *Winesburg, Ohio* (New York: Viking Press, 1960), pp. 243, 241.

9   Stitt, "The Quest for Home," in *The World's Hieroglyphic Beauty* (Athens: Univ. of Georgia Press, 1985), p. 163. Stitt presents a compelling argument for the pervasiveness of the quest motif in Wright's work, especially the quest for a return to "something at least resembling paradise" (163). He goes on to cite parallels between Wright's yearning for the realm of paradise—vaguely remembered in childhood and most generally lost with age—to the thinking of William Wordsworth expressed in the well-known "Ode: Intimations of Immortality from Recollections of Early Childhood."

10  During his conversation with Smith, Wright recalls Frost's conception of the unity of a collection of poems, adding: "That is, in presenting a group of poems in the hope that someone will read them, one ought to be aware of relation between the poems as well as of inner relations that exist in the individual poems" (Smith, "The Pure Clear Word. An Interview," in *Collected Prose*, p. 229).

11  Hank Lazer quite rightly assesses Wright's place among our country's nature poets in this way: "Wright clearly belongs to the American tradition, from Bradstreet to Emerson to Frost to Roethke, that makes nature a symbol of spirit, what James Breslin terms 'visionary pastoralism.' " See Lazer, "The Heart of the Light," *Virginia Quarterly Review* 59 (1983): 721.

12  Wright, *"Far From the Madding Crowd*: An Afterword," in *Collected Prose*, p. 29.

13  After Wright's death, Anne Wright thought enough of "A Reply to Matthew Arnold on My Fifth Day in Fano" to make it the title poem of a limited-edition chapbook. The chapbook, and another titled *Leave It to the Sunlight*, were issued in 1981 by Logbridge-Rhodes, Inc., P.O. Box 3254, Durango, CO 81301. All of the poems included in *A Reply to Matthew Arnold* center on the interaction of a human being, most often Wright himself, with animals; these poems, in addition to the title poem, are "The Turtle Overnight," "Petition to the Terns," "The Limpet in Otranto," "Lightning Bugs Asleep in the Afternoon," "Small Wild Crabs Delighting on Black Sand," "The Fox at Eype," "Entering the Kingdom of the Moray Eel," and "The Journey."

14  Roethke, "Open Letter," *On the Poet and His Craft*, ed. Ralph Mills (Seattle: Univ. of Washington Press, 1965), p. 38.

15  In addition, Lazer's review traces the elements of the mystic's quest for illumination—as identified by Evelyn Underhill in her *Mysticism: Awakening or Conversion, Self-Knowledge or Purgation, Illumination, Surrender, or the Dark Night, and Union*—throughout Wright's final two volumes. Specifically, he argues that "while Wright intends and allows his experiences to be cast in a religious mold, outright theophany does not occur. . . . His 'heart of light,' 'impossibly hovering in the air over everything,' and 'black is the inmost secret of light,' translates traditional, mystical

illumination into his own uncertain natural theophany. Strategically, Wright maintains a secular vocabulary" (722).

16 This version of the prose poem, a kind of epistle of faith in which Wright repeatedly invokes the name of his "master Horace," is gathered with the Wright Papers, file 5.2.4.

17 Nietzsche, *Thus Spake Zarathustra*, p. 20.

18 Stitt, "The Quest for Home," p. 161.

## CONCLUSION

1 James Wright, "Theodor Storm: Foreword," *Collected Prose*, ed. Anne Wright (Ann Arbor: Univ. of Michigan Press, 1983), pp. 76, 75.

2 Wright, in Dave Smith, "The Pure Clear Word: An Interview," in *The Pure Clear Word: Essays on the Poetry of James Wright*, ed. Dave Smith (Urbana: University of Illinois Press, 1982), pp. 3–42; rpt. in *Collected Prose*, p. 230.

3 Wright, "The Terrible Threshold," review of Stanley Kunitz, *Selected Poems: 1928–1958* (Boston: Atlantic Little Brown, 1958), in *Collected Prose*, p. 249.

4 Wright, "The Stiff Smile of Mr. Warren," in *Collected Prose*, p. 242.

5 Wright, "The Stiff Smile of Mr. Warren," p. 240.

6 Wright's handwritten or, more accurately, scribbled draft of "Didactic Poem" appears in the James Wright Papers, file 5.3.1, Kenyon College Libraries.

7 This page also shows that Wright may have considered yet another title for the volume. Next to the other titles, Wright appears to have written "*Two Sides of the Story*," which, given the book's mix of traditional and free-verse offerings, would seem not only an accurate but also an ironic title. See the Wright Papers, file 3.2.11.

8 Wright, "The Stiff Smile of Mr. Warren," p. 241.

9 Wright seems to have been undecided about what to call the book that eventually became *To a Blossoming Pear Tree*; several title pages offer various names for the collection, such as *Hook, Redwings, and Others*, and *Hook: Poems and Sketches*. The last title, especially, emphasizes both the importance of the poem "Hook" to the collection and the integral role of the prose poems Wright here calls "sketches." Finally, several notes indicate that Anne Wright played a part in the final decisions regarding the content and shape of the manuscript. On the page containing the Jonson epigraph, for example, he wrote a note to Anne asking her to help "decide on" the following matters: "(1) Title, (2) Exclusions, (3) Inclusions, (4) Is this a *true book*? Is its shape clear and true?" Later on the same page, he addresses a note to her which gives solid evidence of his movement from despair to joy and of the contribution that Anne Wright had in this transition: "I am marvelously happy! Whatever life means, this is the life I had hoped for! . . . you have given me my own hope" (Wright Papers, file 5.3.2).

10 Matthews, "The Continuity of James Wright's Poems," in *The Pure Clear Word: Essays on the Poetry of James Wright*, ed. Dave Smith (Urbana: Univ. of Illinois Press, 1982), p. 112.

11  Franz Wright, "Some Thoughts on my Father," in *Poets and Writers Magazine* 15, no. 1 (Jan.-Feb. 1987): 21. This issue features a collection of comments from writers whose parents were also writers and some remarks from the parents, as well. Besides the remembrance of Wright by his son Franz, the issue includes pieces by John and David Updike, Kaylie Jones, Adam Below, George and Magda Bogin, David and Yaedi Ignatow, Linda and Rachel Pastan, and Tama Janowitz.

12  Wright, in Dave Smith, "The Pure Clear Word: An Interview," *Collected Prose*, p. 211.

# Appendix

Poems:
*Three Letters in One Evening*
*His Farewell to Old Poetry*
*Just Off the Highway to Rochester, Minnesota*

# THREE LETTERS IN ONE EVENING

> "...on account of his helplessness,
> his terrible loneliness, the
> cruelty of man, the cruelty of
> God, and the absence of God." (Tolstoy)

### 1. To the Mother

Dear Mrs. ......,

Several years ago,

I had the pleasure

Of meeting you.  One brilliant afternoon

In late October, when the maple leaves

Seemed fresher for their falling, you and I

Exchanged a word or two, a pleasant word,

I'm sure, over your daughter's life.  This week,

Riffling a paper to remark the news

Before I fell asleep, I found her name,

The circumstance, the date.

I write you now,

As one wholly a stranger.

Even then,

I knew her slightly.

I must confess I cannot keep in mind

The color of her hair, whether she was

Plump or slender; and yet I am sure you know

How names remain with us, only because

We have so little else.

I notice here

She lived near Shadyside and later moved,

To join her husband.

I trust her children comfort you, if only

To clarify her child's face in your mind.

For my part,

When I think about her face,

I keep nothing but haze

Falling through maples,

October nearly gone.

If only

We held one secret corner of our minds

For those clear faces we might dwell upon.

Ah, well, the Good Lord has clear purposes,

And we have ours.


I tender my regards

To all surviving relatives, her sisters,

Uncle, and you.  With every due respect,

And all condolences,

Of course, very sincerely yours, I am.


                    2.  To the Unmarried Sister


Thank you for writing me.

I can say nothing.

J.... is dead.


Lonely, in danger of the loss of faces,

I will just tell you back the plain details

You had the nerve to write.  I have to keep

My mind on something.

                    I keep wandering over leaves,
As I just wrote your mother.  Early today
I took my stroll among some leaves left over,
Blackened and tough almost beyond the death,
The rot.  They had gone through all that, and come
To lie among stones.  Even the winter rain
Could not affect them now.  One afternoon,
Long past, some years ago, she rose to leave,
Arranged her dress primly as ever, turned,
And stirred the leaves.  Without goodbye, she left.
I sat alone thinking for along time.
Her face, irregular and vulnerable,
Flamed like a maple leaf, the kind we keep
For their quick scarlet that is almost sound,
That falls so richly and turns gray so fast.

Where was I, then?  Oh, yes.  Oh, I can't think
Of anything but leaves.
I climb as far as names,
And afternoons,
And vulnerable faces
Quickened, half-frightened into gentleness,
Turning into gray leaves.  J.... is dead.

I walk all afternoon into the black leaves
Of my own life.

If I could find the path
Where I came into the forest, I might go back
Without a word.
Well, one last word, maybe.  I want to keep
One face, out of the general ruin, clear.
I have to keep my mind on something.

Now:
You were with her.  Her husband had gone out
To fetch the children.
It was three-thirty.  She had done her hair
Up in a bun.
She stood up on a chair,
To hold the rods still
While you lifted the curtains.
You turned
To fold a seam, she lit her cigarette.
She squealed, then she said nothing, then you turned.

Then the fire fell across her gently, soft
As scarlet maple
That is almost sound.
No, no:
I have to keep my mind on something:
Backward, backward,
She fell before you screamed.
She rolled in the light, now
Opening her fingers,
Now lying still,
Humming.  The dress went quickly, and the face.
J....'s face.  A strange darkness.  Sighing and singing.

I think of the sighing and singing, the very high
Thin voice: I suppose, rather like summer dusk,
When you are sitting on damp grass, before
Your house, and dew has come down, and kids play
Hide-and-seek under the streetlights.   Crickets
Are loud far off, and then mosquitoes sing,
Suddenly clear, very faint.  I have to keep
My mind on something.

Then she clawed at her face with a free hand.
You cannot say whether or not she felt.
Do you think I care?
The face was nothing.

I close now.
Through my windows,
I can make out
A black leaf, coiling
On the moon's left arm.
Thank you again.  Yours truly, I remain.

Oh, Jesus.
I think I will keep this second letter
To myself.

3.

J....,

Now I have told them all they want to know.

Deliberate faces,

The emptiness of peace:

Let them eat darkness.


This is the one thousand,

Eighty-fifth letter I have written you,

Since your face, innocent and overwhelmed

With need to love your mother, disappeared

Out of my life and everything that lived

In me.


Not a day,

But I see faces everywhere, the face

Of age caught napping in the sun, the face

Of vapid adolescence sneaking home,

My father's face chiselled a hundred times

Out of its life, and many faces freed

From Continental Can at six o'clock,

Where bodies fall down ramps into a yard

Beside the river.  Faces of headlights flare

Till the gray moths

Of water vanish into a black fire.

And the blast furnaces

Of Benwood hulk their hushed thunderheads

Of coke into the darkness.

When laborers drive home,

Each car-hood is a dark sloop bearing

Living men under water,

Each eye

The dead wick of a blow-torch.

                   Other days, I walk

In leaves.

        J...., the face

Of fine Catullus, whose immense delight

I sang you once, rolls in the sea alike

With the quick eyes of thieving children, lost

In the loud streets of Alexandria,

So many years ago, when bread

Was hard to snatch at, and there was no God

To speak of. J...., J...., the old men

Of the T'ang Dynasty crept sick for home,

Trapped among alien Tartar faces, left,

Starved on the bad wine of barbarians.

One of my brother's children raised his face

Clutched in a hump of agony, and died

Too stupid to believe, after six weeks.

J...., this afternoon,

Dreaming of your annihilated face,

I left my mail in the box, and I came home

Trying to walk with closed eyes without stumbling.

What's more, I nearly made it.

Then I turned me into the wind, and I cried,
This is not my country! this is not my country! This is a strange
Moon's desolation, a disastrous place.
This is a stone my body rolls upon.
J.... is dead.

J....!

Now the amenities of stone are done,
God damn me if I care whether or not
Anyone reads this book, now you will not.
No more, no more.
Atlantis rolls with Alexandria
And my brother's humpbacked child
And your face and my face
In the sea's wound the moon left us...

(J....,
We came so early, we thought to stay so long.
But it is already midnight, and we are gone.

I know your face the loveliest face I know.)

###

HIS FAREWELL TO OLD POETRY

                    _more precious...than the rubies_

I have been here, alone, all afternoon,
Dreaming, of maple leaves I walked beneath
Some years ago, with Philip Timberlake,
Who is dead.  We paused together once beside
The Ohio river flowing past the town
Of Marietta, where the trees, he said,
Held in green shadows many noblest men,
And we might hear their voices quietly.
Now he is buried, but he was the first
To tell me how the Muse survived in trees.
Now I must leave you, Jenny of strange names,
Jenny of maple leaves.  One afternoon,
One later time ago, you rose to bear
Blossom above my own awakening face
In a small room.  Then, as you turned away,
You fluffed your dress primly as ever, turned,
And shook down leaves.  Vanished without goodbye.
I sat alone thinking for a long time.
Your face, so regular and vulnerable,
Flamed on a maple leaf, the kind we keep
For the quick scarlet that is almost sound,
That flares so richly and falls gray so fast.

Jenny, Sir Walter Ralegh and John Donne
Brood in the trees, but they say nothing now.
They sang delicate melodies to your voice
When I was young, but now I grant them rest,
As they walk lightly, kindly past the grave
Of Timberlake, my friend. Some hidden poets
Had names, almost forgotten by the crowd
Of explicating critics now, thank God:
Chidiock Tichbourne, Robert Haymon, and
Peter Hausted, melancholy and fragile,
Who sang only one song that I know of
And slipped away darkly between dark trees.
I think of you, Jenny, singing among
The small grape vines with that anonymous
Poet who sang Ah love they wrong thee much
That say thy sweet is bitter. Let him rest.
Now that I cannot hear your voice, I lose
All the old echoes, Jenny, maple leaf.
Now you are gone, I dream about your face
Quickened, half-frightened into gentleness,
Fallen and printed flawlessly upon
The silence, the dark earth where trees have gone.
I have to go there soon, where it is dark:
You could have told me whether it be death
Or life I hope to find. But where are you?

Now my amenities of stone are done,

God damn me if I care whether or not

Anyone hears my voice, now you will not.

We came so early, we thought to stay so long.

But it is already midnight, and we are gone.

I know your face the loveliest face I know.

Now I know nothing, and I die alone.

###

## JUST OFF THE HIGHWAY TO ROCHESTER, MINNESOTA

Twilight bounds softly out on the grass.
They have come gladly out of the willows
To welcome my friend and me.
We step over the barbed wire into the pasture
Where they have been grazing all day, alone.
And the eyes of those two Indian ponies
Darken.
I would like to hold the slenderer one in my arms,
For she has walked over to me
And nuzzled my left hand.
She is black and white,
Her mane falls wild on her forehead.
At home once more,
They begin munching the young tufts of spring in the darkness.
I think
That if I stepped out of my body I would break
Into blossom.

not Poetry (accepted
in earlier version
— "The Blessing"
and this version
to Kenne.)

not Poetry

Dec.13: Nims still
wants to print the
previous version. Chay-
see how it looks in
print.

it is possible

(The Blessing).

Jan.27:
Use the other Poetry version (The Blessing).

# Index